2995
80E

RECKONERS

RECKONERS

THE PREHISTORY OF THE DIGITAL COMPUTER, FROM RELAYS TO THE STORED PROGRAM CONCEPT, 1935–1945

Paul E. Ceruzzi

Contributions to the Study of Computer Science, Number 1

GREENWOOD PRESS
WESTPORT, CONNECTICUT • LONDON, ENGLAND

Library of Congress Cataloging in Publication Data

Ceruzzi, Paul E.
  Reckoners.

  (Contributions to the study of computer science,
ISSN 0734-757X ; no. 1)
  Bibliography: p.
  Includes index.
  1. Electronic digital computers—History. I. Title.
II. Series.
QA76.5.C4164   1983   621.3819′58′09   82-20980
  ISBN 0-313-23382-9 (lib. bdg.)

Copyright © 1983 by Paul E. Ceruzzi

All rights reserved. No portion of this book may be
reproduced, by any process or technique, without the
express written consent of the publisher.

Library of Congress Catalog Card Number: 82-20980
ISBN: 0-313-23382-9
ISSN: 0734-757X

First published in 1983

Greenwood Press
A division of Congressional Information Service, Inc.
88 Post Road West
Westport, Connecticut 06881

Printed in the United States of America

10 9 8 7 6 5 4 3 2 1

Contents

Illustrations	vii
Tables	ix
Preface	xi
1. Background	3
2. Computers in Germany	10
3. Bessie—The Automatic Sequence Controlled Calculator	43
4. Number, Please—Computers at Bell Labs	73
5. Faster, Faster: The ENIAC	104
6. To the First Generation	131
7. The Revolution?	149
GLOSSARY A: Translations and Equivalents of German Terms	153
GLOSSARY B: Technical Terms Used in the Text	155
APPENDIX: Program Listings	159
Selected Bibliography	167
Index	177

Illustrations

PHOTOGRAPHS

Konrad Zuse and Helmut Shreyer at Work in Zuse's Parents' Apartment, Berlin	20
The Reconstructed Z3 at the German Museum, Munich	32
The IBM ASCC at Harvard	50
Complex Number Computer, One of the Three Terminals	90
The ENIAC	114

FIGURES

2.1	Graphical Representation of $2(ab+cd)$	12
2.2	Automatic Placement of Numbers	13
2.3	Sketch of the Basic Functional Elements of a General-Purpose Computer, c. 1936	15
2.4	Binary Memory Device	19
2.5	The Conditional Combinatoric	22
2.6	Mechanical Implementation of an "and" Statement	25
2.7	Basic Vacuum Tube Switching Circuit	27
2.8	Bistable Switching Circuit	27
2.9	Display and Keyboard of Z3	33
3.1	Sketch of a Decimal Wheel for the Mark I	53
4.1	Using Multiple Key Contacts to Encode Decimal Digits	82

FIGURES (continued)

4.2	Keyboard Layout of the Complex Number Computer	85
4.3	Block Diagram of the Complex Number Computer	88
5.1	Sketch of a Decade Counter	113
5.2	One of the ENIAC's Accumulators	115
5.3	Timing Pulses in the ENIAC	118

Tables

2.1	The Z3	34
3.1	The IBM ASCC	58
4.1	The Bell Labs Model I	86
4.2	Bell Labs Models II through V	95
5.1	The ENIAC	123
6.1	Types of Computer Architectures	141

Preface

> Human agents will be referred to as "operators" to distinguish them from "computers" (machines).
> —George Stibitz, 1945

The modern digital computer was invented between 1935 and 1945. That was the decade when the first machines that could be called true digital computers were put together. This book tells the story of that invention by looking at specific events of the 1930's and 1940's that show the computer taking its modern form.

Before 1935 there were machines that could perform calculations or otherwise manipulate information, but they were neither automatic nor general in capabilities. They were not computers. In the 1930's the word *computer* meant a human being who calculated with the aid of a calculating machine. After 1945 the word meant a machine which did that. From that time on computers have continued to evolve and improve, becoming dramatically cheaper and smaller, but their design has not really changed. So the story of what happened in that ten-year period will reveal quite a bit of the entire history of the computer as it is known today.

I have chosen four projects from that era that best illustrate how the computer was invented. These are by no means all that happened, but they are representative of the kinds of activities going on.

The first is the set of electromechanical computers built in Germany by Konrad Zuse, who because of the war had no knowledge of similar activities in America and England. His independent line of work makes for an interesting and self-contained case study of just how one goes about building a computer from scratch.

The second is the Harvard Mark I, built by Professor Howard Aiken and first shown to the public in 1944. This machine was one of the first truly large-scale projects, and because it was well publicized it served notice to the world that the computer age had dawned.

The third project is the series of relay computers built by George Stibitz of the Bell Telephone Laboratories between 1939 and 1946. These machines represented the best that could be done with electromechanical devices (telephone relays), and as such mark the end of that phase of invention and the beginning of another.

The final project is the ENIAC, the world's first working electronic numerical computer, using vacuum tubes for its computing elements, and operating at the speed of light. With its completion in late 1945 all of the pieces of the modern computer were present: automatic control, internal storage of information, and very high speed.

What remained to be done after 1945 was to put those pieces together in a practical and coherent way. From the experience of building and using those machines there came a notion of what a computer *ought* to look like. The old definition of a computer gave way to the modern one: a machine capable of manipulating and storing many types of information at high speeds and in a general and flexible way. How this notion came about, and especially why the notion of storing the computer's program of instructions in the same internal memory as its data gained favor, are also examined.

This book has a dual purpose. The first is to recount the history of the computer, emphasizing the crucial decade between 1935 and 1945 but including earlier events and more recent trends as well. The second is to explain in simple terms the fundamentals of how those computers worked. Computing has certainly changed since 1945, but the basic concepts have not; I feel that it is easier to grasp these concepts as they were present in earlier, slower, and much simpler computers. I have included brief explanations of some of these concepts in the text of the book; a glossary at the end gives short definitions of many terms of modern computing jargon.

That the computer is having a profound effect on modern life is hardly at issue. Just how and why such a profound change in our society is happening because of computers can better be understood with a grasp of how this technology emerged.

I wish to thank the following persons and institutions for their help with the researching and writing of this book: the Society for Mathematics and Data Processing, Bonn; the Charles Babbage Institute, Minneapolis; the Linda Hall Library, Kansas City, Mo.; the Baker Library, Dartmouth College; and Professors Jerry Stannard, Walter Sedelow, and Forrest Berghorn of the University of Kansas. Konrad Zuse, Helmut Schreyer, and George Stibitz supplied me with personal archival materials and criticized portions of the manuscript. I also wish to thank Bill Aspray, Gwen Bell, and Nancy Stern, who also read portions of the manuscript and gave me helpful advice. Any errors or statements of opinion are of course my own.

1
Background

> All the other wonderful inventions of the human brain sink pretty nearly into commonplaces contrasted with this awful mechanical miracle. Telephones, locomotives, cotton-gins, sewing-machines, Babbage calculators, Jacquard looms, perfecting presses, all mere toys, simplicities!
> —Mark Twain, 1889

Computers have appeared so rapidly on the modern scene that it is hard to imagine that they have any history at all. Yet they do, and it is a most interesting history indeed. The computer has been around now for at least thirty years, maybe more. But there was a much longer period of activity before its invention when important preliminary steps were taken—a period of the computer's "prehistory." It is much more than just the story of specific machines and what they did, although that is at the center of this study. It is also a part of the history of mathematics and science—of the story of how mankind acquired a perception of quantities, and of the long, slow acquisition of the ability to code and manipulate quantities in symbolic form.

The history of computing, if not the history of the digital computer, could begin at the dawn of civilization, when people first sought to measure and keep track of surpluses of food, the management of which freed them from the anxiety of daily survival. The first mechanical aid to calculation was probably a device like the modern abacus, on which numerical quantities were represented by the positions of pebbles or beads on a slab. (The modern version, with its beads strung on wires, has been around at least a thousand years and is still in common use in many parts of the world.)

Or one could begin the history of the computer with Blaise Pascal, who in 1642 built a mechanical adding machine that performed addition automatically. (Like the abacus, it too survives—the cheap plastic totalizer sold in supermarkets to keep track of a grocery bill works the same way.)

But the computer is something more than just a sophisticated adding machine, even though at the heart of every computer is something like Pascal's automatic adder. The computer is a system of interconnected machines which operate together in a coherent way. Only one of those pieces actually does arithmetic. A computer not only calculates: it also remembers what it has just calculated, and it automatically knows what to do with the results of those calculations.

And numbers are not the only kind of information a computer can handle. Letters and words can be coded into numbers and thus made grist for the computer's mill; the same holds true for photographs, drawings, maps, graphs: any information which can be symbolically represented. A computer is a machine which is capable of physically representing coded information (numbers, words, or whatever) and which is further capable of manipulating those values in any combination or sequence one desires. Numerical calculation is of course one form of symbol manipulation, but it is by no means the only one.

By this definition, the history of the computer really begins sometime after 1935, when machines with such general and automatic capabilities first appeared. It is that emergent period of their history—beginning around 1935 and ending about ten years later—that this book examines.

The invention of the computer was the result of a convergence of a number of different social, technical, and mathematical traditions.[1] Some of those traditions are external: the increasing need by governments for statistical information, for example, brought on in the United States by political developments such as the Progressive Era and the New Deal. Other traditions are more internal to the computer: they are literally present as components of the machine itself.

The tradition of mechanizing arithmetic has already been mentioned: its legacy may be found in the "central processor" of any modern computer. The tradition of building devices that control a sequence of mechanical motions can be traced back to medieval cathedral clocks, where mechanical cams directed an elaborate sequence of movements at the striking of every hour. (The cuckoo clock is a much simplified version; one of the most elaborate examples is the cathedral clock at Strasbourg, France.) An electronic version of that mechanism, too, is present in a modern computer.

A computer directs a sequence of activities, senses what it has already done, and modifies its future course of action accordingly. That kind of intelligence has its roots in medieval devices such as windmills which automatically adjusted the pitch of their vanes to adapt to the prevailing winds.[2] Another example of such a device is the fly-ball speed governor that James Watt attached to his steam engine, turning that machine into a reliable source of steady power.

Finally, there is a long tradition of techniques that record information; certainly the invention of writing itself, and of printing with movable type in the 15th century in Europe are part of it. The idea of using holes punched in pieces of cardboard to represent and manipulate data was first successfully employed by Herman Hollerith for the 1890 United States Census. (Punched cards had earlier been used in the silk weaving industry to control the pattern made by a loom, but that belongs more to the tradition of automatic control than to that of data storage.) Punched cards are still the backbone of modern data storage, although much faster electronic devices are used in a computer's main store. More modern storage techniques have appeared which may displace the punched card entirely; for example, the use of bar-codes to identify items in a supermarket.

Each of those traditions forms a separate block that goes to make up a computer. They are revealed whenever a computer is described by a block diagram that groups its functions together. But each tradition developed separately from the others, with a few exceptions—until the 1930's, when they merged and continued on as one.

Despite the general capabilities of computers, their immediate ancestors were machines that performed arithmetic. But their enormous impact on modern life is due less to their numerical abilities than to their ability to sort and handle large amounts of data, and to their ability to direct their actions intelligently. Nevertheless they bear the legacy of their "calculating" ancestry. The word itself reveals that legacy: before 1935 a "computer" often meant a human being who evaluated algebraic expressions with the aid of a calculating machine. That person (who was often a woman—the job of "computing" was thought of much like typing) would be given a mathematical expression—say a formula that evaluated the solution of a differential equation—plus the numerical values that were plugged into that formula. Depending on the "computer's" prior mathematical training, the instructions given to him or her to evaluate the expression would be more or less detailed.

These workers had the use of mechanical calculators which performed addition, subtraction, multiplication, and division to an accuracy of eight to ten decimal digits. (These machines are still in common use, as are adding machines that only add or subtract.) The calculators were driven by turning a crank or by a small electric motor, but all arithmetic done in them was mechanical. The person had one other important aid to computation: a pencil and sheets of paper, on which intermediate results were written down for use later on. With only a few exceptions, the mechanical calculators could not store intermediate results.

Taken together, the person, the calculator, the pencil and "scratch" paper, and the list of instructions formed a system which could solve a wide range of numerical problems, as long as the solutions to those problems could be specified as a series of elementary steps. That human and mechanical system was precisely what the first digital computers replaced.[3]

By 1945 the definition of the word *computer* had changed to reflect this invention: a computer was no longer a human being but a machine that solved computing problems. The definition of *calculator* remained unchanged: a device which could perform the four ordinary arithmetic operations, working with no more than two numbers at a time. (The modern definitions are in the same spirit but a little different; see Glossary B.)

After 1945 the evolution of computing technology followed a single line to the present. With the end of the Second World War the many computer projects that were in progress around the world became known and were publicized to varying degrees. Conference reports and other written descriptions of the first computers became templates for computer designs thereafter.[4] The ideas and writings of one man, John von Neumann, were especially influential, so much so that even today computers are said to have a "von Neumann type" architecture.

So after 1945 there was a more common understanding of the nature of this new invention, what it could do, and what overall structure ("architecture") it should have. There was still little agreement on what its components should be, especially for its memory, but by 1950 it was clear that a computer had to be made of high-speed electronic components (such as vacuum tubes), and it should be organized into functional units that performed the operations of storage, arithmetic, input, and output. Since 1950 those decisions have not changed, even though the components that make up a computer have. So the analogy of a person working with a desk calculator and some scratch paper still holds true, although everything has gotten much more complicated at every stage.

In the following chapters I have chosen four case studies of computer projects undertaken between 1935 and 1945 which I feel best illustrate the emergence of the new technology. These case studies by no means exhaust the subject, but the details encountered represent the major issues well.

The first project examined was one of the first to be completed. It was surprisingly not in England, where Charles Babbage had proposed building an Analytical Engine a century before, nor was it in the United States, where sophisticated calculating and punched card equipment was being extensively used, but rather in Germany, where the story may be said to have really begun. Konrad Zuse, an engineering student at the Technical College in Berlin, began looking for ways to ease the drudgery of calculations required for his coursework—drudgery which the slide rule and the desk calculator could not relieve. Zuse was not well versed in the calculating-machines technology of his day (which may have been a blessing), but by the end of the war in 1945 he had not only designed and built several working automatic computing machines, but he had also laid the foundations for a theory of computing that would independently emerge in America and Britain a decade later. Zuse's electromechanical devices were the first that could be programmed to do sequences of calculations, so they will be examined first.

In America, a similar idea occurred to a Harvard physics instructor named Howard Aiken, who had faced long and tedious calculations for his graduate thesis. The result was a computing machine that used the components of standard punched card equipment that the IBM Corporation had developed. Aiken's "Mark I" was the first large computing device to be made public (in 1944), and as such its name is appropriate—it marks the beginning of the computer age, despite the fact that it used mechanical components and a design that soon would become obsolete.

The third example is the work of Dr. George Stibitz and his colleagues at the Bell Telephone Laboratories in New York, where a series of computers was built out of telephone relays, as were Zuse's machines. These machines, too, would soon become obsolete, but their design and the programming done on them contributed much to the mainstream that followed.

Finally I look at the ENIAC: the first computer that could carry out, automatically, sequences of arithmetic operations at electronic speeds. It was completed in late 1945, and from that time onward the age not only of computing but also of high-speed electronic computing had begun.

For each of the machines examined in the next four chapters I hope to establish the following data: (1) how the machine was conceived, designed, and constructed; (2) how it was programmed and operated; and (3) to what practical use, if any, it was put. (Actually, for all the experimental computers of that day the design specifications were never really "frozen" for long. Someone was always improving and modifying them. I have tried to establish those vital statistics for the machines when they first began solving mathematical problems.)

Where it has been feasible, and in the Appendix, I have included sample programs. The reader who is unfamiliar with modern computer programming may follow these samples; the terms and details of each one are defined and explained as they are introduced. Several early programs have also been rewritten for a pocket programmable calculator, for the reader who wishes to get a better feel for just what the prehistoric computers could do.

The public dedication of the ENIAC in 1946 marked the dawn of the electronic computer age; actually it was more like the herald of the dawn. The ten years from 1935 to 1945 saw the convergence of various traditions to make the computer; the ten years following that saw both a continuation of the projects begun during the war, and an intensive study of the theory of computing itself—not so much how to build a computer as how one ought to build a computer. This activity was made visible as conferences, reports, memorandums, lectures, and short courses in computing that were held throughout America and Europe. John von Neumann was one central figure; others who contributed to this phase of activity were D. R. Hartree, Alan Turing, and Maurice Wilkes in England; Howard Aiken and George Stibitz in America; and Konrad Zuse, Eduard Stiefel, and Alwin Walther in continental Europe, to mention only a few.

What they accomplished can be summed up in a few words: the computer, as before, was seen as a device that did sequences of calculations automatically, but more than that, it was seen as not being restricted to numerical operations. Problems such as sorting and retrieving non-numeric information would be just as appropriate and in fact, from a theoretical standpoint, even more fundamental to computing than numerical problems.

Second, they realized that the instructions that told a computer what to do at each step of a computation should be kept internally in its memory alongside the data for that computation. Both would be kept in a memory giving access to any data or instructions at as high a speed as possible. This criterion allowed the execution of steps at speeds that matched those of the arithmetic unit of the machine, but it also allowed for more than that. The data and the instructions were stored alongside one another because they were not really different entities, and it would be artificial to keep them separate. An understanding of that startling fact, when implemented, made the computer not just a machine that "computed" but one which also "reckoned"—it made decisions and learned from its previous experiences. It became a machine that could think, at least in a way that many human beings had defined thinking.

It was the adoption and recognition of this stored-program concept that would make the computer's impact on society so strong in later years. That recognition was slow in coming—the principle is even today not fully understood. How it emerged, and how it was eventually incorporated into the design of computers after 1950, is the subject of Chapter 6. As with the other chapters, I discuss the stored-program concept and its implications in layman's terms.

In presenting the history of the digital computer in the years of its birth I have several goals in mind. One goal concerns the state of the art today. The fact that computers have such an impact on daily life today should lead us to understand more of their nature and what gives them their power. But for someone unfamiliar with the engineering and mathematical concepts, that task can be difficult, if not impossible. Looking at the history of the computer offers a way out of that bind. The men and women whom we shall encounter on the following pages knew nothing of "computer science" when they began their work—such a science did not exist then. They created computer science, out of their diverse backgrounds and from their experiences in trying to build machines which later generations would call "milestones." By retracing some of their steps, we can learn something of the foundations of modern computer science, for it was then that the foundation was laid.

Another goal, closely related, is to try and get a fresh outlook on the computing world today. It is a crazy world: a mixture of wild speculation, careful theoretical research, technological breakthroughs every few months, fortunes made (or lost) overnight. We frequently hear that these machines are smarter than we are, and sooner or later they will "take over" (whatever that means). Can a computer really think? Indeed, does it even make sense to ask a question like that? And with twenty-five dollar computer games that speak, with computer programs that make accurate medical diagnoses (and with others that only *pretend* to be psychoanalysts), it is hard to find a good vantage point from which to survey the field and get an overall view.

By looking not at those computer programs that dazzle us today, but rather at simpler ones that did more routine problems on the earliest machines, we can get such a view. We shall be examining the computer before it got so complex that, in Alan Turing's memorable words, "I suppose, when it gets to that stage, we shan't know how it does it."[5]

Today we often hear the command that we must learn about computers if we want to keep up with the pace of modern society. We hear further that computers are bringing us a technological Utopia (at last!), but if we do not learn about them, all we can do is forlornly press our noses against the window looking in; we may never enter. I have always felt uncomfortable with that scenario—I do not like to be coerced into doing something I otherwise might never have thought of doing. Nor do I feel that learning about computers is absolutely necessary to manage in the world today. Humans can get by without them, just as many live comfortable lives without telephones or automobiles. Why not learn about computers because they are inherently interesting, and because it is fun to see what makes them tick? They are, after all, "only" creations of ordinary human beings. And learning about them can tell us something about how *we* tick, as well. And that should not threaten or intimidate anyone.

NOTES

1. Thomas M. Smith, "Some Perspectives on the Early History of Computers," in *Perspectives on the Computer Revolution*, ed. Zenon W. Pylyshyn (Englewood Cliffs, N.J.: Prentice-Hall, 1970), pp. 7-15.

2. Otto Mayr, *The Origins of Feedback Control* (Cambridge, Mass.: MIT Press, 1970).

3. George R. Stibitz, "Relay Computers," Report 171.1R, U.S. National Defense Research Committee, Applied Mathematics Panel, Feb. 1945, p. 2.

4. See, for example, Arthur Burks, Herman Goldstine, and John von Neumann, "Preliminary Report on the Design of an Automatic Computing Machine," in John von Neumann, *Collected Works*, vol. 5 (New York: Macmillan, 1963), pp. 34-79; there were also several conferences held at Philadelphia, Harvard, and Cambridge, England, just after the dedication of the ENIAC.

5. Sara Turing, *Alan Turing* (Cambridge, England: W. Heffer and Sons, 1956), p. 98.

2
Computers in Germany

> For about a year now I have been occupied with thoughts about a mechanical brain.
>
> —Konrad Zuse, 1937[1]

In the world of computers Konrad Zuse has not had much influence. There are others, mostly Americans, who had more. But the story of how Zuse came to build a digital computer is not only fascinating in its own right: it can also tell us more about computers than the stories of the others can. Zuse worked independently on his projects, because of the language barrier and because he worked during World War II, when he could not have had any contact with the Americans and the British. That means that his story is almost a laboratory illustration of the major problems in the design and construction of a digital computer, even if the way he solved those problems did not serve as a model for how they would be solved later.

Not only that, but Zuse was the first. He designed and built a working automatic calculating machine by December, 1941, at least a year or two ahead of anyone else.

Konrad Zuse was born on June 22, 1910, in Berlin, where his father was a clerical official with the post office. Shortly after 1910, the family moved to Braunsberg, in East Prussia, where Zuse spent his childhood. (Braunsberg is now the Polish city Braniewo, between Gdansk and the Soviet city Kaliningrad.)[2]

Zuse has since described the school he attended as being traditional and conservative, with more emphasis on Latin than on other subjects such as mechanical engineering. After a few years there he transferred to a more progressive school in Hoyerswerda (in Silesia, near Dresden), which he enjoyed a bit more. By 1927 he had decided on engineering as a career, and that year he enrolled in the Technical College of Berlin-Charlottenburg.

This chapter is revised from an article published in the *Annals of the History of Computing* © 1981 American Federation of Information Processing Societies.

School records from those years show that Zuse was not especially talented or proficient at mathematics.[3] For him, mathematics was a tool with which one could design and build structures, but the structures themselves (buildings, highways, whatever) interested him more. What math he did learn was applied: how to set up and solve equations that described mechanical structures. One particular problem he faced was the analysis of load-bearing structures that are said to be statically indeterminate. If a load is carried by more than two supports one cannot determine how that load is distributed without taking into account the elasticity and strength of the materials involved. Such analysis quickly leads to a system of simultaneous linear equations of sufficient degree to include all those factors. The theory for setting up such equations—for making an analysis of the structures at hand—was already well known by the 1930's. The formulas were in the textbooks.[4]

The problem was that for all but the simplest sets of equations the tedium of manual calculations necessary to solve them was too great. Doubling the number of equations increases the number of calculations not two-fold, but eight-fold. Engineers did those calculations with the aid of a slide rule, or, if one had the money, a mechanical calculator that could perform arithmetic with greater accuracy. Even with those aids, though, the upper practical limit for an individual is about six equations with six unknowns. Beyond that, the number of elementary arithmetic operations becomes impractical; also, the chances for error in copying and retrieving intermediate results greatly increase. One example from that era was the design of a railroad station; the calculation of the stresses on its roof required the solution of a system of thirty equations in thirty unknowns. Its solution took a team of human computers several months to complete.[5]

But it was precisely these kinds of problems that the theory of static structures was designed for. It did not matter that the textbooks gave the method of solution, if that solution was so time-consuming it could never be practically carried out. For Konrad Zuse this imbalance between what he found in his textbooks and how the practical world applied those theories led him to the invention of a computer.

The slide rules or mechanical calculators available at the time were capable of performing elementary arithmetic operations one at a time. But even if those operations could be speeded up it would not break the real bottleneck, which was in the routing of those numbers to and from the calculating instruments, writing down and retrieving intermediate results, and gathering the input data at the right time for each stage of the computation. That logistic problem overwhelms the individual problems of computing the sums, products, quotients, and differences of pairs of numbers. It is the complexity of this "traffic control" that grows exponentially as the size of the problem increases, and it cannot be solved by better or faster calculating machines, or by simply hiring more human computers to do the work. Zuse knew little of the existing technology of calculating machines. But as far as mechanizing the logical part of a problem was concerned the calculating machines industry had hardly progressed at all. Circuits that do arithmetic, though they are found at the heart of every modern computer, make up only part of a computer's power.

Zuse's first thoughts about automating this task were to try to represent the problem graphically. He reasoned that for every problem there could be a preprinted form, with labeled boxes into which the input values would be placed. Each graphical location on the form would correspond to a specific arithmetic operation. The user would not have to worry about those operations but would only need to write the numerical data into the appropriately labeled places. Intermediate results would likewise be placed in boxes corresponding to their role in the overall computation. Thus the labeled form would translate the logic of the solution of a system of linear equations into a corresponding graphical layout. The engineer would only have to write down the input values in the appropriate boxes. Someone else—or a machine—could do the elementary operations. In the graphical scheme Zuse envisioned, values that lay next to each other would be multiplied or divided; those that lay under each other would be added or subtracted (see Figure 2.1).[6] (Zuse's thinking in graphical terms was to characterize much of his later work in computing, especially his work on programming languages after 1945.)

Once the numbers were in their places, carrying out the arithmetic on them would be so routine that it could be automated. One could link calculators to those specific places—the calculators in turn could carry out the correct operations on the numbers they found there, according to their location on the plane. To avoid copying numbers from the form into a calculator, Zuse thought of

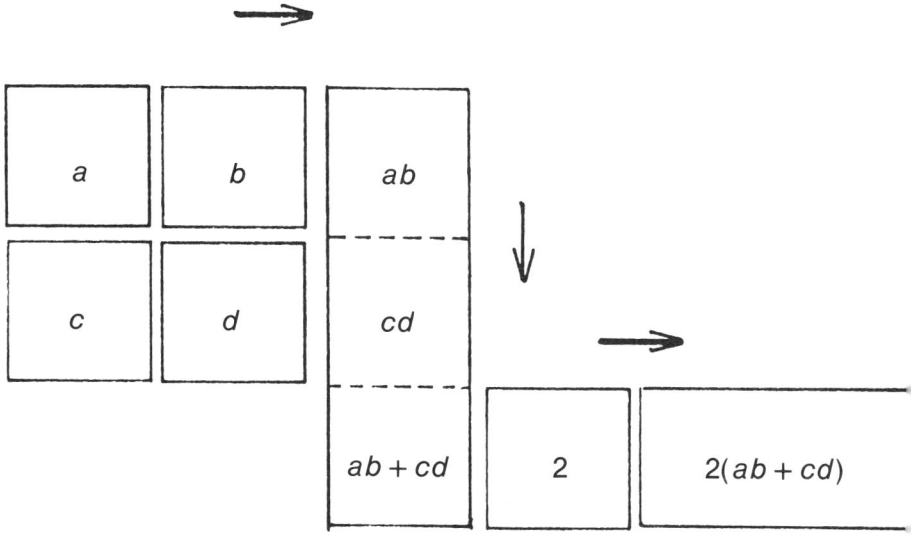

Figure 2.1. Graphical Representation of 2 (ab + cd)

entering those numbers in such a way that a machine could take them directly as input—something like a hand-held card punch that could be scanned over the surface of the form, punching in values as needed. From this idea (he had not at this time actually built any apparatus) he thought of having the numbers entered into a mechanical register directly, using push-button switches that hold their position, but which, unlike perforated media, may be cleared for reuse.

At this stage of Zuse's thoughts on how to automate computation, the only step still requiring a human's judgement was the requirement that he determine where on the form (or "solution surface") each number belonged. But why not make that step automatic, too? A person could key numbers into an ordinary keyboard; then an automatic crane would take each number and place it at the correct position on the surface. (The contraption might resemble the treasure-finding cranes found in amusement parks.) The crane would know where to place the numbers because it would be given the x-y coordinates of the surface for each one. It would receive a list of those coordinates beforehand, corresponding to the specific problem being solved (see Figure 2.2).[7]

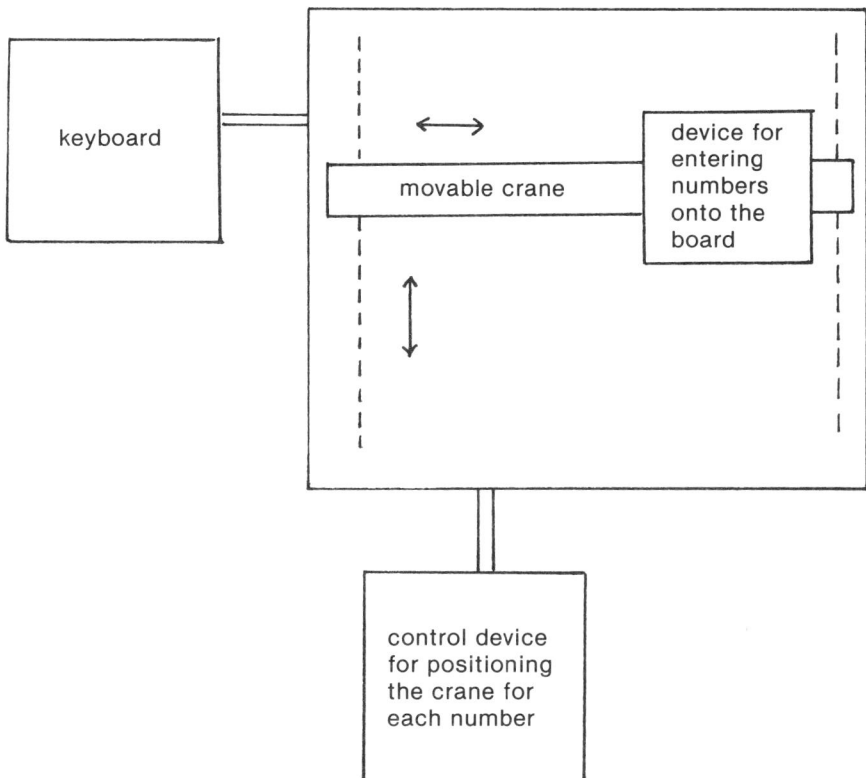

Figure 2.2. *Automatic Placement of Numbers*

To sum up this scheme that Zuse conceived of while a student in Berlin: given a problem in structural engineering, one first translates it into a corresponding mathematical equation or set of equations that will solve it. (This is or should be the most difficult and creative part.) Associated with that particular equation will be a list of x-y coordinates directing the input data to places on a two-dimensional surface. The places correspond to the arithmetic to be performed on each number. Having supplied those coordinates to the machine, the engineer would then key in numbers for the variables in the equation (for example, the length of the span, the weight of the load it is to carry, etc.), and the machine would place them on a surface, where calculators would perform the necessary arithmetic on them.

Now the whole purpose of having the numbers positioned graphically on a surface is to specify what arithmetic operations are to be done on them. But that graphic information is also contained in the coordinates that make up the "plan" of the calculation, so there is really no need to have those numbers represented by a two-dimensional grid after all. The information is redundant. It would be just as easy to connect the individual calculators to the input data via the coordinates themselves, since each one represents a specific arithmetic operation.

What Zuse had discovered, by the back door, was that the plan of a calculation could itself be coded and delivered to a machine—in short, a machine could be programmed to carry out *any* sequence of simple operations. (Zuse used the word *plan*, but he understood it in the same way as the modern definition of program.) Such a machine, since it could carry out any finite sequence of elementary arithmetic operations, would be a general purpose computer; it would not be restricted to any one problem or specific type of problem.

Now (c. 1934-1935) Zuse was ready to begin thinking of how actually to construct a machine that would work that way. Figure 2.3 shows the overall design that he sought to implement.

Rather than have separate calculators for each operation as before, he would employ just one calculator (*Rechenwerk*): one that could perform the four operations of arithmetic. Numbers would be transferred into this calculator from a storage area (*Speicherwerk*), which could also serve as a temporary storage area for intermediate results. A control device (*Programwerk*) would direct the transfer of numbers into and out of the store and would also specify the arithmetic operation performed on each number transferred into the calculating unit. The program unit would in turn be directed by a strip of punched tape (*Lochstreifen*), which contained the overall plan of the calculation.

The design of such a universal calculating machine, which Zuse says he came upon during his student days in Berlin, is not much different from the overall design of a modern computer. In both there is a clear separation of units that perform arithmetic, control, and storage of data. Zuse's design is similar to the first design for a universal computer that was envisioned by Charles Babbage in the 1830's. Babbage never completed his Analytical Engine, but he saw it as being organized around two fundamental units:

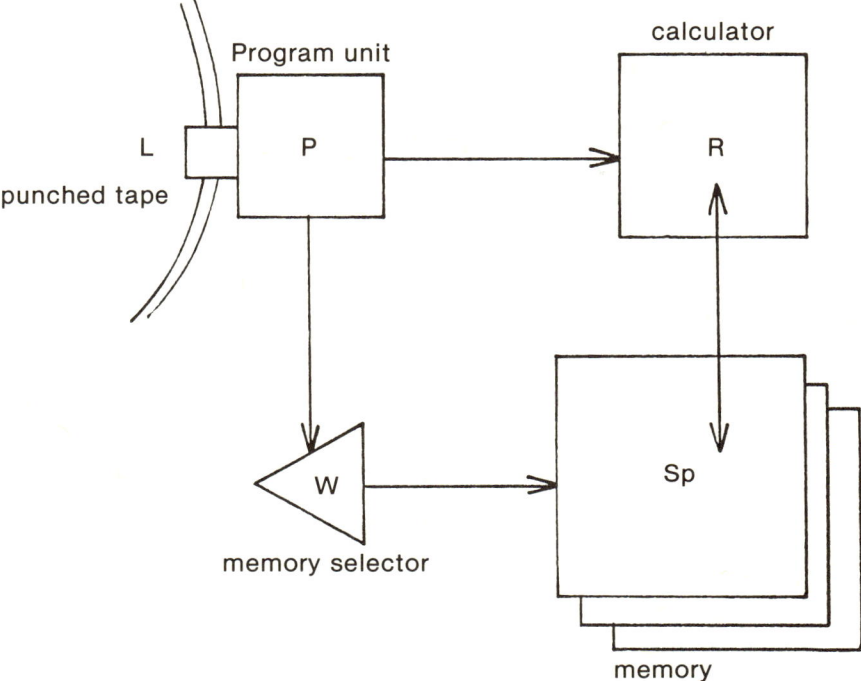

Figure 2.3. Sketch of the Basic Functional Elements of a General-Purpose Computer, c. 1936

First: The Store in which all variables to be operated on, as well as all those quantities which have arisen from the result of other operations, are placed.

Second: The Mill into which the quantities about to be operated on are always brought.[8]

Punched cards borrowed from Jacquard's looms were to control the Babbage Engine; perforated paper tape was to control Zuse's.

Zuse was not aware of Babbage's prior work at first, although he did learn of Babbage in 1939, when he tried to obtain a German patent on one of his first mechanical models. (The patent application was rejected.) By that time Zuse felt that he had progressed so far beyond what Babbage had done that he did not stand to gain much from a study of the Englishman's earlier work.[9]

Zuse graduated from the Technical College in 1935, with a degree in civil engineering, and he began working as a stress analyst for the Henschel Aircraft Company in Berlin. Once there he was faced with the same problem of analyzing indeterminate structures (this time aircraft wings) by solving systems of linear equations. His desire to mechanize the process, first kindled while a student, grew. He began actually constructing a device, turning a portion of the living room of his parents' house on Methfesselstrasse 10 (near the Tempelhof Airport) into a workshop. It was here where his first computers took form.

MECHANICAL CALCULATION, c. 1935

The heart of such a computer would be a calculating machine. How would one build it given the technology of the day? By the 1930's calculators had reached a mature stage of development. (In fact machines of that design continue to be used and sold to the present day.) There were many types available, but they all stored and manipulated numbers by toothed gears or racks, the number of teeth varying from zero to nine according to the decimal digit represented. Mechanical linkages carried a digit from one column to another in the course of an addition (a principle first used by Schickard and Pascal in the early 17th century).[10]

What differences there were among commercial machines centered around the problem of a carry of 1 from one column to the next (or a corresponding "borrow" of 1 during subtraction). Especially troublesome was the case where a carry propagated itself across several columns, as in the sum

$$1 + 99999 = 100000.$$

It was here that the machinery was most likely to jam.

Another difference was in the way the calculators handled multiplication. Most treated it as a repeated addition column by column, building up the partial products step by step. Another method was to compute the partial products directly, just as human beings are taught to do in grade school. The machine is somehow "taught" the multiplication table, using mechanical linkages, metal plates, or whatever, so that it at once generates a complete partial product for each digit of the multiplier.

But just as learning the times table is never easy for most school children, it is mechanically complex to get a machine to know it. So the direct multiplication method was rarely used, even though it was much faster than the method of repeated addition.

These two questions, how to carry digits from column to column, and how to perform multiplication, dominated all discussion of mechanized calculation when Zuse began his work. Others besides Zuse were also thinking of designing fully automatic calculating systems; with few exceptions they all took a mechanical decimal calculator as a starting point, and so these issues were of central concern to them as well.

THE PATH TO THE FIRST COMPUTER

With a degree in civil engineering, Zuse had a command of mechanics and technical drawing, but he knew little of electrical engineering and even less of the principles of mechanical calculators. He was taught the mathematics necessary for his field, but that did not include the recent advances in symbolic logic and set theory that would one day form the heart of computer science. (Germany—especially Göttingen, where David Hilbert taught mathematics—was at the center of those activities.) Zuse's ignorance of calculating machine construction may have been to his benefit; as it turned out, his approach was fresh, original, and not hindered by what experts said could not be done. His ignorance of advanced mathematics may have been a hindrance at first, but it did not remain so long.

The first step he took to implement his ideas turned out to be the most important. That was to abandon the use of mechanical devices which stored numbers by assuming one of ten physical positions, in favor of a simpler system which could assume not ten but only two positions in total. He was thinking of something like a switch that was either on or off, or a lever that was either forward or back.

Thus from the start Zuse was committed to using the binary system of enumeration for his machine. (He never seems to have considered using the decimal or any other base.) He came to the idea not as a mathematician but as a mechanical engineer concerned with keeping the physical apparatus as simple as possible.

The binary system is so central to modern computers that it is hard to realize what a radical and unexpected step it was when first introduced. Our familiar decimal system had been used so long that it was assumed to be almost God-given, a stage on which further arithmetic and mathematics was to be played out. Only when someone provided a mathematical analysis of the decimal system, showing that each digit of a number represents a successive power of ten, did the idea occur that one could use other numbers as a basis, including the simplest case of the base two.

As early as 1680 Leibniz worked out the binary number progression and how to perform arithmetic in that base. He mentioned in his writings that it would be possible to mechanize binary arithmetic, but his famous calculator used the ordinary decimal, not binary, system. (Indeed it was such a successful design that it was used as a model for decimal calculators for centuries thereafter.) For his philosophical writings and for his work on binary logic, not for his construction of a decimal calculator, Norbert Wiener called Leibniz "the patron saint of cybernetics."[11]

Whether or not Zuse got his idea of using binary arithmetic from his knowledge of Leibniz is hard to say. Certainly Leibniz would have been more familiar to a German student than to an Englishman or to an American, but his fame at that time came not from his discovery of binary logic but from his independent discovery of the calculus. Most of his writings on binary arithmetic remained unpublished until recently, when the computer revolution spawned a renewed interest in them. Nor does the fact that Zuse knew of Leibniz's work mean that he would have grasped its significance. A hundred years before, Babbage had studied the works of Leibniz intensively, and had even joined a society at Cambridge devoted to the promotion of Leibniz's work in the calculus. Yet Babbage never considered any but a decimal base for his Analytical and Difference Engines.

One of Zuse's school friends, Walther Buttmann, recalls having searched the library of the University of Berlin (to which he, but not Zuse, had access), for Leibniz's writings on binary arithmetic.[12] So we know that Zuse at least was aware of those first halting steps Leibniz took toward a non-decimal number system.

Why was abandoning the decimal system so advantageous? After all, humans learn not binary but decimal numeration, and would certainly shy away from any machine that did not use a base of ten. One obvious advantage is that it is easier to design and construct mechanical elements that assume only two instead of ten positions. That was the main reason Zuse chose the binary system. The problem of machining the computer's parts to a fine tolerance (the problem which undid Babbage's dreams) is much less acute when only two states are needed.

Another advantage, not nearly as obvious, is that yes-or-no elements can also be used to make up the other elements of a computer, especially those that control it. A computer is not just a calculator; it must also direct the course of the calculations it performs. Control devices, which specify what arithmetic operations the calculator performs on a given number, would not at first glance seem to have anything to do with arithmetic devices, and in a decimal computer that is indeed the case. They do different things and they are made out of different basic elements. But the operations of control, when simplified to their most elemental forms, are also two-fold, yes-or-no decisions, and so can be expressed as binary quantities. So with a binary computer the same physical elements can be used: simple two-position levers or switches throughout. It is much easier to visualize and design a machine to carry out an alternating sequence of arithmetic and control operations that make up the process of computing.

Now in such a long sequence, the machine ought to manipulate and transfer numbers from one of its parts to another without any human intervention. The human operator sees the numbers only at the beginning of a computation, when he supplies the input variables, and at the end, when he gets the answer. Those are the times, of course, when the numbers should be in the decimal form. But in a long computation, those two conversions make up only a small fraction of the total computing that the machine does. Intermediate results remain in binary and need not be converted (they are "among their fellows," Zuse said).[13] He recognized a fundamental difference between a computer and a calculator: the user of a calculator sees and handles all numbers the machine uses; the user of a computer does not. Converting each number to and from binary is time-consuming, but a computer does not have to do that.

In late 1936 Zuse began building a computer. He worked in the evening in his living-room workshop, after a day's work at Henschel. He enlisted the help of a few friends (Helmut Schreyer, Andreas Grohmann, and Walther Buttmann), who had faith in his idea—even if they did not fully understand what he was doing.[14]

Their first task was to build a memory device that could accept and store numbers during a calculation. That was actually the simplest part of the machine, since a memory unit only has to represent binary digits without having to provide for the carry of a digit from one place to another. Zuse devised a system in which slots cut in a metal plate stored a number. The position of a pin in each slot represented a binary digit; on one side it was a binary "1", on the other a binary "0". Another plate could be engaged against the pins to sense their position, thereby "reading" the number stored therein, or "writing" numbers into the memory by moving the pins. A third plate, set at right angles to the second, activated the reading and writing functions, by moving the pins to a position where the read/write plate became active (see Figure 2.4).[15]

Zuse wanted a memory with a fairly large capacity. He decided that the first test device should have an accuracy of sixteen binary digits, corresponding to about four or five decimal digits (less than what ordinary decimal calculators had, but about the same as a slide rule). So he and his friends spent many an evening cutting out the slots in the metal plates—over a thousand were needed.

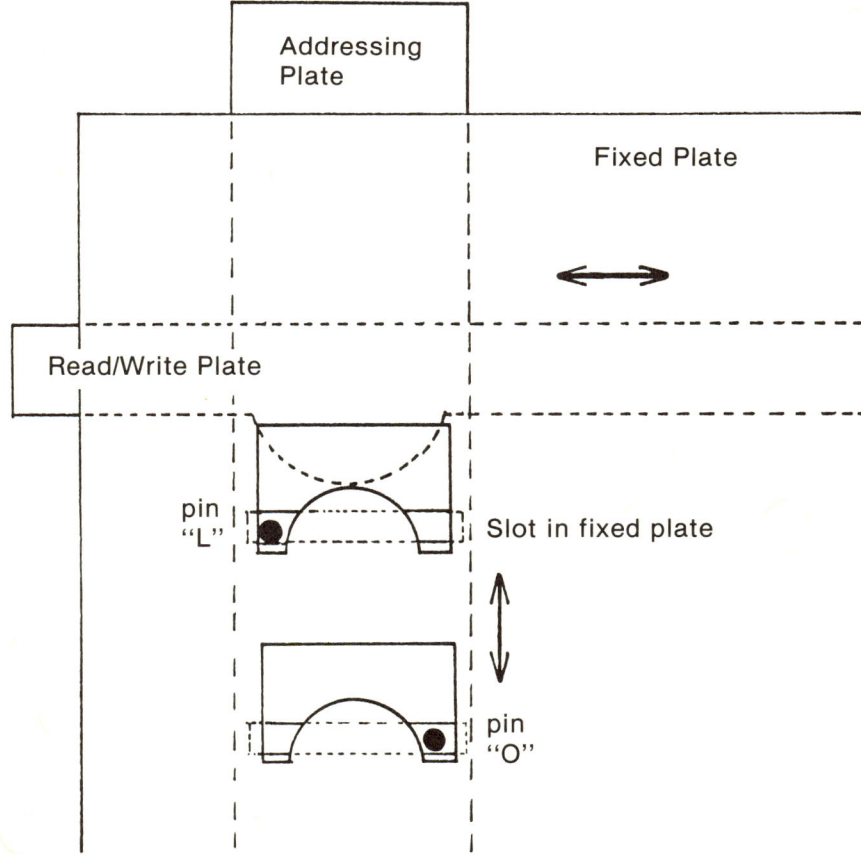

Figure 2.4. Binary Memory Device

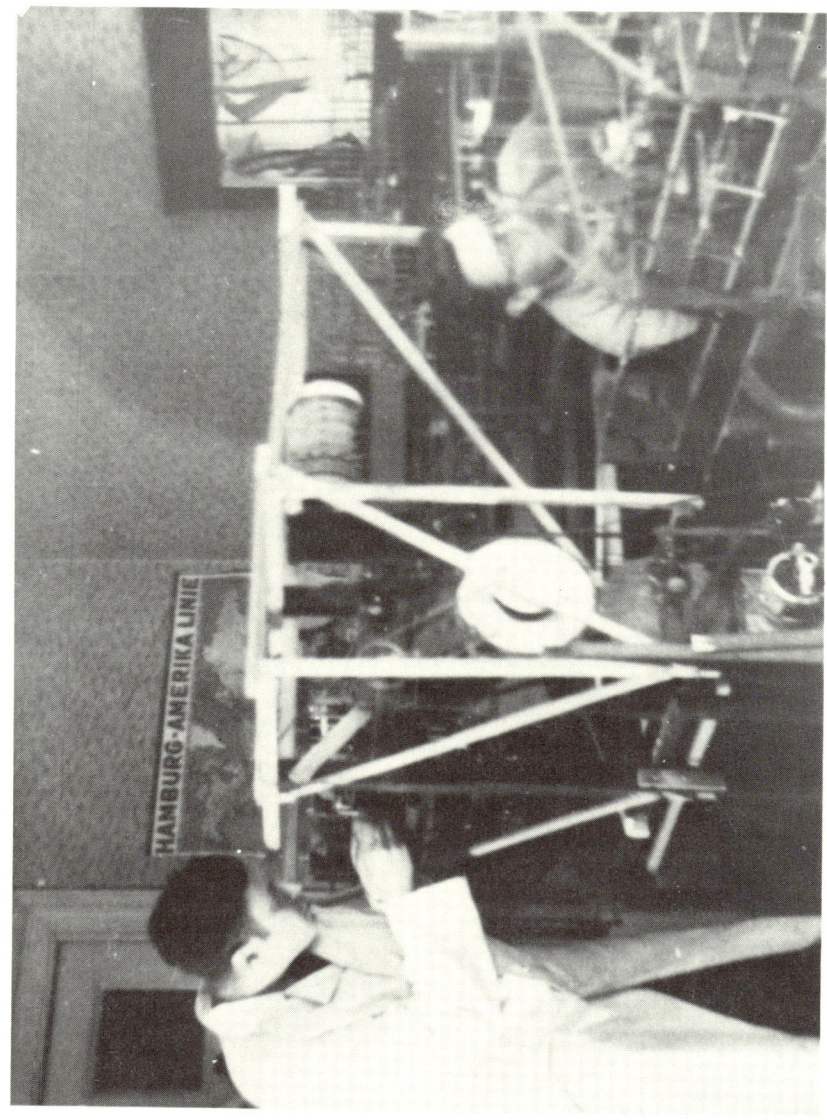

Konrad Zuse (right) and Helmut Schreyer (left) at Work in Zuse's Parents' Apartment, Berlin. Courtesy of Gesellschaft für Mathematik und Datenverarbeitung, Zuse Archiv.

Andreas Grohmann recalls that task, remembering how important was the need to cut the plates accurately:

> Kuno [Zuse] drew the form on paper exactly. I pasted the paper on a plywood board, then placed the desired number of plates between it and another board that lay under it. I then screwed the boards together, and sawed out the form of the relays [slots] with a small electric fretsaw. I made these relays by the thousands.[16]

The memory unit worked. Neither Grohmann nor the others were skilled machinists, and they did not have more than basic hand tools to work with. Their success was due first of all to the modest size of Zuse's machine. But more than that it was due to the simple design that only the binary system can provide.[17]

Building the arithmetic unit proved to be more difficult. Here it was necessary to link each digit with its two neighbors, in the event of a carry during addition.

One place where the use of binary arithmetic does not simplify matters is the case of a carry propagating itself through a whole number. The addition

$$1 + 11111 = 100000$$

is mechanically just as complex as the decimal

$$1 + 99999 = 100000.$$

The question of how to implement multiplication, which so baffled calculator manufacturers, interestingly does not come up at all in binary. The binary multiplication table is so simple ($1 \times 1 = 1$; all other products are 0) that it is trivially easy to teach it to a machine. But the price of this simplicity is that the summing of partial products is much more lengthy in binary than in decimal. All multiplication reduces to the addition of partial products.

Zuse has often told the story of how he approached a manufacturer named Kurt Pannke for financial support. Pannke asked what system Zuse's machine used to perform multiplication—table look-up or repeated addition. Zuse told him the two schemes were identical. By using two as a number base he "solved" the problem, as Alexander the Great cut (he did not untie) the Gordian Knot. Pannke was not impressed; he thought that Zuse might be trying to swindle him. But after Zuse explained binary multiplication to him he recognized the principle, and was sufficiently impressed by it to supply much of the money used to build Zuse's first computers.[18]

There remained the problem of connecting the arithmetic unit to the other parts of the computer. He had already used up all three spatial dimensions for the arithmetic itself; where would he add more linkages to transfer numbers into and out of the arithmetic unit? Whatever he added had to be kept as close to the other elements as possible; at some point the amount of "play" those elements introduced into the system would render it inoperable.

So at that stage of work Zuse began by first making a sketch on paper of the functions and linkages of the arithmetic unit, disregarding for the moment their physical locations in space. He devised a symbolic notation to describe the action of individual two-state mechanical elements, borrowing a notation then in common use to describe electromagnetic relays.

Relays are also fundamentally binary devices, and it would have been possible to build his computer out of them rather than out of mechanical plates. But that was not his reason for using the relay notation, at least not at first. Relays were not cheap, and any computer of adequate size would need thousands of them. They also took up quite a bit of space and would have required a hefty supply of electric power. Besides, Zuse was not as familiar with relays as he was with mechanical devices. He had, after all, already built a reliable and compact mechanical memory.

But just the same, he chose at least the symbolic representation of relays because of its great flexibility. Relay circuits, being linked to one another by wires, do not have to be physically close to one another, as do mechanical linkages.

Using the symbolic notation of a relay, Zuse worked out the basic operations of the arithmetic unit of his computer in terms of elemental yes-no operations. In this way he could set out exactly what he had to build before he began cutting out any metal plates. He called the notation that he developed the "Conditional Combinatoric" (*Bedingungskombinatorik*) (see Figure 2.5).[19]

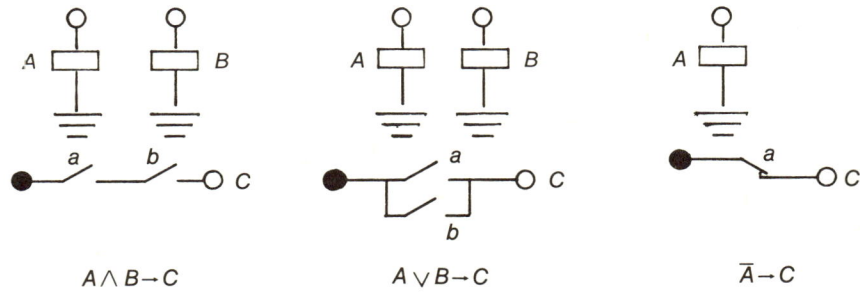

Figure 2.5. The Conditional Combinatoric

So by 1938 Konrad Zuse had made three fundamental decisions that would characterize his work for the coming decade. The first was his overall plan for the structure of a computer (Figure 2.3). The second was his decision to use the binary system. The third was his development of a symbolic notation by which he could express the machine's functions, especially those of arithmetic and control.

His Conditional Combinatoric combined the rules of binary arithmetic with those for expressing simple logical statements. Zuse referred to the binary states of his calculus not as "one" and "zero," implying only numerical information, or "true" and "false," implying only logical information, but as the letters "*L*" and "*O*," implying either. From the standpoint of a mechanical engineer, thinking of levers or relays, there was obviously no difference.

In the Conditional Combinatoric, the expression

$$(A,B) => C$$

would be fulfilled (logically "true," numerically "one") when either *A* or *B* was true. The expression

$$[A,B] => C$$

would be fulfilled only when both *A* and *B* were true. The expression

$$-A$$

would have the opposite value of *A*, whatever that was. The following expression yields the algebraic sign of the product of two numbers, assuming that the value "true" represents "+" and "false" represents "−":

$$[(Lm,Ld), ([Vx,Vy], [-Vx,-Vy])] => Vr$$

The expression says that the sign (*V*) of the result (*r*) is positive for the operations of multiplication (*m*) or division (*d*), when either the signs of *x* and *y* are both positive or both negative. Note that the result of the operation appears at the right, and is indicated by the arrow formed by typing an equals sign and a greater-than sign. This convention indicates the dynamic aspect of what actually goes on in a machine, and is the opposite of the way mathematical functions are ordinarily written (with the function name at the left and an equals sign joining it to an expression on the right). Zuse's convention avoids confusing equality and the assignment of a value, a confusion that many modern programming languages exhibit. (There was an attempt to have a right-pointing assignment statement in the programming language ALGOL, but it was never adopted. This question will be discussed again in Chapter 6.)[20]

The conditional chains intended to form the basis for Zuse's computer were the three primitive logical operations: conjunction (the square brackets), disjunction (the parentheses), and negation (the minus sign), corresponding to the logical "and" statement (true only when both statements are true), logical "or" (true when either statement is true), and logical "not" (true when the statement is false, and vice versa). He also combined those primitive statements into a logical equivalence statement, true only when each elemental part of the statement has the same truth value, both true or both false (as in the example of the sign in multiplication).

Mathematicians knew further that chains of these primitive logical statements could express the laws of ordinary arithmetic as well. Since before the turn of the century there had been an effort to show that *all* mathematics was reducible to a logical basis. As with the discovery of binary arithmetic, that too had its roots in the work of Leibniz. In a remarkable anticipation of the computer age, Leibniz had attempted to construct a universal language, a *Lingua Charactera*, in which both logical and numerical information could be expressed. But like his exposition of binary arithmetic that idea was all but forgotten by 1935.[21]

In Germany in the 1930's, Göttingen was the center of efforts to establish a logical foundation for mathematics. There David Hilbert and W. Ackermann led the "formalist" school of mathematics with their *Foundations of Theoretical Logic*, published in 1928. In the English-speaking world Alfred North Whitehead and Bertrand Russell, in their *Principia Mathematica*, stated an even bolder "logicist" case.

But Zuse was unaware of those works, including Hilbert's, even though those ideas were at the center of a vigorous debate going on concerning the nature of modern mathematics. When Zuse wrote to his former mathematics teacher, a Professor Naumann, and told him of his "Conditional Combinatoric," Naumann informed him that he had just independently rediscovered what Hilbert had already described as the "Propositional Calculus."[22] Naumann further suggested that Zuse study Hilbert and Ackermann's book, which he promptly did, finding in it what would become the theoretical basis for his further efforts to construct a working computer.

So with the help of the Propositional Calculus (nee Conditional Combinatoric), Konrad Zuse could write out the arithmetic and control operations that he wanted his computer to perform, and manipulate those expressions without worrying about how they would be implemented. Only at the final step, after the operations were specified and put into their simplest form, would the "words be made flesh"—put into the form of mechanical pieces that would actually carry out those functions. The mechanical world that he would build would be one generated by mathematical statements—that was a reversal of ordinary applied mathematics, in which the equations described a world already there. Zuse proposed the name "logistic" (as mathematical logic was known in Germany) to describe it; it might well have been called "computer science," which is hardly a better phrase. (In Europe today computer science goes by the name "Informatics.")[23]

CONSTRUCTION OF THE FIRST COMPUTERS

Now to return to the problem of getting metal plates and levers to obey those logical expressions. With the help of the Propositional Calculus it was possible to simplify expressions to the point where they could be made up of *and*, *or*, and *not* statements. That may not be the shortest or most concise form, but those statements are the easiest to implement mechanically, by a system of interlocking bars (see Figure 2.6).

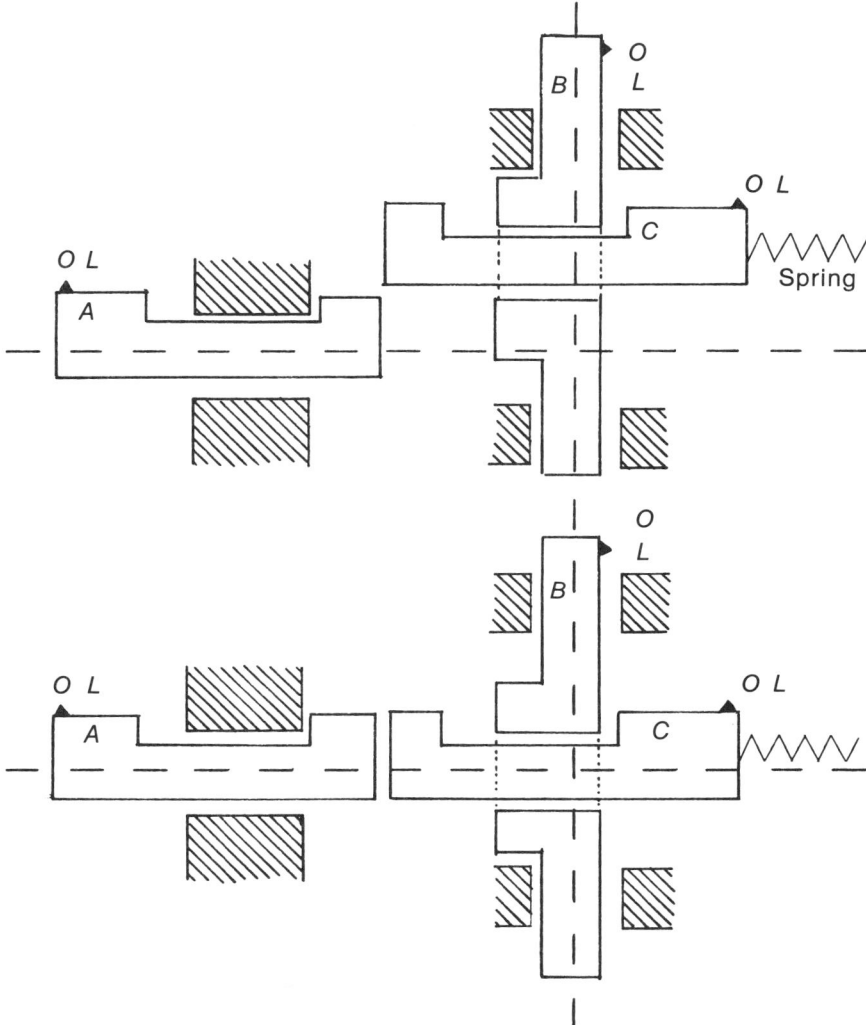

Figure 2.6. Mechanical Implementation of an "and" Statement

But despite the aid of the Propositional Calculus, the job proved to be difficult. Zuse completed a small mechanical arithmetic and control unit in 1938 and joined it to the mechanical memory he had constructed the year before. It did not work very well. But it was a start. (Later on, he called that device his "V1," for the German "Experimental Machine One" [*Versuchsmodell 1*]. After the war he called his machines "Z1," "Z2," etc., to avoid confusion with the V-1 and V-2 rockets that Wernher von Braun had built.) The V1 worked just well enough to convince Zuse that he was on the right track, but it also convinced him that mechanical computing elements were too difficult to get to work reliably. They were all right for the memory, but for the other units of the computer he began looking for a better method.

Throughout those early days in Zuse's home workshop, he could always rely on the help of Helmut Schreyer, a college mate, a student of electrical engineering, and a handsome amateur actor of considerable charm. Schreyer was one of those who helped cut out all the metal plates for the Z1. While a student Schreyer had worked as a film projectionist—he and Zuse were especially fond of the sensational American film *King Kong*, then just released in Germany. He remembered that in a movie projector, the film advances through a gate where each frame is stopped for a moment so that it can be projected on the screen. That was precisely the kind of motion the programming unit of Zuse's computer needed—a quick reading of the calculating plan, one command at a time. From then on Zuse designed his computers to have their programs supplied by perforated movie film instead of paper tape. (Discarded 35mm film was cheaper than commercial paper tape anyway.)[24]

From Schreyer's training as an electrical engineer came a conviction that electrical computing elements could be made to work much better than Zuse's mechanical elements. Schreyer had a confidence and familiarity with telephone relays that Zuse did not have. Telephone relays were not that expensive—a few dollars each—but remember, thousands would be required. Nevertheless he convinced Zuse to adopt them. They managed to find very cheap second-hand telephone relays and they rebuilt them to work in a computer. Zuse had already been using the relay notation as a design aid, so the transition was not hard to make. In 1938 and 1939 Zuse pressed on with that approach: a mechanical memory, an arithmetic and control unit made of relays, and program control by perforated 35mm movie film.

Schreyer went one step further. Why not build the binary functions out of vacuum tube circuits? Up until that time tubes were used to amplify continuous signals, but he knew he could build a tube circuit that would have the same on-or-off properties that relays and mechanical linkages have. Such a "tube relay," as he called it, would switch by moving streams of electrons and would be many times faster than any electromechanical relay.

By that time Zuse was convinced that his chances of success with telephone relays were too good to pass up. There was a lot of developmental work needed to perfect the "tube relay" circuit, which he was not willing to undertake. Schreyer in turn suggested to Professor Stäblein at the Berlin Technical College that an investigation of the electronic switching circuit be the subject of his doctoral thesis. Stäblein agreed, and in 1941 Schreyer was awarded a doctoral degree for his thesis, "The Tube Relay and the Techniques of its Switching." Figures 2.7 and 2.8 show two of the circuits that Schreyer built.[25]

The key to their operation was the use of a gas-filled lamp which conducted only after a certain threshold of voltage was passed; but once conducting, it would

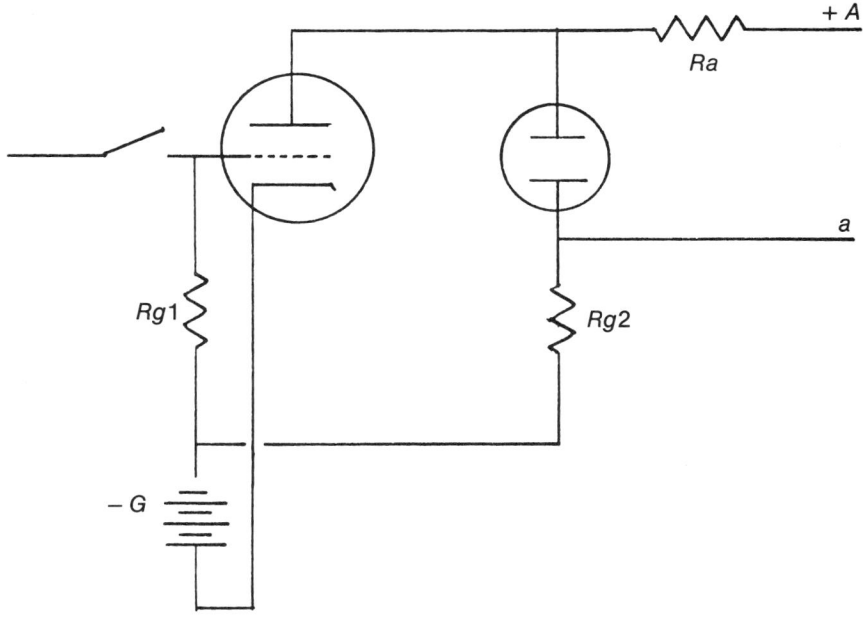

Figure 2.7. Basic Vacuum Tube Switching Circuit

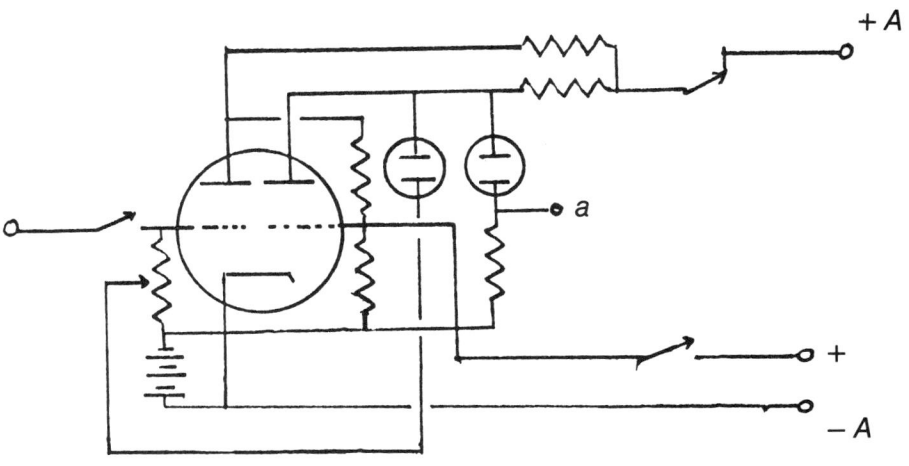

Figure 2.8. Bistable Switching Circuit

continue to conduct with a lower "holding" voltage flowing through it. (The familiar fluorescent light is such a lamp; it requires a "starter" to turn it on.) This threshold effect gives the circuit two well-defined states, analogous to the open and closed positions of a relay and quite unlike the continuous output of an ordinary vacuum-tube circuit.

While Konrad Zuse was going ahead with a calculating unit that used telephone relays, Schreyer proposed to build one out of vacuum tubes, using, of course, Zuse's overall design and the binary scale. He managed to obtain special tubes well suited for his circuits from the Telefunken Company. But when he submitted his proposal for a full-scale computer to the German Army Command (OKH) in 1942, he was turned down. At that time, the German authorities thought the war would be over within the two or three years Schreyer knew it would take to complete the machine. And they did not want to fund anything that would not directly benefit the waging of the war. The proposed machine was to have about 1,500 tubes, and as many glow-lamps.[26]

The story of Schreyer's attempt to build an electronic computer in Germany during the war is one of the more interesting "what-ifs" of that entire period. By 1942 he was working independently of Zuse, and had his proposal been accepted, Germany might have had a working electronic computer before either the Americans or the British. It was true that his circuits were not as fast, nor was his proposed machine as large as the American ENIAC, but with his use of Zuse's elegant overall design, and especially with his use of the binary system, he might have come up with a very powerful computer.

So for a moment, then, Schreyer cracked open the door to an awesome and strange new world, but that door slammed shut before he could pass through. Only after the war did a now-divided Germany enter the electronic computer age, but as a follower, not a leader.

All that Schreyer built was a test model containing about 150 tubes that converted three-digit decimal numbers to and from binary. (It was financed not by the army but by the Aerodynamics Research Institute.) It was damaged in a bombing attack on Berlin in late 1943, and with Schreyer's evacuation from Berlin in 1945, Germany's first steps toward electronic computing came to an end. After the war Schreyer left Germany and abandoned work on computers. (Konrad Zuse was not a member of the Nazi Party, but Helmut Schreyer was: he had joined in 1933. After the war he emigrated to Rio de Janeiro, where he worked for Brazil's telecommunications network, and where he still lives.)[27]

Schreyer has since reflected on what might have been. The American ENIAC project was given a go-ahead in the middle of the war, and its builders were given all the manpower and money they needed to see it through (not without some difficulty, as we shall see). They did not complete their machine until after the war was over either. But by that time no one really cared that it was late—there were other jobs it could do. Getting a machine running in time to help the war effort *would* have been an issue for the Germans, who were losing badly after 1943. Schreyer was never able to assemble a team of qualified helpers, and this, coupled with the lack of money, killed the chances for success. In this regard Zuse made the right choice to stay with second-hand telephone relays, since he could get by with more modest resources. Zuse had already faced the same problems convincing the German authorities of the importance of his work; in the fall of 1939 he was drafted into the infantry and sent to the front, but was soon recalled to work as an aircraft engineer. Schreyer wrote a letter to the German authorities to help get Zuse back to Berlin. The letter describes the potential benefits of Zuse's computer work, and, incidentally, is one of the earliest known documents describing the operation and programming of an automatic computer.[28]

Zuse built a small binary arithmetic unit out of second-hand telephone relays, joining it to the mechanical memory of his "V1." The results were encouraging enough to convince him that a full-scale computer could be built along those lines and would work well. He approached the Aerodynamics Research Institute (DVL) for help. They were not interested in a general-purpose computer, but they did have a computational problem which, as they said, "was burning their fingertips," it was so urgent. That was the wing-flutter problem, one which Zuse had already encountered while at the Henschel plant. At certain high speeds the wings of a plane would resonate—flutter like a flag in the wind. To prevent their failure one had to design the wings so that their resonant frequency was higher than the speeds the plane would ever encounter in flight. Airplane wings are not "static" structures, but the analysis of their resonance can be done by treating the wing like a static indeterminate structure such as a bridge or a roof. In both cases the analysis requires the solution of large systems of linear equations. For an airplane wing the coefficients are complex numbers, taking into account the phase of the pressure waves of air across it.[29]

Zuse invited Alfred Teichmann of the DVL to his parents' apartment to have a look at his machine (now called the "V2"). It ran well enough to impress Teichmann (Zuse claims it never worked again!), and so the DVL agreed to help finance a completely new machine. Before building it Zuse decided to build one more "provisonal" test machine—this one using telephone relays for both memory and for arithmetic—one which would incorporate all the features of his original design for a general-purpose programmable computer. He still relied mostly on his own funds and still worked in his home workshop, but with the encouragement of the DVL, he proceeded at once to build a relay computer that functioned reliably in every respect. It was completed by December, 1941, and was the first fully operational program-controlled computing machine in the world. It is now known as the Z3 computer.[30]

DESCRIPTION OF THE Z3

Like Schreyer's electronic circuits, the Z3 did not survive the war. It was destroyed in a bombing raid on Zuse's workshop in 1945. What little we can find out about that historic machine must be gleaned from the patent applications he filed for it, and from personal recollections from those who saw it in use. In 1961 a replica of the Z3 was reconstructed for the German Museum of Technology, in Munich, and although it is not an exact copy, it does give a good idea of what the original Z3 must have looked like.[31]

The reconstructed Z3 reveals three large units: two relay cabinets, and a keyboard/display panel. Just to the right of the keyboard is the device that read in programs from perforated movie film. The original had two racks of relays for the storage of sixty-four numbers, not just one rack, as the replica has. Each memory cabinet was six feet high and three feet wide. On the whole the Z3 was a modest machine, nothing like some of the "giant brains" that later would be built in America.

The size of the cabinets that held the Z3's memory reveals why Zuse was reluctant to abandon a mechanical approach. He knew that a full-scale computer having sufficient power to do useful work would need far more than sixty-four memory cells—a thousand was a more realistic requirement. But to store 1,024 numbers (as he planned for his next machine) using relays would have required thirty-two cabinets like the one used for the Z3's memory. That would have taken up a lot of room and needed a lot of power. Zuse returned to a mechanical store for his Z4, which eventually stored 512 numbers in a very compact and reliable unit. He never seriously considered building a computer on the huge scale of the ENIAC or the Harvard Mark I.

All computing and storage in the Z3 was done with ordinary telephone relays, although their contacts were carefully adjusted so that their opening and closing times were all within a specific range. This was necessary to synchronize the running of the whole system.

These telephone relays are two-position switches, open or closed. Telephone networks also use other relays, which have more than two positions. (In all but the newest telephone networks, rotary-dial phones make a connection by activating such multi-position relay switches.) The Z3 also used eight of these "uniselectors," as the telephone company called them; they were mounted in the enclosed area at the bottom of the right-hand relay cabinet. These switches controlled some of the detailed sub-operations of multiplication, division, and taking the square root; addition and subtraction were handled entirely by binary relays.

The Z3 had a total of about 2,600 relays: 1,800 for the memory, 600 for the arithmetic, and 200 for the film reader, keyboard, and display. Assuming that the relays cost about two dollars apiece, then Zuse must have spent about fifty-two hundred dollars for relays alone. Other materials costs may have added another thousand dollars. There were also labor costs, although Zuse and his friends donated hours and hours of their time. Considering the materials alone the Z3 probably cost between six and seven thousand dollars, a figure that agrees with estimates Zuse gave to the DVL. (He said that he had spent around twenty-five thousand Reich Marks for the machine.)[32] That is a lot less than the cost of any other comparable device built in those years.

The relays were purchased second-hand, cleaned, and synchronized with one another. They required 60 volts DC, supplied synchronously to all parts of the computer by a rotating drum mounted below the arithmetic cabinet. Each rotation of the drum directed one full operation of the computer, such as the storage of a number into a memory cell.

The drum could be spun at varying speeds, up to a limit of five cycles per second (300 RPM). It could be slowed down to a single step at a time, useful if someone wanted to trace a computation step by step.[33]

The drum controlling the flow of current through the machine was set up so that current was sent to the relays only after they had switched. This so-called current-free (*stromlos*) method of switching prevented arcing at the relay contacts, and so made the machine more reliable. (When any large currents are switched, arcing can occur at the moment of switching, when the connection is only partially made. By having all current switched at the rotating drum, any contact wear is now shifted to the carbon brushes on the drum, and these are inexpensive and easy to replace.)

That principle made the Zuse computers extraordinarily reliable—they could run for months without needing repairs. Telephone relays are simple devices not prone to failure, but to use them in a computer requires more reliability than a telephone system needs. Unlike in a telephone system, the relays in a computer must work every time; furthermore those relays go through more cycles in just one hour of computing than they might in a week of telephone use.[34]

A DETAILED LOOK AT THE Z3

Figure 2.9 shows the calculator-style keyboard and display panel of the Z3 replica. Numbers were keyed in by pressing the appropriate buttons on the lower panel; results were read from the upper panel, which contained small incandescent light bulbs for each decimal digit. In both input and output the numbers were represented in their floating-point, decimal form, with the decimal point assumed to be after the first digit in the first column, and the power of ten indicated by a row of buttons or lamps along the bottom of each panel. The Z3 had a decimal accuracy of four decimal places, with a range of $10^{\pm 9}$ (answers could range farther, to $10^{\pm 12}$).

The keyboard also had buttons for the four ordinary operations of arithmetic, plus square root, divide or multiply by ten, divide or multiply by two, and multiply by -1. (Some of these functions were not built into the replica.) When a number was keyed into the machine, it was converted into its floating-point, binary form before being stored or used for a calculation. On the replica this binary number was indicated by a set of twenty-two lights on the arithmetic relay rack.

Additional lights on the display panel were for special results. Lights at either end of the exponent field indicated when the results overflowed or underflowed the machine's capacity. If the machine was told to take the square root of a

*The Reconstructed Z3 at the German Museum, Munich.
Courtesy of Gesellschaft für Mathematik und Datenverabeitung, Zuse Archiv.*

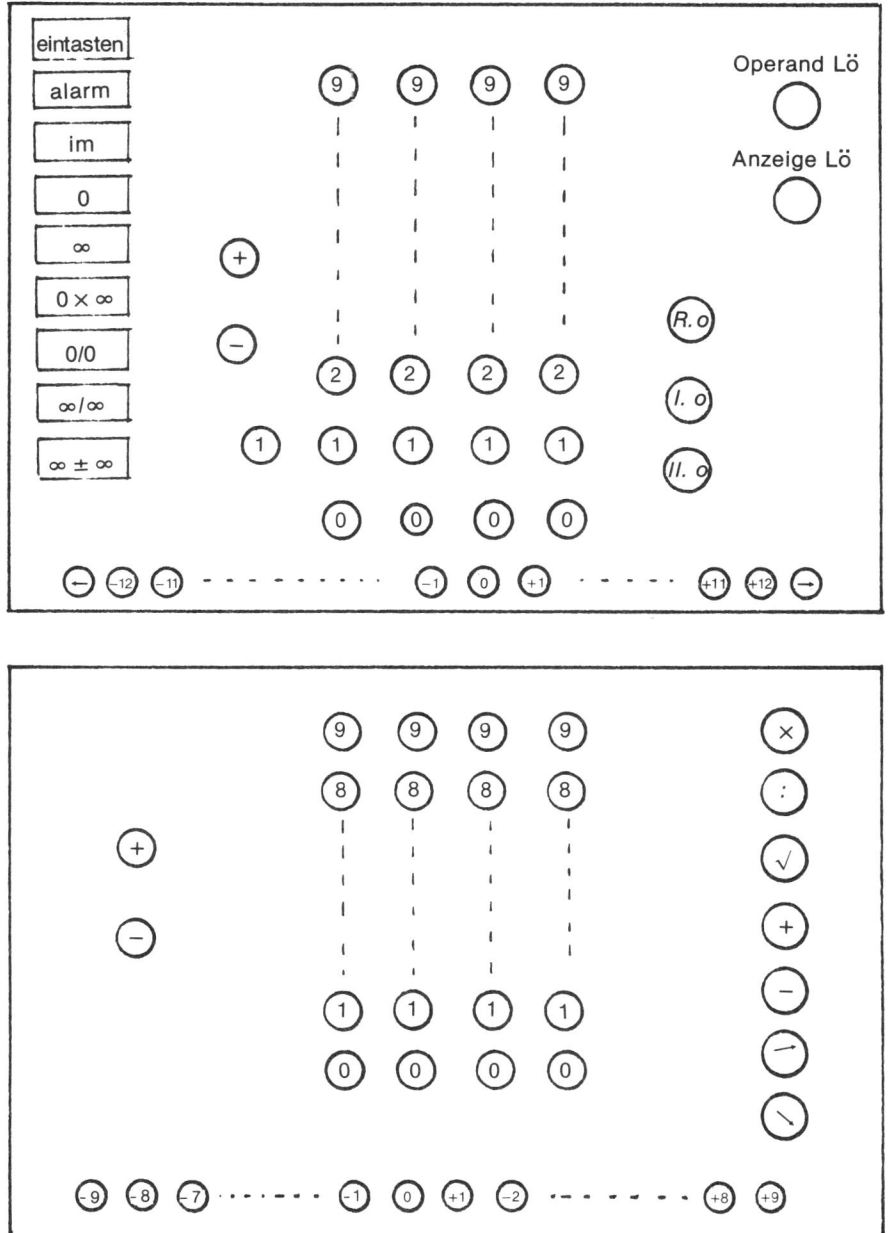

Figure 2.9. Display (above) and Keyboard (below) of Z3

negative number, the display "im" for "imaginary" would light up. (The Z3 did not automatically handle complex numbers, although of course one could write a program to do that. Since the analysis of the flutter problem involves matrices that have one or more complex elements, it was likely that Zuse eventually wanted his computers to handle those numbers).

There was also a special light for true zero, since in floating-point arithmetic, true zero cannot otherwise be represented (0.000×10^0 may mean a number as large as 0.0005).

If division by zero occurred during a computation, a special display for "infinity" would light up (∞). Similar displays indicated indeterminate results such as $\infty \times 0$, $0 \div 0$, or $\infty \div \infty$. In certain cases these quantities would factor out of a computation, so their presence would not necessarily mean a wrong answer. This feature has been implemented in several modern computers, including the CDC 6600, but it has not become universally adopted.[35]

Programs were read into the Z3 by a simple device that sensed the presence of holes in a strip of film. A hole stood for the binary value "1" or " + "; no hole for "0" or " − ." The film was prepared by a simple manual punch having eight buttons, one for each channel of the filmstrip. The holes were staggered slightly to prevent tearing. For example, the number LOOLLLO would be punched into the film as follows:

L O O L
  L L L O

The film sensing device was built in Darmstadt with the help of Alwin Walther and W. de Beauclair, two of continental Europe's other computer pioneers.

Table 2.1 summarizes the specifications of the Z3.

Table 2.1. THE Z3

Technology: electromagnetic relays: 2600 binary: memory		1400
arithmetic		600
misc.		600
20 step switches		
Number System: floating-point binary		
word length: 22 binary digits: sign		1 bit
exponent		7 bits
mantissa		14 bits
Memory Capacity: 64 numbers		
random access		
Input/Output: push-button keyboard, display by incandescent bulbs, one for each decimal digit		
Programming: eight-channel perforated filmstrip, basic commands of +, −, ×, ÷, square root, shift binary or decimal point "zero-addressing" (see text)		

Table 2.1. *Continued*

Dates: completed 1941, destroyed 1945; replica built after original plans, 1963, now in German Museum, Munich
Place: Berlin, Methfesselstrasse 7 (near Tempelhof Airport)
Cost: 25,000 RM, or about $6,500
Speed: 3-5 seconds/multiplication
  clock frequency: 4-5 cycles/second

A person keyed floating-point decimal numbers into the Z3. It converted them into floating-point binary. The twenty-two relays that held a number were divided as follows: the first seven relays held the power of two, the next relay the algebraic sign of the number, and the remaining fourteen relays the mantissa of the number. In floating-point binary the first digit of the mantissa is always "1" (just as in floating-point decimal the first digit is never zero), so that "1" was not stored. The decimal number 398, for example, would be stored as:

$$398 = 110,001,110 \text{ in binary}$$
$$= 1.1000111 \times 10^{1000} \text{ in floating-point binary}$$

or, using Zuse's notation:

$$\underbrace{000L000}_{\text{exponent}} \quad \underset{\uparrow}{L} \quad \underbrace{L000LLL0000000}_{\text{mantissa (with leading L dropped)}}$$
$$\text{sign digit } (+)$$

Representing numbers by floating-point binary in the Z3 was its most interesting feature; it was something no other functional computer would have for years. As an engineer, Konrad Zuse recognized from the start that such a representation was better suited to the kinds of problems he faced, but to get a machine to handle numbers that way was not a simple task. Floating-point arithmetic has an additional effect of making the operation of addition slower (since the exponent has to be adjusted before the mantissae can be added to each other), while it makes multiplication a little faster (since one obtains the exponent of a product simply by adding the exponents of the two operands). In engineering calculations, multiplication occurs more frequently than it does in business or accounting work, so on the whole the Z3 was a more balanced machine given the kind of work it was designed to do.

Zuse called his representation "semi-logarithmic form," since the exponent may be thought of as the characteristic of the logarithm of the number.

PROGRAMMING THE Z3

Programming the Z3 is best illustrated by looking at the problems it was designed to solve, namely the evaluation of the determinant of a matrix. For the matrix

$$\begin{pmatrix} a & b & c \\ d & e & f \\ g & h & i \end{pmatrix}$$

the determinant is given by the following formula:

$$\text{Det} = (aei + bfg + cdh) - (ceg + bdi + afh)$$

To evaluate that expression using only pencil, paper, and slide rule, a person would perform the multiplications, additions, and subtractions as they appear in the formula above, writing down intermediate results along the way. (It is also possible to rearrange the expression slightly to minimize the number of intermediate results that has to be recorded.)

Programming the Z3 to compute the determinant was similar. A film strip having the same sequence of operations coded into it would be fed into the machine. The initial values would be placed manually into memory cells, and other memory cells would be used to store intermediate results for later use. The program would connect the calculating unit of the machine to the correct memory cells for each step of the problem.

The calculating unit did all the arithmetic; the memory unit only stored numbers. If the result of one calculation was needed for the very next calculation, there was no need to store it in the memory only to retrieve it immediately. In that case the number remained in the register of the calculating unit where it was needed anyway. Only numbers needed more than once or needed at some later step had to be stored in memory.

For an operation like multiplying two numbers together, the program would recall both numbers from memory and place them into registers in the calculating unit before it gave the command to multiply. Today this is known as "postfix" notation, in contrast to the more familiar "infix" notation of placing the operation between the two operands. Postfix notation is also found today in some pocket calculators, where it goes by the name of "reverse Polish" notation (after a Polish logician named Jan Łukasiewicz, who first proposed it for writing logical expressions in the 1920's). Zuse's machine was probably the first to employ postfix notation—his Z3 not only specified operations after the operands, it also contained circuits in its calculating unit that ensured that the operands were in the proper order for division and subtraction.[36] The Z3's arithmetic instruction set assumed that the operands were already in place in the calculating unit. In modern terms the Z3 had a "zero-address" coding scheme, since no memory address needed to be specified for an operation. (A sample Z3 program—and the same program for a modern calculator that uses postfix notation—is found in the Appendix, in section 1.)

It was not difficult to produce a coded filmstrip for a problem once the mathematical expression was given. So while only Zuse himself could service the machine, he hired others to program it. Because of the manpower shortages during the war, he wrote to an institute for the blind in Marburg and requested a list of blind people who were gifted in mathematics. From this list he hired August Fast to produce programs. Fast learned the job easily and so became one of Europe's first computer programmers.[37]

The Z3 was designed to test the feasibility of a machine that would solve the flutter problem for the Henschel Company. It passed that test. But it was also a general-purpose machine that could be programmed to solve other problems just as well, since the solution of the flutter problem was similar to the solutions of many other similar ones.

In Germany during the 1930's, H. G. Küssner had worked out a mathematical analysis of the wing-flutter problem by developing an iterative procedure whereby the determinant of a matrix (whose elements were complex numbers) was computed for successive values of approximate forces on a wing. When the determinant becomes zero, Küssner showed that the elements of the matrix equalled the actual forces on the wing. This method computed those forces without having to build a wing and test it in a wind-tunnel, which was the only other way to get that information.[38]

So the method required computing determinants, each time with slightly different matrix elements. In a 1941 report, Alfred Teichmann (who had seen Zuse's V2), compared the numerical method with the wind-tunnel method, saying, "A disadvantage of carrying out the flutter calculations is the huge expenditure of effort which it requires: 100-400 man-hours to calculate a simplified system."[39] Teichmann did not mention computers in that report, but he obviously saw the advantages of having a machine take over the job.

The Z3 was never put into routine use for that or any other problem. But it did run a number of test programs and did so reliably and without error. Several people visited Zuse in his home workshop and observed it in operation. Dr. Alwin Walther, H. J. Dreyer, and W. de Beauclair of the Institute for Applied Mathematics in Darmstadt saw it during a visit to Berlin, and of that visit de Beauclair has said: "On the ground floor of the house we saw it. It demonstrated for us the solution of a determinant. We were very much impressed; we probably never had even thought of this approach—binary, relays, punched tape control."[40] Dreyer remembers the machine as a series of racks on which the relays were mounted, there being a clear separation of units for memory, arithmetic, control, input, and output. He says further:

The Z3 was fully functional. For a series of different calculations there were program tapes available, for example for systems of linear equations. One could key in the coefficients, and the results were displayed. From my recollection it ran without error.[41]

That it was never put into routine use was due to its limited memory, which meant that it could not compute the determinant of large matrices where manual methods were impractical.

Such is the story of the Z3. It lived for about four years and never performed routine useful work, but it stood at the gateway to the computer age nonetheless. How significant was it? The modern computer owes far more to the American and British wartime machines than it does to the Z3. Indeed, its very existence was hardly known to historians or computer scientists until the 1960's.

None of that detracts from what the Z3 was: possibly the first machine to be programmable in a general way, to use the binary system, to use floating-point arithmetic, and to have an elegant logical design.

Actually the Z3 was only one part of the German contribution to computing; besides the prototype electronic circuits that Helmut Schreyer built during the war, there were several other relay machines that Zuse constructed which are also part of the story.

The Z3 was only a test machine, but Konrad Zuse also built a relay device that was put to practical use by the Henschel Company during the war. That was the so-called S1; a machine that carried out a fixed sequence of operations that Zuse permanently wired into its circuits.

The S1 was smaller than the Z3, using about 800 binary and 30 multi-position relays. It too worked in the binary system (fixed point), and had a memory of six cells. The fixed program it carried out was a sequence of sums of products. The computation aided the production of the Henschel HS-293, an unmanned flying bomb that was carried aloft by a bomber and then released and guided remotely to its target.[42]

In normal aircraft production, the wing and rudder surfaces must be machined accurately. But for an unmanned flying bomb that would have been too expensive. Instead, the wings were fabricated cheaply, with the understanding that there would be inaccuracies. These inaccuracies would be measured, and then the S1 would calculate how far the bomb would deviate from a straight path because of them. The wings and rudder could then be adjusted along a movable axis to compensate for the error, but no expensive refabrication would be necessary. The S1 took a set of about 100 measurements of the wing and calculated the resulting aerodynamic performance. When it was put into service at Henschel, it replaced a team of thirty to thirty-five women who worked with desk calculators. Human "computers" were a dying breed.

The flying bomb was successfully produced and deployed in large numbers toward the end of the war, especially against Allied shipping in the Mediterranean after August, 1943. It was also used in the German retreat from Poland in 1945. It made a modest contribution to the German war effort.[43]

Zuse built one other computing machine during the war that ranks with the Z3 as a pioneering computing device. That was the Z4, a full-scale relay machine that he started to build as soon as the Z3 demonstrated the feasibility of the overall design.

The Z4 (or V4, as it was known then) was to have been the full-scale general-purpose computer the DVL wanted for aircraft design. Its construction was begun in 1942, and it used the same design as the Z3, with a few differences.

One difference was that it was to have a longer word length—thirty-two binary digits instead of the Z3's twenty-two. This gave it an equivalent of seven decimal places, with a range of 10^{20} for both input and output.

But the main difference was its much larger memory: Zuse planned a capacity of up to 1,024 numbers, although that was not achieved. For that memory Zuse returned to a mechanical memory device, like the one he first built for his "V1" four years before. So the Z4 would have a memory unit that was about a third the size of one of the Z3's relay memory racks, yet it would have many times the memory. (Eventually a 512-cell store was built, having eight times the capacity of the Z3.) That capacity was far greater than anything being designed in America or England at the time.

Designing the Z4 was straightforward, but its construction was severely hampered by Allied bombing raids on Berlin after 1944. Zuse had to move it three times to different parts of Berlin; at least once he was moving it even as the building was being hit. (In one of those raids, on April 6, 1945, the Z3 was completely destroyed.)[44]

The Z4 was finally moved out of Berlin in early 1945, first to Göttingen (where it performed test computations), then to an underground fortification in the Harz Mountains, then to a village in the Bavarian Alps. There it stayed during the chaotic postwar years, until it was finally refurbished and put to work at the Federal Technical Institute in Zürich in 1950.[45] For a few years it was the only functional computer, electromechanical or otherwise, in continental Europe, and it initiated much of Europe's postwar activity in computing thereafter.

So despite incredible hardships and hard luck, the work of Konrad Zuse, Helmut Schreyer, and their co-workers was not totally lost. The Z4's influence was modest, but the machine worked well and was heavily used at Zürich, even after the computing world had turned from relay machines to the faster electronic technology. During his stay in Hinterstein, the Alpine village where the Z4 rested from 1945 to 1949, Konrad Zuse did not abandon work on computing. Work on the Z4 itself was impossible: even getting enough to eat was difficult in those years, and Zuse lacked the tools and manpower to do much more than just try and save what he had. He turned his attention to the problem of programming computers—pencil-and-paper work that few at the time thought was crucial to making use of a computer's power. Today the cost of writing programs for computers far exceeds the cost of the machinery itself. Now that the computing world faces this "software crisis," it should be remembered that here, too, Konrad Zuse made original contributions. His work on a "Plan calculus," begun in 1945, was one of the first attempts to design a programming language for a computer.[46]

After the Z4 was installed in Zürich in 1950, Zuse founded a private firm that made and sold relay machines to industrial and educational customers. For the Leitz Optical works he built a relay machine that he called the Z5, and after that he built a series of other relay computers, the last being the Z11, built in the mid-1950's. His company also built electronic computers, and for a while it prospered. In the 1960's it had trouble raising capital and was absorbed into the Siemens company. That left Konrad Zuse free once again to pursue the theoretical side of computing. He is still active, a remarkable feat in a field that is so volatile and fast-developing.[47]

So what do we have in the story of the first computers in Germany? They are not the ancestors of the modern computer; that honor goes elsewhere. But their overall design and their use of binary numbers and floating-point arithmetic make them resemble the modern computer far more than an ancestor like the ENIAC does. The German story is a fascinating one, and it has a lesson for us as well. The key concepts of computing were discovered independently in different places by different persons. That the present computer world bears the imprint of the American projects was not inevitable; things could have turned out very differently.

NOTES

1. Konrad Zuse, *Der Computer, Mein Lebenswerk* (Munich: Verlag Moderne Industrie, 1970) p. 68.

2. Zuse, *Der Computer*, pp. 15-16; C. Evans, interview with Zuse, "Pioneers of Computing Series" (London: Science Museum, 1976).

3. Notebook 17, Zuse Archives, Gesellschaft für Mathematik und Datenverarbeitung, Bonn.

4. Konrad Zuse, interview with the author, April, 1978.

5. Wilfred de Beauclair, *Rechnen mit Maschinen* (Braunschweig: Vieweg, 1968), p. 2.

6. For a discussion of the symbolic analysis of Zuse's graphical scheme, see F. L. Bauer, *Between Zuse and Rutishauser—the Early Development of Digital Computing in Central Europe*, Technical University, Munich, Department of Informatics, Report 7629 (Munich, 1976).

7. Zuse, *Der Computer*, pp. 36-39.

8. Charles Babbage, "Passages from the Life of a Philosopher," in *Charles Babbage and His Calculating Machines*, ed. Philip and Emily Morrison (New York: Dover, 1961), p. 55.

9. N. Metropolis and J. Worlton, "A Trilogy on Errors in the History of Computing," *Annals of the History of Computing*, 2 (1980): 49-59.

10. De Beauclair, *Rechnen mit Maschinen*, pp. 11-15; W. Meyer zur Capellan, *Mathematische Instrumente*, 2nd ed. (Leipzig, 1949), pp. 53-55; Friedrich A. Willars, *Mathematische Instrumente* (Berlin, 1926), pp. 28, 48-51.

11. Anton Glaser, *History of Binary and Other Nondecimal Numeration* (Southhampton, Pa., 1971); Hans J. Zacher, *Die Hauptschriften der Dyadik von G. W. Leibniz, ein Beitrag zur Geschichte des Binaeren Zahlensystems* (Frankfurt am Main, 1973), pp. 18-34; "Herrn von Leibniz' *Rechnung mit Null und Eins*," transcription of MS, 1679 (Munich: Siemens A. G., 1966).

12. Quoted in Karl-Heinz Czauderna, "Konrad Zuse—der Weg zu seinem Computer Z3 und dessen Verwirrcklichung," Report 120, Gesellschaft für Mathematik und Datenverarbeitung (Bonn, 1979), pp. 88-89.

13. Konrad Zuse, "Method for Automatic Execution of Calculations with the Aid of Computers," German Patent Application Z 23 139 IX/42m, April 11, 1936, reprinted in Brian Randell, ed., *The Origins of Digital Computers: Selected Papers*, 2nd ed. (New York: Springer Verlag, 1973), pp. 159-166.

14. Czauderna, "Konrad Zuse," pp. 85-89.

15. Ibid., pp. 31-40.

16. Ibid., p. 89.

17. E. Jessen, "Konrad Zuse—Konstructeur der ersten programmgesteuerten Rechenanlage," paper presented at the Advanced Course on General Net Theory of Processes and Systems, Hamburg, Oct. 10, 1979.

18. Zuse, *Der Computer*, pp. 75-76; also Zuse Archiv, Bonn, # 009/002.

19. Zuse, *Der Computer*, pp. 53, 64.

20. F. L. Bauer, *Between Zuse and Rutishauser*, p. 36; see also the discussion by Bauer on the history of ALGOL, Association for Computing Machinery (ACM) *SIGPLAN Notices* 13, no. 8 (August, 1978), p. 40.

21. Morris Kline, *Mathematical Thought from Ancient to Modern Times* (New York: Oxford, 1972), chapter 51; Jean van Heijenoort, *From Frege to Gödel: A Source Book in Mathematical Logic* (Cambridge, Mass.: Harvard, 1967), introduction.

22. Zuse, interview with the author, April, 1978.

23. Konrad Zuse, "Über Programmgesteuerte Rechenanlage für industrielle Verwendung," *Probleme der Entwicklung programmgesteuerte Rechengeräte und Integrieranlage*, ed. H. Cremer (Aachen, 1953), p. 74; Konrad Zuse, "Die ersten programmgesteuerten Relaisrechenmaschine," *350 Jahre Rechenmaschine*, ed. M. Graef (Munich, 1973), p. 55.

24. Helmut Schreyer, "Die Entwicklung des Versuchsmodells einer elektronischen Rechenmaschine," unpublished, Mosbach/Baden, Aug. 1, 1977.

25. Helmut Schreyer, "Das Röhrenrelais und seine Schaltungstechnik," dissertation, Technische Hochschule, Berlin, August, 1941.

26. Ibid., p. 77.

27. Records of party membership were obtained through the Berlin Document Center, Mission of the United States.

28. Schreyer's letter has been translated and published in Brian Randell, *Origins*, pp. 167-169.

29. Alfred Teichmann, "Das Flattern von Trag- und Leitwerken," Deutsche Akademie der Luftfahrtforschung, *Schriften* 49 (1941); Zuse, interview with the author, April, 1978.

30. A letter from the DVL to Zuse, April 22, 1942, Zuse Archiv No. 014/008, states that the "provisory" machine (that is, the Z3) was completed by December 5, 1941.

31. German Patent Application Z-391, applied for in 1941, rejected May 7, 1956; letter from de Beauclair to Czauderna, in Czauderna, "Konrad Zuse," p. 98; letter from Dreyer to the author, July 23, 1978; letter from Zuse, Zuse Archiv, No. 014/001.

32. Zuse, *Der Computer*, p. 82; correspondence between Zuse and DVL, Zuse Archiv, No. 014/008; interview with Zuse by Uta Merzbach, Zuse Archiv, No. 030/002.

33. Czauderna, "Konrad Zuse," pp. 70-73; Wend Goldbach and Rolf Schneider, "Beschreibung der Rechenanlage Z3," *Zuse Forum*, 2 (September, 1963), 19-31.

34. H. Flessner, private communication, October 10, 1979.

35. See, for example, John Ball, *Algorithms for RPN Calculators* (New York: Wiley, 1978), p. 163; Donald E. Knuth, *Seminumerical Algorithms* (Reading, Mass.: Addison Wesley, 1969), pp. 192-193, 205.

36. Ball, *Algorithms*, chapter 1; John Kennedy, "RPN History," paper presented at the Western Calculator Conference, Anaheim, Calif., Sept. 22, 1979.

37. Zuse, *Der Computer*, pp. 83-84, 93-94; Zuse Archiv, No. 017/013.

38. H. G. Küssner, "Flügelschwingungen an Flugzeugen," *Zeitschrift fur Angewandte Mathematik und Mechanik*, 9 (1929), 492-493; H. G. Küssner, "Zusammenfassender Bericht über den instationären Auftrieb," *Luftfahrtforschung*, 13 (1936), 410-429.

39. Alfred Teichmann, "Das Flattern"; letter from DVL to Zuse, May 6, 1943, Zuse Archiv, No. 028/008; Konrad Zuse, "Some Remarks on the History of Computing in Germany," paper presented at the Conference on the History of Computing, Los Alamos, New Mexico, 1976; C. Evans, interview with Zuse, "Pioneers of Computing" series.

40. Letter from de Beauclair to Czauderna, in Czauderna, "Konrad Zuse," p. 98.

41. Letter from Dreyer to the author, July 23, 1978.

42. Interrogation summary of Gerhard Overhoff by U.S. Forces in Austria, Air Interrogation Unit, 8 Nov., 1946, p. 1; correspondence in Zuse Archiv, Nos. 028/009 and 036/012.

43. Rowland F. Pocock, *German Guided Missiles of the Second World War* (New York: Arco, 1967), pp. 33, 44-45.

44. Zuse, *Der Computer*, pp. 87-90, 97, 106; correspondence in the Zuse Archiv, Nos. 002/004, 014/001, 017/009.

45. R. C. Lyndon, "The Zuse Computer," *Mathematical Tables and Other Aids to Computation*, 2 (1947), 355-359; "Applied Mathematical Research in Germany, with Particular Reference to Naval Applications," British Intelligence Objectives Subcommittee (BIOS), Report No. 79, pp. 63-64; "The Development of Theoretical and Applied Mechanics in German Institutions During the War," Great Britain, Field Information Agency, Technical (FIAT), Final Report No. 1167, 1947.

46. F. L. Bauer and H. Wössner, "The Plankalkül of Konrad Zuse: A Forerunner of Today's Programming Languages," *Communications ACM*, 15 (1972), 678-685; Donald E. Knuth and L. T. Pardo, "The Early Development of Programming Languages," *Encyclopedia of Computer Science and Technology*, ed. Jack Belzer, vol. 7 (New York: Dekker, 1977).

47. See, for example, Konrad Zuse, "The Emancipation of Data Processing," paper presented at the Advanced Course on General Net Theory of Processes and Systems, Hamburg, October, 1979.

3
Bessie—
The Automatic Sequence Controlled Calculator

> ...if it should ever turn out that the basic logics of a machine designed for the numerical solution of differential equations coincide with the logics of a machine intended to make bills for a department store, I would regard this as the most amazing coincidence that I have ever encountered.
> —Howard Aiken, 1956[1]

In the summer of 1944, the American press reported the waging of the war: grim news of battles in France, casualties, sacrifices and shortages at home. Among the stories on August 7 was another report that probably did not arouse much attention. On that day a large electromechanical computing machine was publicly unveiled at Harvard University, in a ceremony attended by the presidents of both Harvard and the IBM Corporation. The machine they dedicated that day was called the ASCC, short for Automatic Sequence Controlled Calculator; later it would be known as the Harvard Mark I as other similar devices appeared there. It was not really the first automatic computer. Zuse's Z3 was already in use by then, and there were other top-secret projects in America and Britain that also could have vied for that claim. But nonetheless its dedication is as good a moment as any to mark the beginning of the computer age, for it was on that summer day that the existence of the computer became public knowledge.[2]

The Mark I was well publicized, and the details of its construction were duly reported in the press. It was a general-purpose calculator that could carry out a sequence of operations specified by a program punched in a paper tape. It was not a test machine like the Zuse computer but a full-scale device that was put to work as soon as it was completed (well before its dedication that summer). The public dedication brought news of computing machines to a world still at war, while it also marked the entry of both the IBM Corporation and Harvard University into the business of building and using large-scale digital computers.

Like Konrad Zuse's relay computers, the Mark I was the product of the vision and hard work of one man, although its enormous size and scale required the cooperation of a large team of skilled collaborators. That man was Howard H.

Aiken, Commander in the U.S. Naval Reserve and Professor of Applied Mathematics at Harvard.

Aiken grew up in Indianapolis, Indiana, where he attended the Arsenal Technical High School. He went on to the University of Wisconsin, where he received a B.S. in 1923, and then he worked as a power engineer for the next twelve years.[3] But he returned to school as a doctoral candidate in physics, first at the University of Chicago and then at Harvard, where he submitted a thesis on "The Theory of Space Charge Conduction" in 1939.

He got interested in automatic calculating machinery while working on that thesis. Like Zuse, he found himself spending hours computing sequences of sums and products, aided only by a desk calculator and some scratch paper. What was worse, for many of the problems he was trying to solve (involving the numerical solution of differential equations) he found that the sheer number of individual calculations rendered any solution impossible. He just could not do them all in a reasonable time without making errors. It was not for any theoretical reason concerning the numerical methods themselves.

NUMERICAL METHODS OF SOLUTION

The problems that stumped him were nonlinear differential equations which only numerical methods could solve. To solve those kinds of equations required evaluating an integral: finding the area that would lie under the curve of an equation if it were plotted on graph paper. For many equations one can find a corresponding formula that gives the area directly. They are called analytical solutions; for example, the area under the curve described by

$$y = \sin(x), \text{ between two points, } x1 \text{ and } x2,$$

is given by the formula

$$A = \cos(x2) - \cos(x1)$$

But for many equations, especially those of the complexity that Aiken faced, it is not possible to find such an equation. The area must be found by breaking it up into small rectangular "slivers," whose height and width are known. (The person selects the width in advance; the height of each sliver is given by plugging the appropriate value into the original equation.)

So evaluating an integral by such numerical methods is straightforward; it is the sum of the areas of each individual narrow sliver, whose areas are in turn found by a simple multiplication of a constant width by a varying height.

The difficulty with numerical methods lies in the need to divide the area under the curve into a large number of narrow slices to ensure enough accuracy in the answer. Mathematicians had long ago established guidelines for just how fine this mesh had to be for a given type of integral, but the logistics of carrying out those elementary sums of products became a severe bottleneck as Aiken worked on his thesis: not just the calculations themselves but the writing down, labeling, and accurate recopying of intermediate answers mushroomed to unmanageable proportions.[4]

Aiken saw no reason why the whole process could not be carried out by machinery: specifically by suitable combinations of commercial accounting and tabulating equipment. Especially if intermediate results could be punched into cards rather than written down, the errors of copying and reentering numbers would be reduced.

The first element of the system would be a card reader that would supply the values of the function to be integrated. (Someone would have to punch the cards, but by the 1930's many tables of mathematical functions were already being supplied as decks of punched cards in addition to the more familiar form of books of printed tables.) The values of the function would be taken from the card reader to a multiplying punch, where the area of each sliver would be computed and punched onto another deck of cards. This deck would be taken to an accumulating punch that would sum up the areas, and punch the results onto cards. Finally those cards would be fed into a printer that would print the results automatically.

In this method of computing, each part of the whole sequence of operations is performed for all the values of the independent variable before the deck of cards is transferred to the next station: first the values of $f(x)$ are supplied, then all the multiplications are done, then all the additions, and so on. Intermediate results take the form of decks of punched cards that are physically carried (by hand) from one station to another.

But Aiken felt that the intermediate steps of punching cards should also be eliminated. Why not connect the various machines to one another by wires and not use cards or printing except for the first and last steps? But to do that would require a change in the way the computations were carried out. Instead of doing first all the multiplications, then all the additions, and so on, the machines would have to do the entire sequence of calculations for each value of the independent variable: for each x, find $f(x)$, then find the area of the narrow segment under the curve at $f(x)$, then add that value to the sum of the areas obtained thus far. The machine would have to perform *sequences* of elementary calculations, in contrast to the parallel method suggested by the way that existing machinery operated.

(Consider evaluating $f(x) = x^3 + 3x^2 + 4x + 4$, for $x = 1, 2, 3,\ldots,10$. Using punched card equipment, a multiplier would first be set up to produce the cubes of the x's: $1, 8, 27,\ldots, 1000$, punched into a deck of cards. Another multiplier would be set up to produce the next term: $3, 12, 27,\ldots, 300$, and so on. Finally the decks of cards representing the values of those terms for all values of x would be fed into an accumulating punch, which would sum their values to produce and punch the list of values of $f(x)$ on a deck of cards. That deck could be fed into a printer if desired. By contrast, a sequential calculator would compute $f(x)$ by performing the individual operations for each value of x, one at a time: $f(1) = 12$, $f(2) = 32, \ldots, f(10) = 1344$. Hence the name "Automatic *Sequence* Controlled Calculator" that he gave to his project.)

In 1937, while still a graduate student, he wrote a proposal for such a machine.[5] This proposal began by summarizing the reasons such a machine with its novel way of computing sequentially was needed, and the various attempts that had been made in the past to construct such a device. It discussed in particular the unsuccessful attempt by Charles Babbage a century earlier to build an Analytical Engine—a machine Aiken recognized as a genuine ancestor to his proposed sequence calculator.

Most of his proposal dealt with how the calculator differed from the punched card machinery of the day. The major difference was of course that the devices for addition, multiplication, reading cards, and punching or printing results would each be connected to one another and would sequentially carry out a computation. (Aiken called the method computing in "lines" instead of "columns," thinking of how a numerical solution would be arranged on a page.)

Other features his machine would have were the ability to handle positive and negative numbers equally well; an ability to supply, automatically, tables of commonly used functions such as sines, cosines, logarithms, and probability functions; and the ability to automatically increment the value of the independent variable each time a sequence is carried out.

That last requirement is useful for numerical integration, where the width of each rectangle is a small constant. There is no reason why the machine should not supply those values automatically once it has been given a starting value and the size of the constant increment. Implicit in that requirement is the need for the machine to stop incrementing the x-value when it reaches the endpoint of the integration.

The remainder of the proposal describes how a general-purpose sequential calculator could be built out of only a few basic components: out of machines that could perform the four basic arithmetic operations, that could read selected values of functions from punched cards or tape, and that could store and retrieve intermediate results on mechanical registers.

The picture painted by Aiken's 1937 proposal is one of equipment racks on which are mounted individual subassemblies—the innards—of standard business equipment. Each of these assemblies would be connected to the others by a switchboard of wires. Other equipment would supply constants such as *pi* or *e*, or specific constants pertaining to a given computation. A standard printing device would print the results directly, thus avoiding copying errors.

The sequence of operations would be controlled by punched cards or by a long punched tape, as well as by physically wiring the individual units to one another through a plugboard. That was the way that Babbage wanted to control the operation of his Analytical Engine—borrowing the idea from the silk-weaving industry, where by the 1830's punched cards were widely used to control the pattern woven into the cloth. (The idea is usually attributed to J. M. Jacquard, who successfully employed the method in his looms in Lyon in 1805; cruder versions had been known in France since the 1720's.)

So Aiken proposed to use perforated media for both numerical storage (as business machines used cards), and for control (as Jacquard looms used them), in a single machine. The idea was a novel one (actually it originated with Babbage, but it was not picked up again until Aiken's proposal). The business machines industry had developed the use of punched cards from the work of Herman Hollerith, who first applied them for the U.S. Census of 1890. But Hollerith was probably not influenced by either Jacquard or Babbage, and the industry that grew up around his invention never used the cards for anything but data storage. Whatever control those machines had was done by plugboards. It was left to Howard Aiken to see what had been clear to Babbage but strangely had been neglected since: that punched card equipment could not only calculate: it could also direct the sequence of those calculations automatically, using perforated cards or tape for each.

To ensure enough accuracy of the results of any calculations done on such a calculator, Aiken proposed that the machine be able to handle numbers of up to twenty-three decimal places in its individual registers. That was over twice what commercial business equipment handled, but Aiken recognized a fundamental difference in the kinds of problems his machine would be solving. Business calculations are carried out to dollars and cents: two and only two digits to the right of the decimal point. Few businesses dealt with amounts of money in the range of millions of dollars, so seven or eight decimal places to the left of the decimal point were almost always more than adequate. Business equipment and desk calculators therefore had a capacity of eight to ten decimal digits, with the decimal point fixed two places from the right of the register.

But scientific calculations could range throughout the number fields, positive and negative, with very small quantities just as likely to occur as very large ones. Zuse had met that problem by adopting floating-point arithmetic, with part of each number set aside to store the position of the radix point. But that complicated the construction of his machines; it would have been intolerably complex had he not taken advantage of the simplicity of the binary scale of enumeration. But Aiken was committed to modifying commercial business equipment, which operated in the decimal system and had a fixed decimal point. So he proposed a register that could hold twenty-three decimal digits, with the decimal point fixed at the middle, giving a decimal range of at least $10^{\pm 10}$. The breakdown of the digits was to be:

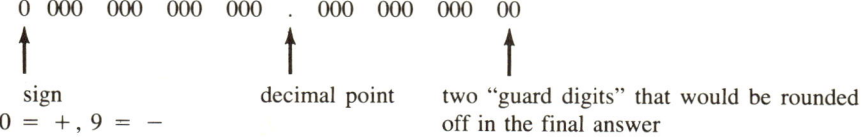

So Aiken retained the simplicity of registers with a fixed decimal point while giving them a much longer "word length" to allow his machine to handle quantities more typical of scientific calculations.

If Aiken drew the inspiration for his proposed automatic machine from Charles Babbage's Analytical Engine a hundred years earlier, he also knew that Babbage never completed more than fragments of that Engine.[6] Babbage was known to some in the 1930's not as a man of great vision but rather as a failure: an impossible, irascible dreamer who could not anchor his dreams in the reality of iron, brass, and steam. Aiken felt that Babbage's "principles were theoretically sound," but he felt that the problem lay in the Englishman's having to rely on a machine-tool industry which was not up to the demands of the project. The Analytical Engine was to have been powered by a steam engine. Today that seems faintly ludicrous; if he had been successful, would we see today's computer designer doing his business with an oilcan and an adjustable wrench instead of with a voltmeter and an oscilloscope? But Babbage had no alternative to steam: in 1830 electricity was still a mysterious force, and practical motors that harnessed it were still half a century away. Aiken of course could draw on the experience of forty years of business machines and commercial calculators (both industries were established after 1890), but he still had to face skepticism from his peers. His proposed machine was much more complicated than the business machines he was to build it out of. There certainly was the risk that he would fail, just as Babbage had failed, in getting all those individual pieces to fit and work together as a system.

But Aiken succeeded. The Mark I was completed only a few years after he proposed building it in 1937. Whatever else may be said about its design, it worked. It succeeded where Babbage had failed, and its dedication in 1944 served as an existence theorem for the large-scale digital computer. (By 1944 there was at least one other large-scale computing machine that had been built— that was the Differential Analyzer which was built under the direction of Vannevar Bush at MIT. But it was an analog, not a digital computer, and so its existence did not resolve the question of whether or not Babbage's century-old dream of a general-purpose large-scale digital computer would ever be more than just that—a dream).

Aiken first sought assistance from the Monroe Calculating Machine Company to build the computer. But they turned him down. The Harvard astronomer Harlow Shapley suggested to Aiken that he go to the IBM Corporation. Shapley knew that Professor T. H. Brown of the Harvard Business School was on good terms with President Thomas Watson of IBM. Through Brown, Aiken was introduced to Watson. So began not only Harvard's but also IBM's involvement in computers.[7]

Watson had already begun exploring the use of his company's computers for scientific applications, with the establishment of a Computing Bureau at Columbia University (under Wallace Eckert) in 1934. He did not believe that scientific work would ever displace the more mundane business data processing as IBM's bread and butter. But he was sufficiently impressed by Aiken's proposal to commit his company's resources to the building of the calculator, although most of the money used for its construction came from the U.S. Navy.[8] What IBM contributed most was the experience and skill of a veteran team of engineers from its Endicott, New York, plant, where its punched card equipment was designed and built. The senior engineer put in charge of the project was James W. Bryce, who had been with the company over thirty years; during that time he amassed a long string of patents covering many aspects of the company's line of punched card equipment. Bryce in turn assigned Clair D. Lake, Frank E. Hamilton, and Benjamin M. Durfee to the project at the Endicott plant. Aiken's own role was not as an engineer, even though he had experience in engineering. It was rather as a consultant to IBM's own engineers: Aiken would sketch out what he wanted the machine to do; Hamilton, Lake, and Durfee would match those needs with what they knew existing IBM machinery could do. Aiken spent the summers of 1941 and 1942 in Endicott, but in the early years of the war he also entered active duty as a commander in the Navy, stationed at the Navy School of Mines in Virginia. At least some of that time was spent performing duties entirely unrelated to computers. Nevertheless, Aiken seems to have fitted himself well into that role; he was a self-disciplined man who wore his Navy uniform well. And though he had very specific ideas about how his computer would function, he was glad to be able to use the resources of IBM and that company's engineers to realize those objectives. Unlike Konrad Zuse, Aiken did not immerse himself in the details of building the components of the machine.[9]

The Automatic Sequence Controlled Calculator was completed by January, 1943, in Endicott, where it secretly demonstrated its abilities. It was then disassembled and moved to Cambridge, to a room specially prepared for it in the basement of Harvard's Cruft Laboratory (a few years later the Harvard Computation Laboratory—and the Mark I—got their own building). It began doing serious work for the Navy's Bureau of Ships in May, 1944, three months before its public dedication.

Before that unveiling, the ASCC was covered with a polished stainless steel and glass enclosure: not an easy matter given the wartime shortages of those materials. Watson insisted on it, although Aiken preferred leaving the case off to make the computer easier to maintain and modify. Watson's decision reflected his attitude toward the project and the IBM Corporations's general approach to computing machinery.[10] He did not see much future in making scientific computers, but that is not to say that in the 1940's IBM was content to provide machines that only did simple tabulating and counting. In fact, IBM had already developed machines that had quite a capability for advanced numerical processing by 1944.

A decade earlier the company had designed and marketed an electromechanical multiplier, the Type 601, that accepted two eight-digit decimal numbers

The IBM ASCC at Harvard. Courtesy of IBM Corporation.

punched into a card and computed and punched their product in the remaining columns of the card. (What was interesting about the 601 was that it computed products not by repeated addition, as most mechanical calculators did, but rather by looking up an internally stored multiplication table for the 10 x 10 decimal digits.) By the late 1940's they were working on replacing the electromechanical parts of the 601 with vacuum-tube circuits that could operate much faster. In 1942, under the direction of R. L. Palmer, they had developed a prototype "cross-footing" punch that multiplied electronically.[11] Work on electronic computing circuits continued at a separate lab in New York City; after 1945, research and development of electronic devices was centered at a laboratory in Poughkeepsie, New York. (Endicott remained a center for electromechanical research and development.) When IBM unveiled their Type 603 Multiplier in 1946, it was one of the first commercial devices anywhere that calculated with electronic circuits. (The 603 could perform up to sixty multiplications per second, which was about a hundred times faster than the 601.)

Now a suitable combination of IBM's commercial equipment, including the 601 multiplier, coupled with tabulating, card reading, and printing machines, could certainly do some scientific calculations just as easily as Aiken's Sequence Controlled Calculator. Indeed, Wallace Eckert had been using those machines at Columbia for astronomical calculations with great success (where, among other things, he calculated the orbit of the moon).[12] These standard punched card machines that IBM produced could be programmed to do short sequences of arithmetic, using plugboards to determine which operations would be performed on selected fields of the punched cards. What they could not do was execute an arbitrarily long sequence of operations, the kind Aiken wanted his proposed machine to do. But of course that was precisely the point—the Mark I's completely flexible programming made it a general-purpose computer—not just a fancier calculator, but something qualitatively different. The engineers and executives at IBM, and elsewhere too for that matter, did not see that distinction as clearly in 1944 as it is seen today.

So while IBM engineers took on building the ASCC, they did so because of its status as a military project, not as a potential prototype for a future line of commercial products. The U.S. Navy supplied most of the estimated $300,000 construction cost of the machine, with IBM providing additional money for maintenance and support. The total cost was probably over a million dollars; hardly in the same range as the rental costs of IBM's existing lines of business equipment.[13]

The gulf between Aiken's and Watson's perception of the future of computing was hardly evident at the dedication ceremony, but it was deep. In accepting the machine from Watson, Aiken and President Conant of Harvard graciously acknowledged their debt to Watson and IBM, but although Aiken would go on to build other large scale computers at Harvard, he did so without IBM's help. And for the company that was to dominate the computer industry after 1955, the Mark I was really a reluctant step into a new world.

DESCRIPTION OF THE MARK I

The public dedication of the Mark I in 1944 brought a wide response from other mathematicians and engineers, who saw in it a way to solve problems they too were facing. So in contrast to other wartime projects that were kept strictly classified, the Harvard Computation Laboratory felt the need to provide a detailed description of the Mark I and how it was programmed. Only the specific military problems for which it was first used remained secret. Of course any publicity about the machine would also reflect upon the expertise of the IBM Corporation, even if they were not offering that kind of product to their customers.

The staff of the Computation Laboratory prepared a detailed *Manual of Operation for the Automatic Sequence Controlled Calculator* in 1946, listing Aiken and Lieutenant Grace Murray Hopper as principal authors. It is from that manual that we can get a detailed picture of how the machine worked and what it could do.[14] The *Manual* describes the machine as it existed on September 1, 1945; after the war it was fitted with a so-called Subsidiary Sequence Mechanism, which extended its powers, but by that time it was already fast becoming obsolete.

The fundamental calculating element of the Mark I was a wheel that could assume one of ten positions, for the ten decimal digits, just like a desk calculator. (Some wheels had up to twenty positions: ten decimal digits, and others for control, carry, and transmission of numbers from one wheel to another.) A mechanical desk calculator indicates numbers by digits printed on the wheels themselves, but that was not the case with the Mark I. It stored and counted numbers mechanically, but it transmitted and read those numbers electrically. A wiper attached to each wheel made contact with one of ten wires, one for each decimal digit, and that indicated the wheel's position. And the wheels were turned not by a mechanical linkage but by an electric motor that advanced the wheel to a position that corresponded to the number it was supposed to represent.[15] Hence the description of the Mark I as an *electromechanical* computer.

In a desk calculator, number wheels are engaged by their contact with the keys that the operator presses. If the operator keys the number 6 in a certain column, the wheel corresponding to that column will move six and only six additional places from its initial position (it may also initiate a carry if the wheel passes through zero). In a mechanical device first the keys are pressed, then the number is "loaded" onto the wheels by pulling a lever that moves each wheel the appropriate number of places.

In the Mark I that transfer was accomplished electrically, by a clutch attached to each wheel. A 5-hp electric motor drove a long shaft that ran the full fifty-foot length of the machine. When, say, the number 6 was to be loaded onto a wheel, the clutch would couple that wheel to the shaft for a precise interval of time, until the wheel had moved the six places. Then the clutch would disconnect the wheel from the shaft (see Figure 3.1).

The timing pulses for the clutch relays were supplied by a series of cams connected to the same rotating shaft. The cams could have up to twenty lobes

THE AUTOMATIC SEQUENCE CONTROLLED CALCULATOR

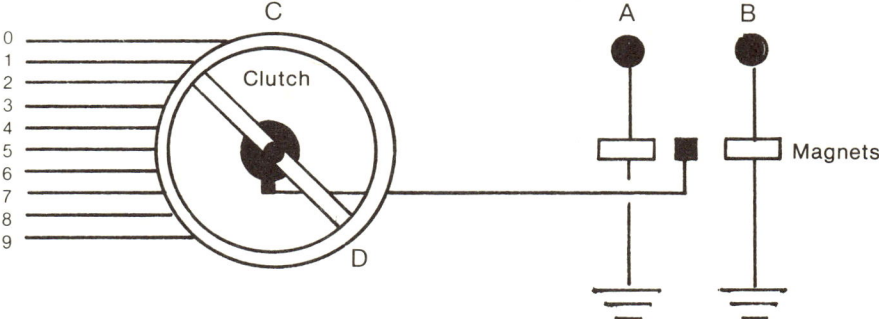

A: "pick-up" relay; engages wheel
B: "drop-off" relay; disengages the clutch
C: clutch and clutch arm connected to constantly rotating shaft
D: rotor arm; makes a connection with the contacts along the wheel

Figure 3.1. Sketch of a Decimal Wheel for the Mark I

depending on their function. To add the number 6 to a register, an electrical signal would be routed through a six-lobed cam, which would pick up the clutch on the wheel for six units of time before dropping it off, while also keeping track of any carry digit produced.

Should a number be subtracted from an accumulator (as the cells were called), an electrical signal was sent to another cam having the "complement" of the number's lobes (the difference between the number and nine: for example, the complement of six is three). The shaft and the wheels always turned in the same direction, but by adding the complements of numbers, with an appropriate carry adjustment, the machine could subtract any number from an accumulator. (An explanation of subtraction by complements is given in Glossary B.)

Note that when a number is added to a wheel, that wheel passes through all the digits in between its original position and the sum. If the wheel was at the position for number 3, and the number 6 was added to it, it would be connected to the motor for six units of time, during which the wheel would pass through the positions 3, 4, 5, 6, 7, 8, and 9, where it would come to rest. That is the way all mechanical calculators work (at least all that use decimal numbers). When human beings perform addition they usually proceed directly to the sum of two digits, previously having memorized the addition table. Occasionally a person forgets that table and has to add the numbers unit-by-unit on his fingers. (From the Latin word for finger comes the word *digital* itself. A digital machine, whether it be a computer or anything else, operates with discrete units.)

For that reason the storage cells of the Mark I were called *accumulators*, since they accumulated numbers in them one unit at a time. An accumulator furthermore does not distinguish between storing a number and adding a number; when a number was transmitted to a cell of the Mark I, it was automatically added to whatever quantity was already in that cell from a previous operation. That property follows from the way electrical impulses advanced its counting wheels. (Also, any carry digits produced must be transmitted from one column to another; the cells of the Mark I, built from pieces of standard punched card equipment, had that ability as well.) Simply to store a number in an accumulator required that it be set to zero beforehand; that was done by subtracting whatever number was in it from itself just before instructing the accumulator to accept a new number for storage.

Modern terminology is often not as strict about preserving this distinction between an accumulator and a *register*, which is the name given to a memory cell that simply writes over any number in that cell when a new number is sent to it. Computers today use binary arithmetic; their design favors doing all arithmetic in a central processor (as the Zuse machines did). With few exceptions, modern memory units can store but not accumulate sums; hence the term *register* to describe them. The main difference between those registers and the "accumulators" also found in the processors of modern computers is that the former do not contain carry circuits. But nowadays that distinction is not strictly adhered to. Aiken often referred to the accumulators of the Mark I as registers, when they were being used only for storage of a number. (Both terms should be further distinguished from a *counter*, which can also accumulate sums, but which can only be fed numbers from its right-most column. An automobile odometer is a counter; miles are added to it only a tenth of a mile at a time. An accumulator can add quantities to any column. These terms are further explained in Glossary B.)

The fact that addition (and subtraction) was done in the accumulators had an important bearing on the overall architecture of the machine. The Mark I had no real "central processor" like the Zuse computers or like most modern computers. Any memory cell could be used for addition and subtraction—and there were seventy-two such cells. Only multiplication and division were done in a separate processor unit. That design reflects the Mark I's legacy: punched card accounting equipment that was mainly used to tabulate and accumulate totals.

The Mark I's seventy-two accumulators could perform addition and subtraction, as well as ordinary storage, by first clearing their contents to zero. Accumulator number 71 (they were numbered from 1 to 72) was constructed so that it could be split in half to handle two twelve-digit numbers. Transferring the contents of the other accumulators through it allowed the machine to store twice as many numbers, each having half the precision. Aiken noted that trade-off was useful for statistical problems "where the quantities dealt with are large in number and of low accuracy."[16] That such a feature was built into the Mark I suggests that the twenty-three digit word length was probably too long for many applications, meaning that the full capacity of the accumulators often was wasted. But at the same time, the Mark I also had the ability to link accumulators 68 and 69 to each other, giving the machine a double precision of forty-six digits plus sign.

The need for that kind of numerical precision arose in one type of work that the Mark I was especially designed to do—to compute and print tables of mathematical functions to many decimal places of accuracy.

Accumulator 72 was fitted with another special circuit that gave it interesting properties. I have already mentioned that the Mark I performed subtraction by adding complements—by adding the difference between the subtrahend and 999999..., then adding the digit 1 (the so-called end-around carry) to the unit's place, viz.:

```
    45793           45793
  − 15342         + 84657      the 9's complement of 15342
  ───────         ───────
    30451          130450
                      + 1      the end-around carry; the 1 at
                   ───────     the left-most column drops
                    30451      away
```

But if the result of a subtraction is a negative number, there is no end-around carry produced at the left-most column. What happens instead is that the digit 9 (which stood for − in the Mark I) would appear in the sign-field, followed by the complement of the true answer:

```
     5793            5793
  − 15342         + 84657      complement of 15342
  ───────         ───────
   − 9549           90450      last four digits are the comple-
                                ment of the difference = 9549

                 sign digit = 9    no end-around carry
```

Accumulator 72 could detect when no end-around carry took place, and then it would stop the machine. In that way, a function could be evaluated by repeated iterations; after each cycle the value would be tested against a tolerance value stored in cell 72. When the numerical accuracy of the Mark I exceeded that tolerance, the machine would stop, "knowing" that further evaluation of the function would not increase the accuracy of the result.[17]

Thus the Mark I could automatically direct the course of its sequence of calculations, at least in this limited way. The question of whether or not the early computers could "choose" their paths of computation is a controversial one, central to the distinction between what a computer is and what it is not, even today. The Mark I had that capability, if only in a limited sense: it could sense the results of its previous calculations and act on that knowledge (that is, stop if programmed to do so by its operator). What it could not do was go to a different sequence of operations depending on the number in cell 72. That capability, which is really what is meant by the term *conditional branching* as it is applied to computers, was only added to the Mark I after 1945 (as it was added to Zuse's Z4 computer when it was installed in Zürich after 1949).

Aiken does not seem to have recognized the importance of that kind of logical decision making beyond his use of cell 72. In another description of the Mark I by Richard Bloch, the "register" is said to "permit the choice of one function if the value of the independent variable is less than a given quantity."[18] But it is not clear if Bloch meant that the computer could turn to a completely different sequence of operations automatically depending on the value in register 72.

Given the way that the sequence of operations was fed into the machine—by a long strip of punched paper tape—it is clear that full conditional branching capability could not have been built into it without some difficulty. There was only one paper tape reader on the Mark I to read operations (three others read tapes containing data). The readers ran the tapes in only one direction. Branching to a different sequence would have required the tape to skip over instructions without executing them. It probably would have also required that the tape be able to back up and repeat a group of instructions in a loop. There would have to be a way for the tape to sense both where it was in a sequence and where the next part of the sequence was located—two pieces of information not part of the Mark I's repertoire. In short, coding instructions by a single continuous strip of tape does not lend itself well to conditional branching. When the Mark I was fitted with that capability after the war, it was done by adding a completely separate tape reader, on which were mounted coding tapes that were repeatedly executed.

Aiken wanted a machine that could evaluate long sequences of operations in which only the argument is changed each time by a small increment. For that work there is less need for flexible branching. Even today many computer programs do little more choosing of their operations besides stopping the machine when the sequence is finished.

At least one of Babbage's writings on his proposed Analytical Engine mentions conditional branching capability. The Analytical Engine was to be capable of sensing when a computed value exceeded a certain tolerance, after which the machine would advance or back up to another part of the instruction sequence (delivered to the Engine by special "operation cards," not by a tape).[19]

In 1841 Ada Augusta, Countess of Lovelace, a daughter of Lord Byron and a gifted mathematician, learned of Babbage's computer and quickly mastered its operating principles. Two years later she translated into English a description of the Engine written by an Italian named L. F. Menabrea. To that translation she added a long set of notes, longer than the original description itself, in which she discussed the importance of the machine's ability to choose its own course of computations depending on what it had just computed.[20] In particular, she stressed the ability of the Analytical Engine to reverse its operation cards and repeat a loop of operations again and again, until a certain limit was met—precisely the ability added to the Mark I and to the Z4 after the Second World War. Countess Lovelace's notes on Menabrea's description of the Analytical Engine stand as one of the first thorough studies of the nature and power of digital computers, written a hundred years before any working computer existed.

Aiken was familiar with Babbage's writings, although he may not have been aware of Ada Augusta's commentary on the Analytical Engine. But in any case Aiken did not feel that a full branching capability was a necessary part of his Sequence Controlled Calculator.

The Mark I was built with the technology of the 1930's business machines industry, but that industry was by no means a static one. Research was constantly going on at the Endicott plant, and no doubt the Mark I benefited from that. The accumulators were based on the accumulators used in standard IBM equipment. Other components of the Mark I were taken directly from IBM's product line, modified only to the extent that they had to be in order to be coupled to the rest of the machine. Card readers, card punches, and electric typewriters could be plugged into the machine at various places. The multiplier unit of the machine computed the partial products directly, one digit at a time, and was based on the ingenious design of the IBM Type 601 multiplier first marketed in 1933.

Other parts of the computer were especially designed for it. The tape readers, for example, supplied numbers or instructions by sensing the presence of holes punched into twenty-four columns of stiff paper tape. If the tape was to supply a number, each digit was coded into a group of four holes: four consecutive lines of tape for each digit, by twenty-four columns for the full twenty-three-digit number plus sign. The four lines were punched as follows for the ten decimal digits:[21]

Decimal Digits—Up to 24 Columns

```
          0 1 2 3 4 5 6 7 8 9
Line #    ─────────────────────
  4       0 0 0 0 1 0 0 1 0 1     ◇ direction of tape movement
  3       0 0 0 1 0 0 1 0 1 0
  2       0 0 1 0 0 1 0 0 1 1     1 = hole in tape; 0 = no hole
  1       0 1 0 0 0 1 1 1 0 0
```

The machine read the bottom line first, twenty-four columns across.[22]

If the tape was to supply an instruction, a different coding scheme was used; it will be described later. The readers themselves were physically identical to one another despite their being used for different purposes. It is conceivable that the Mark I's designers could have recognized that instructions and data in a computer are fundamentally equivalent to one another. That is of course the essence of the stored program principle; it will be discussed at greater length in Chapter 6. But there is no mention of that concept in any contemporary descriptions of the Mark I. In later years, as the stored program principle became more widespread, Aiken was reluctant to acknowledge its advantages for computer design.[23]

In addition to the instruction and the value tape readers, the Mark I also had a tape reader that read in values of functions for selected arguments. Those values could be connected to a device called an Interpolator, which could calculate the value of the function for any arguments in between the values punched into the tape, using familiar methods of interpolation.[24] In this way the Mark I could supply—or generate—tables of the most common logarithmic and trigonometric functions, and their inverses, as needed in more advanced calculations.

The physical layout of the computer was determined by the common driveshaft that synchronized the accumulators. Like a 19th century New England textile mill, all the components of the Mark I were aligned on a common axis to be driven by the rotating shaft. That layout ensured a precise synchronization in a straighforward way. So the machine was long and narrow: fifty-one feet long, eight feet tall, and only two feet deep. Photographs of the Mark I always show it polished and neat, occupying a back wall of an equally well-polished room at Harvard.

Finally it must be said that the Mark I had a distinctive sound unlike that of any modern computer. It did its computing by electromechanical relays, not by invisible and silent electrons in a microscopic silicon chip. There was no mistaking when the Mark I was running, although it did not make a deafening clatter. It sounded rather more, as one observer put it, "like a roomful of ladies knitting."[25]

Table 3.1 summarizes the specifications of the Mark I in 1945.

Table 3.1 THE IBM ASCC (HARVARD MARK I)

Inventors:	Howard Aiken, C. D. Lake, F. E. Hamilton, B. M. Durfee.
Place:	Endicott, New York; moved to Cruft Laboratory, Harvard University; then to the Harvard Computation Laboratory.
Dates:	Proposed 1937; construction begun 1939; completed January, 1943; placed in operation spring, 1944; dedicated August 7, 1944. In use until 1959.
Cost:	$300,000–$500,000, exclusive of R & D.
Technology:	Electromechanical, 3,000 decimal storage wheels. 1,400 rotary dial switches, 500 miles of wire.
Size:	51' x 8' x 2'; 19 panels; weight 5 tons.
Number Registers:	Decimal system, 23 digits plus sign (0 = +, 9 = −); provision for half- or double-precision arithmetic; subtraction by 9's complements; parallel transfer of all numbers.
Memory:	72 accumulators; 60 constant registers (set by 10-position switches); 3 value-tape readers.
Processor:	Multiplier and divider, multiplication by table look-up; all addition and subtraction done in accumulators; special circuits for log and antilog (to base 10), sine, and interpolation of functions.
Programming:	1 sequence tape reader, using two-address code: out-field, in-field, miscellaneous, other sequencing by plugboard; 1 "choice register" and 1 "check register," allowing internal logical control.
Speed:	Cycle time: 300msec. (one rotation of shaft); multiplication time approx. 6 sec.
Input:	3 value-tape feeds, 2 card feeds, plugboard, switches.
Output:	1 card punch, 1 tape punch, 2 automatic typewriters.

THE MARK I IN OPERATION

How the Mark I actually solved problems may be considered separately from what it was physically made of; the latter is the machine's "anatomy," while the former is its "physiology." Although the Mark I's components were similar to those of commercial business equipment, it obviously worked in a different way. In fact, its physiology was remarkably similar to other contemporary computers, even if they had completely different physical anatomies.

A paper tape, called the sequence tape, supplied the instructions that commanded the computer. This tape had twenty-four channels across its width—the same as one line of a number tape. But unlike the number tape, a complete program step could be coded into one line of tape (recall that a number tape needed four lines to code a full twenty-three-digit number). The twenty-four channels were divided into three groups of eight channels each. The first field specified from which part of the machine a number was to be taken (the "out-field"), the second where a number would go (the "in-field"), and the third initiated an operation. Thus the Mark I was a two-address machine, but not in the same sense as the term is used today. The operation specified by the code in the last eight channels did not always specify an arithmetic operation to be performed on the numbers given in the two preceding fields. Most of the out-and in-codes referred to numbers in the accumulators; since those devices automatically added quantities introduced into them, there was no need to give an "add" command in the operation field to perform that most basic of the computer's operations. The operation field would have to be punched with the command for the machine to advance to the next line of coding, however; this was done by punching a hole in the seventh place (from the right) of the op-field.

So the operation, "Take the contents of Unit 5, add it to the contents of Unit 6, and go on to the next instruction," would be coded as follows:

out-field	in-field	misc. or op-field
_ _ _ _ _ 0 _ 0	_ _ _ _ _ 0 0 _	_ 0 _ _ _ _ _ _
8 7 6 5 4 3 2 1	8 7 6 5 4 3 2 1	8 7 6 5 4 3 2 1

Holes punched in columns three and one indicate the fifth accumulator; holes punched in columns three and two indicate the sixth.[26] Note how this coding is different from the coding of the number tapes. The eight columns for the in- and out-fields were more than enough to address the seventy-two accumulators, sixty constant registers, and other devices.

For multiplication, the third field functioned as a true operation-code field, although multiplication was not done in a single step. First two steps loaded the numbers to be multiplied from their locations (given in the out-field of two successive lines of coding) into the multiplier unit of the machine (its code given in the in-field of the two lines). After the numbers were loaded, a command was given in the op-field to multiply, with the in- and out-fields left blank. The next line of coding gave the address of a special register designed to handle up to the forty-six digits of the product.

All in all, then, it required at least four lines of coding to perform a multiplication. Depending on the length of the numbers themselves, it took from ten to twenty machine cycles to perform the operation. Thus the maximum multiplication time was 20 × 300msec., or about 6 seconds.[27]

If the sequence did not immediately require that product, the programmer could specify other operations on the lines of coding between the command to multiply and the command to store the product. That was, in fact, often done. So although Aiken always emphasized the sequential nature of computations in his machine, the Mark I was capable of a lot of parallel computation as well—a consequence of the dual storage and addition capabilities of the seventy-two accumulators.

Interpolation, consulting function tables, and other related functions were handled in the same way; the function tables and constant switches were also given addresses, although of course those addresses made sense only if punched into the out-field of the tape. In the same way the output facilities such as the typewriters and card punches were given addresses that could be punched into the in-field.[28]

The functioning of the Mark I is best illustrated by an example. The following problem is probably too simple to justify using the computer for its solution, but it is representative of the types of problems the Mark I handled. The example is taken from the *Manual of Operation*, p. 292:

Evaluate the polynomial

$$F(x) = x^4 + 3x^3 - 3x^2/4 - 22x + 3$$

by successive multiplication, in the interval $5 \leq x \leq 10$, with

$$\Delta x = 0.01 \text{ (that is, for } x = 5.00, 5.01, 5.02,\ldots 10.00).$$

The first step is done mentally by the programmer. That is to rewrite the above expression in such a way as to minimize the number of multiplications required:

$$F(x) = (((x + 3)x - 3/4)x - 22)x + 3$$

This so-called nested parenthetical form reduces the number of multiplications from ten to only four, including one division. Inasmuch as multiplication is a time-consuming operation, it is imperative that this form be used on any problem of appreciable size.

The next step is to initialize the computer by storing the coefficients 3, $-3/4$, -22, and 3 in the switch (constant) registers. Other registers that are to be used in the course of the computation have to be cleared to zero—a simple matter of coding the same address in both the in- and the out-field, plus the operation to continue (the machine automatically interpreted this command to subtract the number in the accumulator from itself, leaving zero).

Finally the starting value of the independent variable, 5.00, the ending value 10.00, and the increment 0.01 are also stored.

After coding the tape to initialize the machine, codes for the actual computation can begin. That consists of a sequence of elementary operations to evaluate the polynomial for each value of x.[29] Once calculated, the result is sent to an output device, the value of x is incremented by 0.01, and the sequence is run through again. When all values of x have been run, the operator would stop the machine manually by pressing a button. Appendix section (2) lists the actual 36-line coding for this problem on the Mark I, followed by that same program rewritten for a pocket calculator, using the same flow of data and instructions as the original.

ERROR CHECKING AND ACCURACY

Assuming the computer has successfully run through the sequence of calculations and has printed out the successive values of x and $f(x)$, the programmer now faces the question of whether or not those results are accurate. The Mark I was an enormously complicated device, containing three-quarters of a million individual parts. Even a simple program like the one just listed would exercise many of those parts, and they all had to function correctly if the answers were to be correct. Actually there are several different ways that errors can occur, and for each a separate treatment may be required. In his analysis of the reliability and accuracy of the Mark I, Aiken recognized four different types of errors:

1) Errors inherent in the mathematical formulas themselves; the equations yield only an approximation of the phenomena they describe.
2) Round-off errors caused by a repetition of the four basic operations of arithmetic to only a finite decimal precision (23 digits on the Mark I).
3) Mistakes made by human operators: pressing the wrong buttons, setting the constant registers improperly, etc.
4) Errors resulting from a mechanical or electrical failure within the calculator itself.[30]

The first type of error is part of all mathematics, whether or not one is using a computer. It was a problem that computer users faced, but then so so did every other mathematician. The other sources of error are more directly consequences of using a computer, although to a limited extent they appear even when simpler mathematical instruments such as slide rules, planimeters, or desk calculators are used. In 1944 there was no general agreement on what would be the best way to detect and minimize these errors, and so the pioneers in computing each tried a number of different approaches.

Errors of the second kind, round-off errors, are inherent in any physical process that must necessarily handle numbers of a finite length. Aiken sought to minimize these errors by providing the Mark I with an extraordinarily long word length of twenty-three digits; yet there were times when he felt that even that was not enough, and he resorted to a doubling up on accumulators to get forty-six digits. Later generations of computer designers would find ways of minimizing round-off errors while carrying fewer digits in the machine's registers—a careful analysis of the problem beforehand often would reveal just how many digits were needed to give the desired accuracy, and in many cases that proved to be far fewer than twenty-three decimal digits.

Human errors of programming, setting switches, feeding stacks of cards, and the like are much more difficult to detect—the person who makes the error often repeats it when he goes over his work again. By careful attention to details, double-checking by another person, and mechanical safeguards built into the machine they may be kept to a minimum. One obvious test is to run the program as set up with data that were known to give a certain answer beforehand; if the machine does in fact deliver that answer, then it is safe to say that the operation sequence was coded onto the tape correctly (this test does not always work, of course, but it is good enough when combined with other checks). In all of those approaches, Aiken and his staff were exploring unknown territory in what would become an important branch of modern computer science.

The last type of error, due to machine malfunctions, was also difficult to detect and prevent. A machine as complex as the Mark I had thousands of places where something could go wrong at every step of a computation. Aiken stressed one approach to that problem—an approach which curiously reveals his knowledge of the history of computing and his sense of his own place in that history.

The approach was to repeat the computation, using a subset of the input data, but not using the same formulas as before. If the machine yielded the same results as before while using different registers, accumulators, switches, and tape units, then it was safe to say that the original computations were correct for all their input values. If they did not agree, then further calculations could localize and evenutally isolate the defective components. (A good computer programmer is like Sherlock Holmes—when a program does not work the programmer has to be able to piece together bits of strange and seemingly incomprehensible evidence to find the culprit.)

The alternate method Aiken chose to evaluate polynomials was that of finite differences—the same method that started Charles Babbage on his long, frustrating road to computers in 1822. So Aiken not only acknowledged Babbage as the inspiration for his plans to build a sequence controlled calculator, but he also incorporated some of Babbage's very methods into his machine as a way to check its reliability.[31]

The link between Babbage and the modern computer age is a complex one. Other computer pioneers from the 1935-1945 era knew of Babbage: Zuse in Germany, Vannevar Bush at MIT, perhaps a few others. But Aiken, and probably only he, consciously saw his own role as one of picking up where Babbage had left off a century before.[32] In his published descriptions of the Mark I, Aiken always gave generous credit to Babbage as the true pioneer in computing.

Most accounts of the history of the computer mention Babbage's Analytical Engine as the machine that began the computer age. That is because in it one finds all the functions that a true computing system requires: program control, memory, arithmetic unit, and input/output facilities. The Analytical Engine was furthermore consciously designed to be a general-purpose computer, and that, too, is a central feature of today's computers. But Babbage came to the idea of building the Analytical Engine after first building a test model, then planning a full-scale model, of a more modest Difference Engine. (The test model of the Difference Engine was the only machine that he ever finished.)

The Difference Engine was to have computed the values of polynomials by summing up finite differences: by mechanizing only the operation of addition (obviously much easier than mechanizing all the arithmetic operations). The method of finite differences could nonetheless evaluate precisely the same kinds of functions that the Mark I was planned to evaluate. Thus it was a good way to check the Mark I's circuits, as the additions could be programmed in any of the seventy-two accumulators, checking the answers yielded by the multiplier, divider, and other more complex parts of the machine during a regular run of a program. Aiken conceived of the Mark I as the direct successor of the Analytical Engine, and the Mark I was a general-purpose computer. But the spirit of the Difference Engine lived in it as well.

THE METHOD OF FINITE DIFFERENCES

Values of higher-order polynomials like the one given above may be evaluated using only simple additions, once certain initial values have been calculated. That was the secret of the Difference Engine: it could be mechanically simple, yet mathematically sophisticated, by an ingenious linking of its wheels to one another.

The following table lists the values of the function given above:

$$F(x) = x^4 + 3x^3 - 3x^2/4 - 22x + 3$$

for the integer values of x from 5 to 10:

x	$F(x)$	1st diff.	2nd diff.	3rd diff.	4th diff.	5th diff.
5	874.25					
		913.75				
6	1788.00		540.5			
		1454.25		174		
7	3242.25		714.5		24	
		2168.75		198		0
8	5411.00		912.5		24	
		3081.25		222		
9	8492.25		1134.5			
		4215.75				
10	12708.00					

The numbers in the columns to the right of $F(x)$ are obtained by subtracting the two adjacent values in the column immediately to the left (for example, the first entry in the column labeled "1st diff.," 913.75, is the difference between $F(6)$ and $F(5)$, the two numbers immediately to its left). The first entry in the column labeled "2nd diff." is the difference of the first two entries in the first-difference column, and so on.

Note that the fifth difference is zero, and that the fourth difference is a constant value (24). For any polynomial of the nth degree (the degree is the highest exponent that appears in the expression), the nth difference will be constant. (It is in fact

$$n!(\Delta x)^n a_n$$

Where $n!$ is the product $n(n-1)(n-2)(n-3)\ldots(1)$, Δx is the increment value of x, and a_n is the coefficient of the highest exponent of x. In the above example the increment of x is 1, the coefficient is 1, and the degree is 4, so the fourth difference is 4!, or 24.)

So by calculating the constant nth difference, plus a few initial values of the intermediate differences (that would have to be done by hand), one can construct a table like the one above for more complex equations, using only the operation of addition. Furthermore, those polynomials could approximate, as accurately as one wished, any equations that one encountered in descriptions of real-world phenomena—including the far more difficult and refractory transcendental functions such as exponentials, logarithms, trigonometric functions, as well as the more exotic Bessel and elliptic functions that would be the grist for the Mark I's mill throughout its lifetime.

Hence Babbage's Difference Engine would have been a powerful mathematical tool had it been completed. Even though it was limited to ordinary polynomials, given enough levels of differences it could have approximated just about any function a mathematician would have required—accurately, tirelessly, mechanically. In Aiken's own words: "Thus the calculus of finite differences has become the bridge between mathematical analysis and numerical computation."[33]

In 1864, long after Babbage had given up hope of ever completing either of his computing engines, he wrote:

Half a century may probably elapse before any one without those aids which I leave behind me, will attempt so unpromising a task. If, unwarned by my example, any man shall undertake and shall succeed in really constructing an engine embodying in itself the whole of the executive department of mathematical analysis upon different principles or by simpler mechanical means, I have no fear of leaving my reputation in his charge, for he alone will be able to appreciate the nature of my efforts and the value of their results.[34]

Howard Aiken chose that quotation to introduce the *Manual of Operation* of the Mark I.

The Mark I evaluated functions directly. The method of finite differences was used only as a check since it used different parts of the machine and was coded in a different way without any multiplications. Results of the two methods were compared in register 72, using its comparison feature: the machine stopped if the two answers did not agree.[35] Computations were checked frequently: as often as every twenty minutes to ensure that the machine was not spewing out volumes of nonsense. Besides using that check, problems were often recorded and run again using the same direct evaluation method, but using different parts of the machine. In all, the checking of the machine for errors was an important, time-consuming part of the work of the Harvard Computation Laboratory.

At its public unveiling, the Mark I was hailed as "Babbage's dream come true." Aiken succeeded in building the Analytical Engine that Babbage failed to build. But there were important differences between the two. Their anatomies were different: the Analytical Engine was to have been powered by steam, the Mark I was driven by electricity. Numbers in the Mark I were transmitted by wire, not by mechanical linkages. But there were also more fundamental differences. Their physiologies were different as well; had Babbage completed his machine it would have been programmed differently (more like modern computers than like the Mark I, actually). That is the result of the Mark I's arithmetic having been spread out through its memory units.[36]

Howard Aiken probably did not perceive those differences, or if he did, he did not think they were important. It is not clear exactly how much Aiken really drew from his knowledge of Babbage besides the general idea. His 1937 proposal said that the Analytical Engine was to have evaluated algebraic formulas "by the method of finite differences," which was not true. Others have pointed out how, if Aiken had been familiar with Babbage's writings, and especially with Ada Augusta's comments on his work, he would certainly have recognized the importance of fitting his machine out with full conditional branching capabilities—something he did not do until after the Second World War when he learned of other computers that did have them.[37]

But the spirit of Babbage lived in the clicking relays of the Mark I. By 1959, when the machine was dismantled, those relays seemed as quaint and old-fashioned as Babbage's "store," "mill," and Jacquard control. Babbage once remarked that he would gladly give up the rest of his life for the opportunity to live a few days in the distant future.[38] Had he been granted his wish and come back to earth in the 1980's, when executives are stuffing computers into their attaché cases while their children are stuffing quarters into computer games at the local mall, he might be bewildered by it all. But if he could have returned in 1944 to the Harvard Computation Laboratory, where he could have seen the Automatic Sequence Controlled Calculator gobble up paper tape and whack out long tables of Bessel functions on a typewriter, he would have felt right at home.

HOW THE MARK I WAS USED

The various magazine and newspaper articles which announced the dedication of the Automatic Sequence Controlled Calculator in 1944 accurately described its size, weight, storage capacity, and other physical specifications. But they were necessarily vague as to the intended use for the computer. Most said only that it would be used for classified problems by the Navy. Later accounts said that the Navy used it "for ballistics and ship design...also...some problems in lens design."[39] No doubt the ballistics work included the preparation of firing tables. The wartime need for those tables was a major force behind the development of computers in the United States. It was the sole purpose for which ENIAC was built. One other problem for which the Mark I was used was "a highly secret, mathematical simulation of the first atomic bomb." That calculation is still classified, but it might have been a calculation of the bomb's blast effects.[40]

But the main use for the computer was for the preparation and printing of tables of mathematical functions—the same use Babbage intended for his Difference Engine. *Time* magazine devoted a cover story in 1950 to the new computers; in that story the Mark I had acquired an affectionate nickname from its programmers—"Bessie"—because she computed Bessel functions.[41] By 1950 the urgent wartime problems were gone; other military work was better done on the newer and faster computers at Harvard and elsewhere. "Bessie" settled into a daily routine of computing and printing tables of the various Bessel functions, and that would remain her work until she was dismantled in 1959.

BESSEL FUNCTIONS

It was the desire to solve differential equations that started Howard Aiken on his path to the design of an automatic computer. Such equations describe physical phenomena in terms of a rate of change of a quantity that varies with time: hence the name "differential." One particular differential equation arises frequently in the study of vibration and periodic motion, and it involves not only rates of change but also second derivatives, that is, rates of rates of change. This equation takes the form:

$$x^2(d^2y/dx) + x(dy/dx) + y(x^2 - n^2) = 0$$

There are two families of solutions to this equation (since it contains a second-order derivative), and these are usually called solutions of the first and second "kinds." For each kind there are many different solutions depending on the value of the parameter n, which is usually a small positive integer but in fact may take on any positive real value.[42]

Besides the two basic families of solutions, there are also functions that resemble a combination of the solutions of the first and second kinds. These are sometimes called *Hankel Functions of Order N*, and I mention them because the first tables that the Mark I computed were of those functions.[43] There are also classes of solutions defined for complex values of the independent variable, and finally, *integrals* of all the various Bessel functions of the various kinds.

It was the job of the numerical analyst or engineer to determine which of the above functions (if any) was applicable to a particular problem at hand; appropriate values of n and x also had to be selected. That was often the most difficult part of the analysis of a physical problem. But there still remained the problem of evaluating the Bessel function itself. The Bessel functions resemble the trigonometric functions in that they are periodic and often regularly pass through the zero value (the so-called zeros of the Bessel functions). But there is no easy way to evaluate them. The analyst had to select a polynomial approximation that fit the Bessel function closely enough for the interval he or she was interested in—using techniques already well known in Babbage's time. Obviously it would be advantageous if the engineer or mathematician could consult a table of those values rather than compute them every time they were needed. It was the task of the Mark I to compute (using appropriate polynomial approximations) and print tables of the various kinds of Bessel functions for a wide range of arguments. The many different kinds of functions and the range over which their values were tabulated ensured that the Mark I would be busy for many years—even after other more advanced computers had long made its design and technology obsolete. The computations themselves were long and involved, but they suited the abilities of the Mark I well, and they were not hindered by the machine's limitations.

Bessel functions are used throughout the sciences and engineering. A typical application might be the vibration of a plate that is fixed at its perimeter (like a drum-head). The vibration at any point is a function of the elasticity of the material, its tension, and the distance of that point from the fixed perimeter. Another common application is the analysis of radio transmissions, especially FM signals, in which the regular vibration of the carrier wave is modulated by a signal that carries the voice or other information. Even the structure of the DNA molecule, consisting of a periodic repetition of a basic chemical structure, was unraveled with the help of Bessel functions.[44]

That was how the Mark I was used. In the years following the war, Harvard University Press brought out a series of those tables, and they are available in libraries throughout the world as the *Annals* of the Harvard Computation Laboratory, volumes 2 through 36. The first of them, the tables of Hankel Functions of Order One-Third, was coded on the machine in August, 1944, and was run successfully that fall and winter. The entire set of tables contained over 70,000 eighteen-digit quantities and took the equivalent of forty-five days to be computed. Because that work had to be sandwiched in between the other war-related computations, the Harvard staff could not compute the tables in a long continuous run, and so they had to retype the numbers by hand before they could be published. Subsequent tables were printed directly from the output of the Mark I's output devices, which greatly reduced errors in copying and typing long strings of digits. (Such errors were frequent in any tables set by hand—Babbage saw the elimination of that step as a decisive advantage of his Difference Engine).[45] The tables themselves were computed by evaluating suitable polynomial approximations for given intervals, and then checked by alternate methods of direct evaluation (not, however, by the method of finite differences).

In his review of the speed and power of the machine, L. J. Comrie observed that though the tables were useful and their evaluation took a lot of effort, the work could nevertheless have been done by teams of human beings equipped with desk calculators. He asked, "Does the calculator open up new fields in mathematical and numerical analysis?"[46] That is hard to say: it did do more than compute tables. But for the most part it performed yeoman service for mathematicians and engineers. It never did anything glamorous like crack codes or design secret weapons, but the Mark I represented a breakthrough in computing nonetheless. The tables themselves were well-used, although by 1959 other tables of the same functions were also available. Sales of the volumes brought in money for the Computation Lab, money that financed the construction of other computers at Harvard.

Whatever else it did, it spelled the end of the era of computing tables by hand. Even today, when computing power is cheap and widespread, there is still a need for tables of the more complex functions. After the war the National Bureau of Standards undertook a compilation of the most frequently used tables (using the Mark I's work for the Bessel Functions). The NBS's *Handbook of Mathematical Functions* became a staple of many a working mathematician's library. A numerical analyst today can compute the desired values of one of the simpler Bessel functions at his desk, using a pocket calculator or personal computer, but there are many times when that procedure is neither practical nor accurate enough. The computer itself has brought the field of numerical analysis to a new level, where even more tables, more accurate and more elaborate, are needed. All of that activity may be said to be part of the legacy of Howard Aiken and the Automatic Sequence Controlled Calculator.[47]

POSTWAR COMPUTING AT HARVARD

The rift between Aiken and IBM that surfaced before the dedication ceremony grew after the war. It was not just the dispute over whether the ASCC was to be covered or not. Thomas Watson felt that Aiken was unwilling to share any credit for the success of the project. In 1944 IBM was not the industrial giant it is today. Aiken felt that the computer was his idea; whoever happened to build it was of little import. The Harvard Lab continued building computers under Aiken's direction—but not with IBM's help. (The Harvard machines took on the names "Mark I," "Mark II," and so on.)[48]

Aiken was never convinced that vacuum tubes would make good computer components, and so his machines continued to use relays long after much faster electronic computers were completed elsewhere. He did use tubes in the Mark IV, but only for a few units where speed was absolutely needed; everywhere else he used relays.[49] But by 1950 other pioneers were arguing that computers should use only vacuum tubes, handle numbers in binary not decimal form, and store their programs internally. On all those features Aiken swam against the stream, and he did not prevail.

Meanwhile, Watson and IBM had a bitter first taste of large-scale computing, but they were smart enough to remain involved in the new technology. They of course continued to develop and market faster punched card machines, like the 603 electronic multiplier already mentioned. One of their customers, the Northrop Aircraft Company, hooked up an improved type 604 multiplier to an IBM 402 accounting machine, and with that they had a reliable automatic calculator of modest power. IBM recognized Northrop's ingenuity and followed in 1949 by marketing their own Card Programmed Calculator based on that lashup.[50]

But the CPC was not capable of fully general program control like the Mark I, although its reliability and low cost made it a very successful product. The company also went on to build a large-scale computer along the same lines as the Mark I, which they called the Selective Sequence Electronic Calculator, built in Endicott and dedicated in 1948. As the name suggests, the SSEC could branch to different sequences in its instruction set, but despite its name, it was more a relay calculator like the Mark I than a true electronic computer. It used vacuum tubes only for a central high-speed processing unit; electromechanical parts were used elsewhere. It handled numbers in the decimal system, and despite the fact that it could store (and even modify) some of the instructions in its high-speed memory, its architecture owed more to the punched card, plugboard technology than to the new ideas about stored-program computers that were current by 1948. (Nonetheless, it must be given credit as the first machine to function with a stored-program capability.) The SSEC was dismantled in 1952, but it maintained IBM's foothold in large-scale computing at a critical time, and that foothold would be vital to the company's entry into the mainframe computer business a few years later. (The company marketed its first true stored-program electronic computer, the 701, in 1952.)[51]

The SSEC was installed in a prominent place at IBM's New York offices on 57th Street, in full view of passers-by. (When the machine needed maintenance, curtains had to be drawn to prevent the public from seeing the machine with its panels down.) Like the Mark I it was well publicized, and the SSEC gave ordinary people their first glimpse of what a real computer looked like. One little-known fact is that it alone among the early computers was available for private use, at a charge of $300 an hour. All the other machines were used primarily by the military, with only "extra" time, if there was any, allocated to civilians.[52] IBM deserves credit for that innovation as well.

In conclusion, Aiken's work at Harvard was an impressive first step into the computer age. But it did not contribute directly to the mainstream after 1950. The fact that his laboratory was publicized meant that he became a clearinghouse for correspondence and information about computers for those who were not privy to other sources of knowledge. As a result he was always at the center of later computer activity, even though his aversion to electronics and to the stored program principle meant that his ideas had little influence. The Computation Laboratory was perhaps his most lasting achievement. It provided a place where a new generation of students could learn about computers, and many of his students went on to become pioneers in their own right—to be sure, in ways that Aiken might not have understood. (Ken Iverson, the designer of the language APL, and Fred Brooks, who worked on the IBM 360, were two of Aiken's students.) He remained on the staff until his retirement in July, 1961, after which he did some private consulting. He died in 1973; by then his reputation as a pioneer was quite secure.

NOTES

1. Howard Aiken, "The Future of Automatic Computing Machinery," *Elektronische Rechenanlage und Informationsverarbeitung* (Darmstadt, 1956), p. 33.

2. William Rodgers, *Think: A Biography of the Watsons and IBM* (New York: Stein and Day, 1969), p. 172; "Giant New Calculator," *Science News Letter*, August 12, 1944, cover; August 19, 1944, p. 111; Volta Torrey, "Robot Mathematician Knows All the Answers," *Popular Science Monthly*, 145 (October, 1944), 86-89, 222, 226, 230.

3. Henry Tropp, "The Effervescent Years: A Retrospective," *IEEE Spectrum*, 11 (February, 1964), 70-81.

4. Anthony Oettinger, "Howard Aiken," *Communications ACM*, 5 (June, 1962), 29.

5. Howard Aiken, "Proposed Automatic Calculating Machine," *IEEE Spectrum*, 1 (August, 1964), 62-69.

6. Howard Aiken, "Historical Introduction," *A Manual of Operation for the Automatic Sequence Controlled Calculator, Annals* of the Harvard Computation Laboratory, vol. 1 (Cambridge, Mass.: Harvard, 1946), p. 8; Tropp, "Effervescent Years," pp. 72-73.

7. Brian Randell, *The Origins of Digital Computers: Selected Papers*, 2nd ed. (New York: Springer, 1973), p. 127; Rodgers, *Think*, pp. 166-169; Charles and Ray Eames, *A Computer Perspective* (Cambridge, Mass.: Harvard, 1973), pp. 114, 173.

8. Rodgers, *Think*, pp. 169-171.

9. *Manual of Operation*, preface, forward; Tropp, "Effervescent Years," p. 73; Rodgers, *Think*, p. 169.

10. Rodgers, *Think*, pp. 169-171.

11. Byron E. Phelps, "The Beginnings of Electronic Computation," Report TR OO.2259, IBM Corporation, Systems Development Division (Poughkeepsie, N.Y.: IBM, Dec. 9, 1971).

12. Wallace J. Eckert, *Punched Card Methods in Scientific Computation* (New York: Thomas J. Watson Astronomical Computing Bureau, Columbia University, 1940).

13. *Manual of Operation*, preface; Richard M. Bloch, "Mark I Calculator," *Annals* of the Harvard University Computation Laboratory, 16 (1947), 23-30.

14. "Giant New Calculator," p. 111; Thomas G. Belden and Marva R. Belden, *The Lengthening Shadow: The Life of Thomas J. Watson* (Boston: Little, Brown, 1962) pp. 258-261; Rodgers, *Think*, pp. 169-171.

15. Edmund C. Berkely, *Giant Brains, or Machines that Think* (New York: Wiley, 1949), pp. 89-93; J. H. Curtiss, "A Review of Government Requirements and Activities in the Field of Automatic Digital Computing Machinery," *Theory and Techniques for Design of Electronic Digital Computers*, Lectures Given at the Moore School, July-

August 1946 (Philadelphia, 1947), lecture 29; *Manual of Operation*, p. 22; Margaret Harmon, *Stretching Man's Mind* (New York: Mason/Charter, 1975), p. 118.

16. Howard Aiken and Grace Hopper, "The Automatic Sequence Controlled Calculator—I," *Electrical Engineering* 65 (1946), 384-391; Bloch, "Mark I Calculator," pp. 23-30.

17. Aiken and Hopper, p. 205; Bloch, pp. 24-25.

18. Bloch, pp. 24-25.

19. Randell, *Origins*, pp. 11, 187-188; Grace Hopper, "Computer Software," *Computers and Their Future* (Lladudno: Richard Williams, 1970), pp. 7/3-7/26; Berkeley, *Giant Brains*, pp. 90, 112.

20. Philip and Emily Morrison, eds., *Charles Babbage and His Calculating Engines: Selected Writings by Charles Babbage and Others* (New York: Dover, 1961), pp. 245-295.

21. Berkeley, *Giant Brains*, p. 96.

22. Randell, *Origins*, p. 216.

23. *Manual of Operation*, p. 45.

24. Howard Aiken and Grace Hopper, "The Automatic Sequence Controlled Calculator—II," *Electrical Engineering*, 65 (1946), 449-454.

25. Jeremy Bernstein, *The Analytical Engine* (New York: Random House, 1964), p. 54.

26. Berkeley, *Giant Brains*, p. 98.

27. *Manual of Operation*, pp. 32, 111-119, 296; "Mark I," *Encyclopedia of Computer Science*" (New York: Petrocelli/Charter, 1976), pp. 852-853.

28. Howard Aiken and Grace Hopper, "The Automatic Sequence Controlled Calculator—III," *Electrical Engineering*, 65 (1946), 522-528.

29. *Manual of Operation*, p. 16.

30. Aiken and Hopper, "Automatic Sequence...—III."

31. Joseph O. Harrison, Jr., "The Preparation of Programs for the Mark I Calculator," *Proceedings of a Symposium on Large-Scale Calculating Machinery, Annals* of the Harvard Computation Laboratory, vol. 16 (Cambridge, Mass.: Harvard, 1948), pp. 208-210.

32. N. Metropolis and J. Worlton, "A Trilogy on Errors in the History of Computing," *Proceedings First USA-Japan Computer Conference*, Tokyo, 1972, pp. 684-685.

33. *Manual of Operation*, pp. 10, 296-304.

34. Morrison and Morrison, *Charles Babbage*, p. 142.

35. *Manual of Operation*, pp. 10, 296-304.

36. L. J. Comrie, "Babbage's Dream Come True," *Nature*, 158 (October 26, 1946), 567-568; Tropp, "Effervescent Years," p. 73.

37. Randell, *Origins*, pp. 187, 192; Metropolis and Worlton, "Trilogy," pp. 684-685.

38. Morrison and Morrison, *Charles Babbage*, p. xxxi.

39. *Science News Letter*, August 12, 1944, p. 11; *Time*, August 14, 1944, p. 72; Eames, *Computer Perspective*, p. 122.

40. "Mark I," *Encyclopedia*, p. 853.

41. *Time*, January 23, 1950, pp. 54-60.

42. M. Abramovitz and I. Stegun, *Handbook of Mathematical Functions* (Washington, D.C.: National Bureau of Standards, 1964), pp. 358-494; Frank Bowman, *Introduction to Bessel Functions* (New York: Dover, 1958).

43. Published as the *Annals of the Harvard Computation Laboratory*, vol. 2, 1945.

44. Bowman, *Bessel Functions*, pp. 122-134; Francis Crick, "The Double Helix: A Personal View," *Nature*, 248 (April 26, 1974), p. 766.

45. The tables were reviewed in *Mathematical Tables and Other Aids to Computation*, 2 (1946), 176-177.

46. *Annals of the Harvard Computation Laboratory*, vol. 2, introduction; Comrie, "Babbage's Dream," p. 568; Morrison and Morrison, *Charles Babbage*, p. 314.

47. Herman H. Goldstine, *The Computer from Pascal to von Newmann* (Princeton: Princeton University Press, 1972), p. 17.

48. Rodgers, *Think*, p. 178; Randell, *Origins*, p. 188.

49. Oettinger, "Howard Aiken," p. 298.

50. John W. Sheldon and Liston Tatum, "The IBM Card-Programmed Calculator," in Randell, *Origins*, pp. 229-235.

51. Cuthbert Hurd, "Early IBM Computers: Edited Testimony," *Annals of the History of Computing*, 3 (1981), 168; Belden, *Lengthening Shadow*, pp. 258-261.

52. *Time*, January 23, 1950, p. 59.

4
Number, Please—
Computers at Bell Labs

> The Bell Telephone Laboratories general-purpose relay computer is probably the best mechanical brain made up to the end of 1947....
> —Edmund Berkeley, 1949

A telephone network does two things. First, it transmits voices from one person's phone to another's. Second, it allows a person to select the caller he or she wishes to speak with—by letting the caller "dial" a phone connection. Obviously the first is the essence of what a telephone is—that was what Alexander Graham Bell invented in 1875. But the second is just as important to the telephone system as it is used today. The two functions are basically different: one is concerned with continuously varying signals generated by the human voice, the other is a cascading of yes-or-no switches that establishes a path between two subscribers. One is an *analog* process, the other *digital*.

Between 1937 and 1946 engineers and scientists at Bell Telephone Laboratories built a number of digital relay computers, among the first working programmable machines anywhere. Their experience with the technology of switching—that second aspect of telephony—was the basis for Bell's entry into digital computing. But the first aspect—the transmission of analog voice signals—played a role too, as we shall see. The invention of the computer at Bell Laboratories, like its invention elsewhere, resulted from a convergence of technical skill, social need, and talent. Those preconditions were there by the mid-1930's. It remained for one of Bell's employees, Dr. George Stibitz, to serve as the catalyst to bring them together.

BACKGROUND: BELL LABORATORIES

A telephone codes information (the sound of the human voice) into electrical signals, transmits those signals over wires, and decodes them into sound at the other end. The engineers who worked on this form of "data processing" (of course they did not use that term) in the early days had little theory to guide them. For short distances it was easy enough to send voice signals; indeed Alexander Graham Bell's original circuit was terribly inefficient from a modern standpoint, yet it worked well enough to launch the industry.

But for long distances the problem of keeping the signal intelligible became acute. The first circuits were limited to a range of a few miles before the signal faded out.

With that restriction on the telephone's use, it did not compete with Western Union, the dominant telecommunications company of the late 19th century. Western Union handled digital information (dots and dashes) that could be regenerated by "repeaters" along a line, thereby allowing coast-to-coast communication. But telephone signals vary continuously over a large spectrum. As they lose their strength they cannot be regenerated by a repeater. They have to be amplified instead.

So the telephone coexisted with the telegraph in its first few decades of existence. Its personal service, using the human voice and not a code, suited it well for local urban traffic. Western Union's telegraph handled long-distance messages.

The Bell company was not satisfied with that state of affairs. It introduced a number of improvements to increase the distances over which telephone signals could be sent: the two-wire circuit in the 1880's, the "loading coil" after 1900, and others. But it was the adoption and perfection of the vacuum-tube amplifier after 1912 that finally made amplification, and hence transcontinental service, practical. (The first transcontinental call was made in July, 1914.)[1] Establishing reliable (and cheap) long distance service launched Bell into a period of steady growth until it had all but relegated the telegraph to a back corner of the telecommunications world.

So the success of the Bell System depended on its ability to transmit and amplify telephone messages over long distances. That success in turn came from recognizing the potential value of the "audion" vacuum tube (invented by Lee DeForest in 1906) and improving it to the point where it would function as a reliable amplifier. DeForest had not really understood the fundamentals of his own invention; a strong research effort by Bell Telephone revealed the nature of the tube's function—and turned it into a practical device.

It was for that purpose that a laboratory for basic research was established in 1911, as a branch of Western Electric, Bell's manufacturing company.[2] In 1925 the lab was incorporated as the Bell Telephone Laboratories, and given charge of basic research for the Bell System, which by then had become a powerful monopoly under the leadership of Theodore N. Vail. Thus began an institution that has become synonymous with fundamental and exciting research at the frontiers of physics, chemistry, and other branches of modern science.

Research on the physical problems of long-distance telephony was what started Bell Laboratories, but by the 1930's it was busy with that other aspect of telephony, switching, as well. The earliest networks used human operators to route a caller to the desired callee, and indeed there are places in rural America where calls are still placed that way.[3] But from the beginning of personal phone service there was an effort to automate the call-selection process. Many historical accounts mention that an undertaker named Almon B. Strowger invented the automatic rotary dial in 1891 to prevent operators from being bribed to divert business to his competitors.[4] Whether or not that story is accurate, it does show that the telephone system was closely linked to automatic switching from the start. After 1921 the dial began replacing operators in significant numbers. It is still in wide use today, although the push-button "dial" is now replacing it.

The engineers who designed the first switching circuits were, in effect, using electromagnetic relays to implement "logical networks," although they did not consider their work in those abstract terms. Some of the circuits they developed were quite sophisticated: for example, if all the major trunk lines between two cities were busy, a call would be automatically rerouted through another line, perhaps through a third city, all automatically. While the switching equipment was setting up this path, other banks of relays would store the dialed number and then retrieve it when the call was ready to go through. These two functions—automatic selection of a circuit depending on the present condition of the network, and temporary storage and retrieval of numbers—are of course also central to the operation of computers.[5]

In retrospect it seems inevitable that someone at Bell Laboratories would adapt that switching equipment to function as a digital computer. But for what purpose? The switching circuits were already doing their job well; why adapt them to function as a general-purpose computer unless there was an obvious need for one? The Laboratories were committed to basic research in a variety of fields, and in 1925 that was something remarkable for an industrial laboratory in America. Nevertheless they were always mindful of the original purpose for which the labs were set up: in Theodore N. Vail's memorable phrase, "one system, one policy, and universal service."[6] Bell's engineers would build a digital computer only if they believed it would further those goals.

By the 1930's they saw the possibility of using relay circuits to perform ordinary arithmetic, as commonly performed with mechanical calculators.[7] Telephone switching circuits did not perform arithmetic in the ordinary sense, but they did convert numbers from their dialed code of pulses into other pulses that actually did the switching. It would have been an easy matter to have those conversions mimic the familiar laws of addition and subtraction of numbers. But there was no point in building a calculator out of relays, since existing mechanical calculators already worked well, and there was no reason to believe that relay calculators would be better—or cheaper. But a calculator that took advantage of the relay's ability to perform logical switching as well—something mechanical calculators could not do—would be justified, if there was a mathematical problem demanding that capability.

As it turned out, such a problem was being faced by the other division of Bell Labs—the division that worked with long-distance transmission of analog voice signals. Dr. George Stibitz, a research mathematician at the Labs, was the pivotal figure who matched the needs of that group with the capabilities known to the switching engineers. The result of this marriage was the Complex Number Computer, completed in 1939, which though not a programmable general-purpose computer, nonetheless inaugurated Bell's involvement in the computing field.

COMPLEX NUMBERS

The Complex Number Computer performed the four ordinary operations of arithmetic, but on complex rather than simple numbers. Complex numbers were used in the design of filters and amplifiers for long-distance telephone lines. The function of those devices was to maintain the strength of the desired voice signal, while at the same time keeping the level of unwanted signals (for example "noise") low. But the engineers had to be concerned with more than just the amplitudes of the signal and noise. They were also concerned with the "phase" of the signal—the relationship of the ever-varying voice signal with time. Filters and amplifiers introduced time-delays into the circuit, and unless those delays were accounted for, the resulting signal might be reduced rather than increased in strength. (One familiar example of phase effects is found in home stereo systems. The two loudspeakers, which deliver the left and right components of the reproduced sound, must be in phase with each other. If the phase is incorrect, the sound from one speaker will cancel out the sound from the other, regardless of the power of the amplifier. A similar situation occurs in telephone circuits.)

Engineers found that they had to represent a signal by a pair of numbers, one corresponding to its amplitude, the other to its phase, in any mathematical model of the physical processes they were dealing with. The key to the success of this method was that by following certain rules for the addition, subtraction, multiplication, and division of these pairs of numbers, the mathematical results corresponded closely to what happened when electrical signals combined with one another in a circuit.

Long before the first telephone line had been built, mathematicians had devised rules for working with pairs of numbers that arose in the solutions of certain algebraic equations. In devising those rules for "complex numbers," they wanted something useful for the work they were doing, but they were also concerned with making those rules logically consistent. That is, the rules for complex arithmetic were an extension of, and did not contradict, those of ordinary simple arithmetic.[8]

Historically the study of complex numbers arose from the study of quadratic equations, in which certain solutions could only be gotten by taking the square root of a negative number. Thus the "imaginary" quantity i, the square route of -1, was introduced. The second number of the pair that makes up a complex number was thought of as being multiplied by this quantity.

For electrical engineers it did not matter how this theory arose, or even what i stood for, for that matter. (They did not use the letter i either, since it might be confused with the symbol for electrical current, so they used j instead.) What did matter was that the rules for manipulating those numbers were consistent with ordinary arithmetic, and that they were useful for the analysis of electrical signals. The history of mathematics has many other examples of a theory finding unexpected applications that its creators never anticipated. (Probably the most famous example was Apollonius's study of the conic sections, written in the third century B.C.: it was lost to the West for centuries, then in a breathtaking leap—twenty centuries later—Johannes Kepler used those curves to explain the motions of the planets around the sun.)

The mathematicians who developed complex arithmetic lived too early to see its application to telephone circuits, but at least one of them, Carl Friedrich Gauss, would not have been surprised—he built Europe's first telegraph in 1833, connecting his house with his laboratory at Göttingen!

Incidentally, the use of complex arithmetic as a tool for the analysis of electrical circuits was pioneered by Charles P. Steinmetz, an immigrant to America who worked at the General Electric Laboratories on power distribution. Years later the analysis of telephone signals yielded to that same theory (despite their being more complicated than power currents).[9]

The engineer used a pair of numbers to represent the amplitude and phase of a signal, not the real and imaginary parts of the solution to an equation. When two signals were combined their addition corresponded to the addition of the two complex numbers:

$$(a,b) + (c,d) = (a+c, b+d)$$

Similarly for subtraction:

$$(a,b) - (c,d) = (a-c, b-d)$$

In physical terms, when two signals are added to each other, their amplitudes and phases are added separately.

Multiplication and division are less easy to visualize, but they represent what happens to signals when they pass through various stages of amplification and filtering. In establishing a coast-to-coast telephone line in the 1930's, Bell Labs was engaged in the design of filters and amplifying circuits, whose operation introduced phase delays into a signal. The analysis of those circuits required complex multiplication and division.[10]

The rules for multiplication and division are:

$$(a,b) \times (c,d) = (ac-bd, ad+bc)$$
$$(a,b) / (c,d) = [(ac+bd)/(c^2+d^2), (bc-ad)/(c^2+d^2)]$$

Note that in each of the above rules, when the second (phase) term is zero, the rules reduce to those of ordinary arithmetic. Complex arithmetic extends the range of arithmetic; it does not replace it.

Bell Labs employed a staff of about five to ten women who worked full-time computing products and quotients of complex numbers. (Addition and subtraction were presumably simple enough for the engineers to do for themselves.) For the arithmetic they used electromechanical desk calculating machines.

We see from the above formulas that multiplication of complex numbers requires four simple multiplications, one simple subtraction, and one simple addition. Complex division requires six multiplications, two additions, one subtraction, and two divisions of ordinary numbers. In each case several intermediate results appear—they have to be written down and retrieved later on.

George Stibitz saw that the switching circuits the relay engineers were working on in one part of the Labs could compute complex products for the voice circuit engineers in another part of the Labs. That relays could do arithmetic was already known; Stibitz had constructed a simple adder out of binary relays as early as 1937. That alone meant little. But if the relays could also perform the sequencing and temporary storage that complex arithmetic demanded (and which ordinary calculators could *not* do), then such a calculator would have a practical use. He later remarked that as a research mathematician he was familiar with complex numbers but not with relay circuits. On the other hand relay engineers were probably less familiar with complex numbers since these did not arise in their work very often.[11] That may be an exaggeration, but remember that switching circuits were designed in a trial-and-error fashion; there was little theory for them in 1935. Complex arithmetic was a child of pure mathematics—the nomenclature "complex," "imaginary," and "square root of minus one" does not help make this tool more accessible to someone not mathematically sophisticated. In any case, Stibitz made the connection.

GEORGE R. STIBITZ

George Robert Stibitz was born on April 20, 1904, in York, Pennsylvania, and spent his childhood in Dayton, Ohio, where his father was a professor of theology at a local college. He showed a talent for engineering and science at an early age, and so he attended an experimental high school set up in Dayton by Charles Kettering, the inventor of the automobile starting system.[12] He attended Denison University in Granville, Ohio, receiving a B.Phil., and then went on to Union College in Schenectady, New York, where he received an M.S. in 1927. Schenectady was of course the home of General Electric's research laboratory (cf. Steinmetz's work with complex numbers), and for a while Stibitz worked there. He returned to school, however, and received a Ph.D. in mathematical physics from Cornell in 1930, after which he went to New York City to work for Bell Labs. His doctoral dissertation concerned the study of the vibrations of nonplanar membranes.[13]

From 1930 to 1941 Stibitz worked for Bell Laboratories—that was when he pioneered the use of relays for automatic computation. During World War Two he was a member of the National Defense Research Committee (NDRC), where he worked on computing and other projects. At the end of the war he moved to northern New England, where he has lived ever since. He worked as a private consultant in Burlington, Vermont, and since 1964 he has been a professor of physiology at the Dartmouth Medical School in Hanover, New Hampshire. He is still active there in projects involving the use of computers in medicine.

In the fall of 1937 Stibitz was working with a group of mathematicians who were designing relay switching equipment. He took a few relays home one evening and assembled a device that could add two binary digits as indicated by lamps which glowed for the digit 1 and were dark for the digit 0. (In later years the computer world would take notice of these milestones, and so just as the mechanical devices Zuse built in his parents' flat would later take on the name "V1," and then "Z1," Stibitz's "breadboard" circuit would later be given the whimsical name "Model K"—for the kitchen table on which it was assembled. Neither Stibitz nor Zuse knew of each other's relay circuits until after the end of the war, by the way.)[14]

Years later Stibitz was asked to recount his first steps toward building a relay computer. He said he first learned of binary arithmetic from an algebra textbook he read as a schoolboy in Ohio—a textbook that his mother, who had taught algebra, gave him.[15]

Of course binary arithmetic follows naturally from the on-or-off nature of a telephone relay, as Zuse recognized, but remember that telephone networks also used a number of ten-position relays that Stibitz certainly knew of. The few other contemporaries of Stibitz (and Zuse) who were modifying telephone equipment to do arithmetic also regarded the relay as a substitute for the ten-position decimal wheels of a mechanical calculator; so they used multi-position relays.[16]

Only after he had built some of these test circuits for binary arithmetic did Stibitz seriously think of applying them to a complex number machine. Another Bell Labs mathematician, T. C. Fry, mentioned the problem of complex arithmetic to him later that year, and that was how the project got going.[17]

BUILDING THE COMPLEX NUMBER COMPUTER

Consider once again the formula for multiplying two complex numbers:

$$(a,b) \times (c,d) = (ac-bd, ad+bc)$$

where the letters a, b, c, and d stand for ordinary decimal numbers of up to eight digits precision. For the moment disregard the position of the decimal point in each number. (Another way of writing the complex number (a,b) is $(a+bi)$, where i is the square root of -1. If one were to carry out the product of $(a+bi) \times (c+di)$ just like an ordinary polynomial, the result would be:

$$\begin{array}{r} a + bi \\ \times \quad c + di \\ \hline ac + bci \\ + \qquad\quad adi + bdi^2 \\ \hline ac + (bc+ad)i + bdi^2. \end{array}$$

But since $i^2 = -1$, we have $ac + (bc+ad)i - bd$, or $(ac-bd) + (bc+ad)i$, which is the equivalent of the other definition of the complex product.)

Carrying out that multiplication on a machine would require the following steps, in a similar order:

Operator's actions:

1. Key in a, store in machine.
2. Key in b, same way.
3. Key in c, same way.
4. Key in d, same way.

Machine's actions:

5. Multiply a by d, store product temporarily.
6. Multiply a by c, same way.
7. Multiply b by d, same way.
8. Multiply b by c, same way.
9. Add the results of steps (5) and (8), above, giving the imaginary part of the product. Store this result temporarily.
10. Subtract the result of step (7) from step (6), giving the real part.
11. Display or print the real part, above.
12. Display or print the imaginary part, from step (9).
13. Stop the machine, and prepare it to accept new input data, if necessary.

There are, then, thirteen basic steps in multiplying two complex numbers automatically. Note that the above order can be varied: by careful attention to detail it is possible to telescope some of those steps together, and minimize the number of temporary storage registers needed.

One important aspect of complex multiplication is that there are no choices involved in the computation: the sequence proceeds the same way each time regardless of the outcome of previous steps. Another aspect is that, of the thirteen steps outlined above, six involve input or output operations—almost half the total. That is a much higher ratio than was found in either the Zuse computers or the Harvard Mark I.

That aspect of complex multiplication meant that if the machine were to handle numbers in the binary scale, a considerable amount of computing would be required to convert numbers to and from the decimal scale for each input or output step. For the Zuse computers that was less of a problem, since they were designed to handle arbitrarily long sequences in which the numbers were "among their [binary] fellows."[18]

The Complex Number Computer was not programmable. A combination of relay circuits permanently controlled its sequence of operations. Those relays were of the same type as the ones used to handle the numbers, but the machine did not have a separate, clearly defined part that handled the "control" of the computing sequence. (Later Bell Labs computers did.) The concept of programmability arose at Bell Labs only after the Complex Number Computer was built, after its builders saw that its basic computing elements were unduly restricted by its marriage to control circuits tying it to nothing but complex arithmetic. (Besides complex arithmetic, they tried to get the machine to perform polynomial arithmetic, of which complex arithmetic is a special case, cf. above. But the machine was too restricted for that.)

The practical consequence of the machine's permanent program was that it would not make sense to convert numbers into binary for internal handling. So although the first relay circuits Stibitz built were binary, he retained decimal arithmetic for his proposed complex number machine. But he did not want to abandon the simplicity of the binary relay and go over to ten-position relays. So he chose to represent each decimal digit by a tetrad of binary digits. (Four binary digits can express quantities up to $2^4 = 16$.) In this way a group of only four binary relays handled each digit, thereby retaining the simplicity of the binary system at least in the physical construction of the machine. By using the so-called *Binary Coded Decimal* (BCD) form, Stibitz said, "most of the advantages of the binary system are retained without its disadvantages."[19]

At one time he thought of training the machine's operators to think in binary, but Stibitz quickly saw that the difficulties of training human beings to work in a different number base would defeat the whole purpose of automating the process in the first place. A few modern computers, especially the very small ones, still must be programmed in binary or a related base, such as 8 or 16.[20]

Actually, telephone engineers had hit upon binary coding before Stibitz gave it a formal treatment. Switchboards have panels of lights that indicate telephone numbers. The easiest way to construct the panel is to have one wire for each light, or a total of ten wires for each decimal digit, seventy wires for a seven-digit telephone number. But engineers realized that the same information could be carried by only twenty-eight wires, coding each digit on a group of four wires. By the 1930's such an arrangement was standard for the design of telephone switchboards.[21]

Four wires can code more than ten digits—they can represent up to sixteen. For decimal digits there is a choice of which codes to use and which to ignore. The obvious code would be to have each decimal digit represented by its binary value, that is:

0 coded as 0000
1 coded as 0001

2 coded as 0010
3 coded as 0011
 •   •
 •   •
 •   •
9 coded as 1001

The decimal number 345, for example, would be coded as:

0011 0100 0101

Translating each digit into its BCD equivalent is simple and direct. Each digit key can have a set of four contacts that make the proper coded connection whenever the key is pressed (see Figure 4.1).

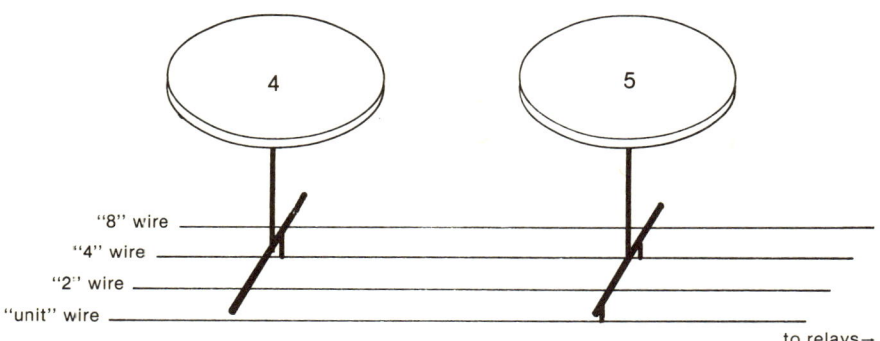

Pressing the 4-key would cause current to flow only in the third wire from the bottom, giving a binary code of 0100. Pressing the 5-key gives a code of 0101, and so on.

Figure 4.1. Using Multiple Key Contacts to Encode Decimal Digits

The disadvantage of BCD is that it is slightly less efficient than pure binary. Representing a decimal number in pure binary requires a little over three times the number of binary digits, but it takes four times the digits with BCD.

Since $2^4 = 16$, there are many other ways of encoding a decimal digit by a tetrad of binary digits besides the obvious one of using the direct binary equivalent. In fact there are over 29 billion possible ways (the permutation of sixteen items taken ten at a time, which is exactly 29,059,430,400). Whether or not any of those codes offer advantages that the direct binary code does not has been intensively studied in recent years, but in 1938 Stibitz had little theory to guide him.[22]

One factor that influenced his choice was the need to have a carry signal; when the sum of the decimal digits was greater than 9, he wanted the code to indicate that somehow. The binary code for 10 is 1010. To have that code initiate a carry would require extra circuits, it seemed.

In a pure binary register, a carry would occur after the number 1111 (decimal 15). That is six greater than the corresponding BCD value of decimal 9 (binary 1001). So Stibitz proposed distributing this difference for his decimal code. In other words, he coded each decimal number by the binary representation of three greater than that number, leaving a gap of three binary numbers at the beginning and at the end of the scheme, viz.:

> nothing coded as binary 0000 to 0010
> 0 coded as 0011 (0+3=3)
> 1 coded as 0100 (1+3=4)
> 2 coded as 0101 (2+3=5)
> 3 coded as 0110 (3+3=6)
> . .
> . .
> . .
> 9 coded as 1100 (9+3=12)
> nothing coded as 1101 to 1111

Adding 1 to 9 now looks like:

$$\begin{array}{r} 1100 \\ +0100 \\ \hline \end{array}$$

0000 plus a carry signal

That is a much easier way to detect a carry than one in which some digits are converted but others are not, depending on the particulars of a specific computation. Since 0000 has no numerical value in excess-three coding, it is easy to recognize when a carry has taken place.

Another advantage to using the excess-three code is that the complement of each digit (the difference between the digit and nine) is obtained simply by exchanging all the ones and zeros:

> 0011 = the code for 0; its complement is 9, coded as 1100
> 0100 = the code for 1; its complement is 8, coded as 1011
> 0101 = the code for 2; its complement is 7, coded as 1010
> . . . .
> . . . .
> . . . .
> 1100 = the code for 9; its complement is 0, coded as 0011

As we have seen with the Harvard Mark I, most machines do subtraction by adding complements. With the excess-three code those complements are easily obtained, by inverting the state of each relay. So with one stroke, Stibitz preserved a lot of the simplicity of the binary system, while gaining the advantages of handling decimal numbers.[23]

The remarkable advantages of excess-three arithmetic are not due to any deeper mathematical property of numbers, as far as I know. Modern electronic calculators use BCD, for the same reasons Stibitz used it—calculators have to display their results and receive new numbers frequently. And most of them use the excess-three coding. (Computers, on the other hand, use pure binary, although many of them can be set up to handle binary-coded decimal as well.)

THE COMPLEX NUMBER COMPUTER

Sometime in the fall of 1937 Stibitz drew up plans for a complex number computer using the above coding scheme. Bell Labs approved, and construction began in November, 1938, under the direction of Samuel B. Williams. Stibitz's role was one of developing the logical flow of numbers and operations that the machine was to carry out, and of translating those expressions into designs for relay circuits. Williams in turn applied his knowledge of relay technology to decide how best to construct the circuits that Stibitz had designed. The two men's skills complemented each other. But their roles were not so specialized that each did not help out with the other's work.

Besides deciding on the excess-three, binary-coded-decimal representation, Stibitz also chose to fix the decimal point at the beginning of each number, for example, −.xxxxxxxx. The operator would have to adjust the decimal points of the inputs accordingly. At first he proposed that the machine have a precision of seven decimal digits, but later he increased it to ten digits, of which eight were displayed and the other two were used as "guard digits" and thrown away.[24]

Most of Stibitz's work at that time consisted of writing out the logical expressions for binary arithmetic, then simplifying them until they were in a form suitable for relay implementation.

He did not know that in Berlin Konrad Zuse was doing almost the exact same thing, only for a pure binary, not a decimal, computer. Stibitz did know that Claude Shannon also had studied the correspondence of statements of symbolic logic with binary relay circuits while a graduate student at MIT. Shannon wrote his graduate thesis (published in 1938) on that subject, and then went to Bell Labs, where he and Stibitz learned of each other's work. But Shannon was not actively involved in the design of the Complex Number Computer. Clearly the idea of using relays to implement binary logic was common in the late 1930's. (Also in the 1930's there was a similar discovery in Japan, but that, too, was unknown in both Germany and America.)[25]

Sam Williams implemented those designs using the latest relay technology available to him. He adapted ordinary ten-digit keyboards for the numerical input, another bank of keys for the control commands, and an ordinary teletype machine for the printed output (Figure 4.2).

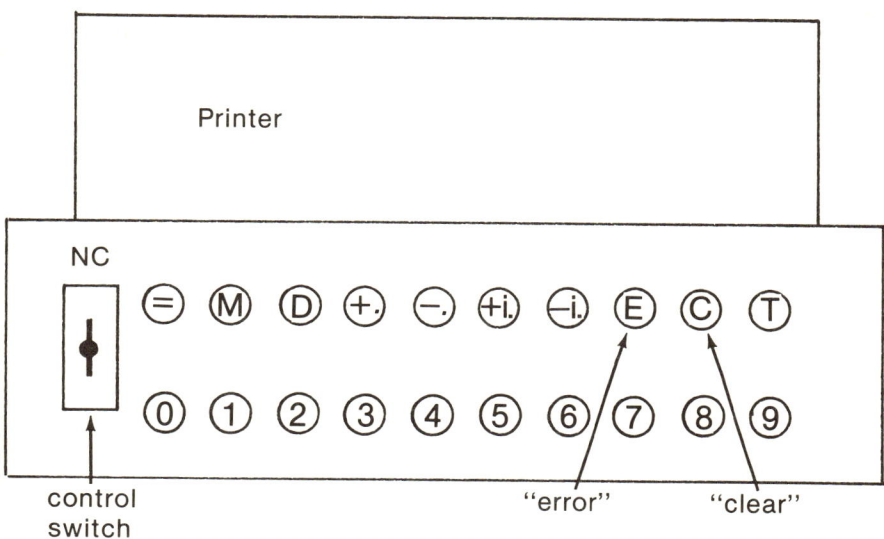

Figure 4.2. Keyboard Layout of the Complex Number Computer

Probably his most important contribution was to use the newly-developed *crossbar* switch to store the four numbers that comprised the input. Crossbars were developed to replace the Strowger rotary switches then in common use; instead of the six or eight contacts that a binary relay could handle, a crossbar had a matrix of switching elements that could switch up to 2,000 individual contacts.[26]

Construction of the Complex Number Computer began in April, 1939, at the old Bell Laboratories Building at 463 West Street in Manhattan. (Bell Labs moved to New Jersey after World War Two. The old buildings in Lower Manhattan have since become artists' lofts, and the dreary industrial neighborhood now goes by the fashionable name of Westbeth.) The machine was completed in October of that year. It began doing routine calculations for the Labs in January, 1940, and remained in service until 1949. As Bell Labs built other relay computers during the war, its name changed from Complex Number Computer (or "Complex Computer") to "Model I."[27] Table 4.1 lists the full specifications of the machine.

Table 4.1 THE BELL LABS MODEL I

Builders:	George R. Stibitz, Samuel B. Williams.
Place:	Bell Laboratories, 463 West Street, New York.
Dates:	Authorized 1938. Construction begun April, 1939. Completed October, 1939. Began operation January 8, 1940. Demonstrated to the public September 11, 1940, Dartmouth College. Dismantled 1949.
Cost:	Approx. $20,000.
Technology:	400–450 relays, 10 crossbar switches. 6–8 panels (approx. 8' x 5' x 1').
Arithmetic:	8-digit precision (10 internally), range ± 0.99999999. Binary-coded-decimal, excess-three code. Fixed decimal point at beginning of number.
Programming:	Fixed program to perform the four operations of complex arithmetic. Sequential operation; i.e., each relay or set of relays would commence its operation immediately after the relays before it in the sequence were finished. There was no synchronizing clock.
Speed:	Approximately one minute per multiplication.
Input/Output:	Ordinary teletype with a modified keyboard. Teletype connected to processor by a multiple-wire buss; therefore remote operation was possible. Up to three teletypes were connected to the arithmetic unit; an interlock permitted only one to be active at a time.

EVALUATION OF THE MACHINE—ANATOMY

The Complex Computer used relays as its basic building block—that was its "anatomy." Its appearance was deceptively simple: a metal rack for the relays, teletype keyboards for the input and output.

In a relay computer the structure is in the way the wiring is routed from one relay in the cabinet to another. One cannot discern the functions of those relays simply by looking at their position on the rack. The Harvard Mark I's layout by contrast was constrained by the need to have its elements arranged along a common driveshaft. Its structure was more revealing of the way it functioned, but at the same time it was not easy to modify that structure later on.

The Complex Computer was originally designed to compute only complex products and quotients; sums and differences were thought easy enough to be done manually. But soon after the machine was completed Williams realized that if the machine's registers were not cleared immediately after a multiplication it could accumulate sums as well. He added that modification with little difficulty—

to add or subtract complex numbers the operator disabled the clearing function, keyed in the number to be added or subtracted, then "multiplied" it by either $+1$ or -1 (in complex form $(1, 0)$ or $(-1, 0)$) to add or subtract.

Stibitz and Williams made another modification to the machine shortly after it was completed. They found that by disabling another clearing relay, the machine would multiply a number by a list of other numbers without having to key in the first number again and again. Stibitz first improvised this constant function by jamming a toothpick (!) in the relay that did the clearing; later the function was permanently wired in, with an appropriate button on the keyboard to activate it.[28] (It is surprising how frequently computer users today modify their million-dollar machines in the same kind of *ad hoc* ways, not always with the blessings of the computer manufacturer—recall Thomas Watson's desire to have the Harvard Mark I enclosed in steel and glass. But mechanical brains are, after all, machines, and there is no reason why their brass cannot be bent to serve man's will. Just the same, it takes some courage to make a so-called kluge modification to a computer, as Stibitz did.)

Using crossbar switches as number registers no doubt simplified the computer's construction, but it also limited its flexibility. Crossbar switches were much more complex than simple relays; they were also slower. All of the later Bell Labs relay computers used only simple relays for their construction.[29]

The binary-coded-decimal scheme is a hybrid, and it shares some of the properties of both binary and decimal arithmetic. Fundamentally, a decimal machine is a decimal machine, regardless of the code used for the individual decimal digits, since that is the way arithmetic is done internally. For example, the registers of the Complex Number Computer initiated a carry after the number 9, not after 1. The machine performed multiplication by repeated addition, but in its preliminary design phase there was some discussion over whether or not a table look-up might be better (cf. the Mark I). We have already seen with the Zuse computers that with a pure binary representation there is no difference between the two methods.

Some aspects of the machine's number handling were more suggestive of the binary system, however. When two numbers were added to each other, the register proceeded immediately to their sum, as a binary register does (and as human beings do). It did not pass through all the intermediate numbers before arriving at the sum. The Complex Number Computer thus computed sums in registers; it did not accumulate them like the Harvard Mark I. That was in part a consequence of the binary nature of the relays used in the machine; like the Zuse computers it handled numbers by applying the rules of symbolic logic. That is one step further removed from our ordinary intuitive concept of number.[30]

Figure 4.3 shows the structure of the Model I in block form. Of course the machine had no separate programming unit, so the circuits that directed the sequences of operations do not show up in the diagram, as they were scattered throughout the other units.

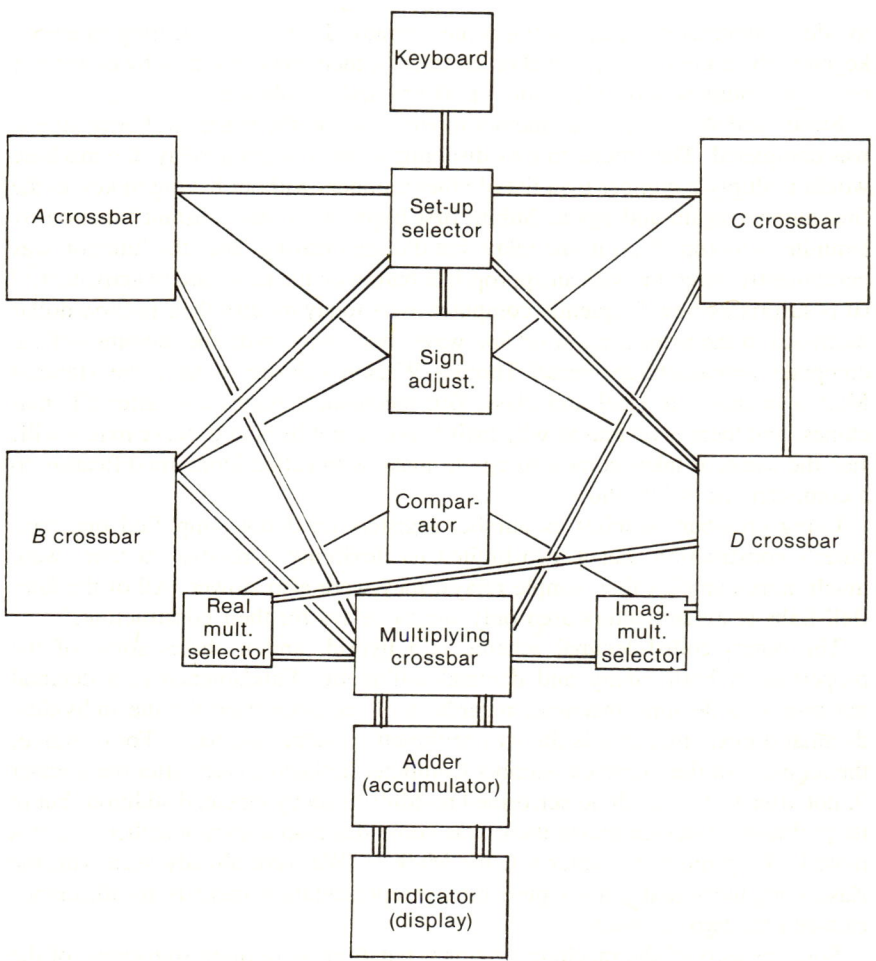

Double lines indicate transfer of a full number, up to ten decimal digits.

Single lines indicate transfer of control or sign signal.

Triple lines indicate transfer of digits, sign, and format information (e.g., whether number is real or imaginary).

Figure 4.3. Block Diagram of the Complex Number Computer

EVALUATION OF THE MACHINE—PHYSIOLOGY

The best way to see how the Complex Computer worked is to follow a typical problem and trace the steps it takes to solve it.

Assume the operator wants to divide the complex number (0.33 + 0.99i) by (−0.370 + 0.91i). This example is one Stibitz himself gave in a public demonstration, using the letter i to indicate the "imaginary" part of the number. Note also that he had already put the numbers in "normalized" form, with the decimal point at the beginning, since that was where the machine assumed it would be. In most problems the operator had to mentally scale the numbers until they were in that form—that was a limitation of the machine's power, and one which Stibitz and Williams recognized as being a serious one. But they chose not to modify the machine to let the decimal point float, as that would have required too much redesign. But even as the Complex Number Computer was performing its first calculations, they were working on a proposed "Model Two" that would have floating point.[31]

The operator was seated at a modified teletype terminal (see Figure 4.2, above). In the Bell Labs Building there were three of those terminals, each connected to the computer. The computing unit itself was kept in an unattended room in the building; few persons who used the machine actually saw it. The operator connected her terminal to the computer by flipping a switch on the left of the keyboard (I use the feminine pronoun because men seldom operated the computer). If another terminal was already in use, hers would be "locked out" —access denied—as a telephone caller gets a busy signal when the person being called is already on the line to someone else. As a rule, they used the machine only for brief sessions, perhaps a few multiplications or so, so the operator would usually wait a few minutes and try again. This early example of remote, multiple access illustrates the kind of flexibility and easy access that relay computers often had.

Having gained access to the machine, the operator would key in the problem as follows:

Problem: (0.33 + 0.99i) / (−0.37 + 0.91i)
Keyed as: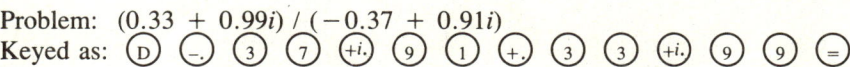

Note that the order is not the same as that in which the problem is usually stated. Pressing the key D told the machine that a division was to be performed, and would close certain relays that prepared the machine for that operation. The Complex Number Computer used "Prefix" notation—the operation was keyed in *before* the operands, not in between them, as a division is usually written, nor after them, as the Zuse computers did.

In a division the operator keyed in the denominator before the numerator, as

*Complex Number Computer, One of the Three Terminals.
Courtesy of Baker Library, Dartmouth College.*

the example shows—again the opposite of the way it is usually written. That was because in the formula for complex division, the quantity $(c^2 + d^2)$ is required for both parts of the answer. Keying in the denominator first got those numbers into the machine first, so that it could begin computing the "norm" $(c^2 + d^2)$ while the operator was keying in the numerator. Like the Mark I, the Complex Computer had quite a bit of parallel computing capability, and that helped speed up the operation of division. By keying the (+i) key, the operator alerted the machine that she was finished keying in the real part, that the imaginary part was to follow, and that the imaginary part was positive. The decimal point after the *i* appeared on all the sign keys, since all numbers had to begin with a decimal point.

After keying in the imaginary part of the denominator, the operator keyed (+), which told the machine that the real part of the numerator was to follow. As soon as she pressed that key the machine would begin computing the norm, since it "knew" that all the digits of the denominator were in the machine. (It automatically added trailing zeros into the registers; for instance, −.37 was stored as −.37000000, but the operator did not have to key the trailing zeros in.)

Finally the operator pressed the (=) key, upon which the machine would immediately begin printing the quotient in the following format:

$$-.37000000 + i.91000000 \setminus +.33000000 + i.99000000$$
$$= +0.80704663 - i.0.69077720$$

Note the special reversed division sign. I say that the machine began printing its answer immediately because as soon as the first number, −.37 was entered, printing began. The input numbers were printed while the answer was being computed. The average speed was estimated as "three times as fast as a human being equipped with a desk calculator," or about half a minute for a division.[32]

Some other samples of the machine's abilities were published in *Science News Letter* in September, 1940, including the following:

$$+.45632450 + i.45367899 \setminus +.31612848 + i.20028853$$
$$= +0.56785431 - i.0.12564532$$

The machine truncated, not rounded, its results to eight digits; otherwise the last digit of the complex part of the answer would be a 3, not a 2.

The article also showed how the machine would multiply 2 × 2:

$$+.20000000 + i.00000000 \times +.20000000 + i.00000000$$
$$= 0.04000000 + i.00000000$$

The operator had to adjust the decimal points accordingly.[33]

THE DARTMOUTH DEMONSTRATION

The Complex Computer was not really a computer by the definition I have been using throughout this book; it was not programmable. Nonetheless it rightly belongs among the early computing devices because of other things that made up for that deficiency. First of all, it marked the beginning of Bell Labs in the computing field; later on they would build relay devices that did have flexible programming facilities, including conditional branching and subroutines, as we shall see. Second, the "Model I" just described introduced the idea of automatic digital computing to the mathematics community at an early date, well before the Z3 or the Harvard Mark I were operational. That was in the summer of 1940, at a meeting of the American Mathematical Society at Dartmouth College in Hanover, New Hampshire. This public demonstration was a pivotal moment in the history of computing—it not only was a demonstration of a working digital calculating machine; it was also the first example of remote access to a computer, something that would not be repeated for another ten years. It marks a beginning of "telecommunications"—the use of telephone lines to carry not voice messages, but coded computer data.

The computer was finished by January, 1940. After it had demonstrated its worth for a while, T. C. Fry at the Labs suggested that Stibitz present a paper on it at the summer meeting of the American Mathematical Society. Fry further suggested that Stibitz actually demonstrate the machine at the meeting by having someone dictate problems over the phone to New York, then receiving the answers as the machine computed them.[34]

Gradually through the summer of 1940 that idea progressed to the notion of having one of the teletype machines actually set up in Hanover, so that the participants could key in the problems themselves. The summer meeting was not to be held until September, so there was time to make the necessary modifications.

Stibitz was not sure he would be able to demonstrate the machine without some human intervention in New York, but that was his goal. He and Fry worked up to the eleventh hour completing the necessary circuits. AT&T set up a twenty-eight-wire teletype link between Hanover and New York, and coders and decoders were built at each end. Williams remained in New York during the meeting in case anything went wrong, but everything worked fine without his help.[35]

The Society met in McNutt Hall on the Dartmouth campus from the 10th to the 12th of September, 1940. New Hampshire is usually at its prettiest in September, but in 1940 the events in Europe dampened everyone's spirits. The meeting was attended by most of the prominent American mathematicians of the day—John von Neumann, G. D. Birkhoff, Norbert Wiener—as well as by John Mauchly and many others who would later be involved in computing projects. (Many participants were, strictly speaking, foreign mathematicians who had taken refuge in America—for example, Richard Courant, Paul Erdös, and John von Neumann. By 1940 many of them had obtained American citizenship. As far as I can tell, there were no German mathematicians who returned to Germany before America's entry into the war.)

On September 11 Stibitz delivered a paper which briefly described how he came to build the Complex Computer, and why there was a need for it at Bell Laboratories. After reading the paper, he and Fry showed how problems were entered on the keyboard by running a few sample ones. The machine took about a minute for each, and it ran without error. Following that demonstration, the audience was invited to submit their own problems via the keyboard. It was available to all from 11:00 A.M. to 2:00 P.M. that day.[36]

There is no doubt that this demonstration made an impression on many who witnessed it. Norbert Wiener, for example, played with it for a while, testing its logic by trying to divide by zero and the like. But he was unable to get the machine to give an incorrect answer, and later, in his autobiography, he recounted that experience at length. It must have been one of his first exposures to the "thinking" properties of machines. Later on he submitted his own proposal to Vannevar Bush for a digital computer, but he was turned down. He spent the war years at MIT doing work that was related more to analog than to digital computing.[37] The Hanover demonstration was also reported in the popular press, but it is clear that Bell wanted most of all to introduce its computer to the mathematics community.

Remote access to computers is common today, but after the Dartmouth demonstration it was not done again until 1950, with the SEAC in Washington, D.C. The demonstration also foreshadowed a time when high-speed data (as opposed to voice) communications would be an integral part of the Bell System's traffic—not to mention that of Bell's competitors. In fact, it is in the area of telecommunications, not voice traffic, where Bell is presently most seriously threatened by competition. But that is another story.

AFTER THE MODEL I: LATER DEVELOPMENTS

Bell Labs took only a moderate interest in Stibitz's work. They were interested in machines that could solve specific problems, but they did not see building general-purpose computers as a worthwhile goal in itself. As the Complex Number Computer was nearing completion, Stibitz was designing machines with more advanced features such as floating point and suppression of leading and trailing zeros. Above all he recognized that it would not be difficult to program future relay computers by paper tape and so not restrict them to only one specific problem.

His proposal to build a successor to the Model I, a relay computer that would be programmable by paper tape, was at first rejected. Then the United States entered World War Two in December, 1941. Bell Labs found itself facing a new set of priorities. Domestic phone service was not among them, but projects involving computing were.[38]

Bell Labs began working on devices that aimed antiaircraft fire. The result was the famous M-9 Gun Director, an ingenious combination of electronic circuits (rugged enough for the battlefield), electric motors, electrical sensors, and mechanical linkages that helped a gunner track a moving target in the sky and hit it (like shooting ducks only a *lot* more complicated). The M-9 was ingenious, and it worked well. It was especially effective in blunting the effect of the German V-1 "buzzbomb" over England and the Low Countries in the later years of the war—the buzzbomb had no pilot and so could not take evasive action against Allied antiaircraft fire.[39]

In this and other computing projects the government was willing to underwrite development costs for new and untried technology. Stibitz moved to the National Defense Research Committee (NDRC), under the supervision of Warren Weaver, but he still kept close ties with Bell. For the duration of the war his main job concerned the design and use of programmable digital calculating machines.

Bell Labs paralleled IBM's building of the Mark I in its first steps into the large-scale computer world: both considered the computer as being far outside their normal sphere of business, but both entered that field and built computers that contributed to the war effort. But the projects themselves were funded mostly by the United States government.

The machines designed by Stibitz and built by Bell Labs after 1940 exhibited two significant qualities: programmability and reliability. All in all, Bell Labs built six more relay computers after the Complex Number Computer, and a chronicle of their development shows a steady progression toward more flexible programming and better techniques for detecting and correcting errors.

For the testing of the M-9 Gun Director it was necessary to run it through a simulated firing, then see whether it in fact kept the gun aimed as it was supposed to. That led to a lot of calculations, especially ones involving the reading of tables of function values and the interpolation of intermediate values from those tables. Stibitz proposed building a relay machine to interpolate function values, and in 1943 the so-called Relay Interpolator was the result. (Later it would be called the Bell Labs Model II.)

The relay interpolator performed only addition and subtraction but by repeated addition it could multiply a number by a small integer as well. However, it could be programmed by paper tape, unlike the Model I, so it had quite a general capability. After the war it was kept in service and used for a few other problems besides interpolation.[40]

Stibitz then desgned two more special-purpose relay machines for the NDRC: the Ballistic Computer and the Error Detector Mark 22. Both machines were concerned with detecting and minimizing the error in aiming antiaircraft fire at a moving target and having the shell explode at precisely the right moment. (They were later renamed the Bell Labs Models III and IV respectively.) Like the Model II, they used a standard five-channel paper tape for the input of data and instructions; unlike the Model II, they were often used for many other problems besides the specific ones they were built to solve. Their memory and arithmetic units had modest capabilities: only six decimal digits of precision, a memory of ten numbers for each machine. They performed multiplication by referring to an internal table of decimal products, unlike the slower method of repeated addition used on all other Bell Labs machines. The result was that they were well-balanced machines whose power, speed, reliability, and ease of programming allowed them to tackle tough problems. Those who used the Models III and IV always spoke well of them; the machines seemed to have just the right balance of features for their relay technology—in contrast to the Models I and II, which were too limited in power, or to the Model V, which was designed for work that was really more appropriate for electronic computers.[41]

Stibitz built one more machine for the NDRC: the Model V, a large-scale general-purpose relay computer in the same league as the Zuse Z4 or the Harvard Mark I. It was not completed until after the war, in 1946, after which Stibitz left that government agency. Two identical copies of the Model V were built, one installed at the Aberdeen Proving Ground in Maryland, the other at the National Advisory Committee on Aeronautics' laboratory at Langley Field, Virginia.

Bell Labs built one more machine, the Model VI, which was a simpler version of the Model V. The Model VI was the only relay machine besides the Complex Number Computer that they kept for their own use; the others were for the military. Table 4.2 summarizes the specifications of the Models II through V.

Table 4.2. BELL LABS MODELS II THROUGH V

	Model II	Model III	Model IV	Model V (two copies)
Date completed	7-1943	6-1944	3-1945	12-1946, 8-1947
Date dismantled	1961	1958	1961	1958
Place installed	Wash., D.C.	Ft. Bliss, Texas	Wash., D.C.	Langley, Va. Aberdeen, Md.
Also known as	Relay Interpolator	Ballistic Computer	Error Detector Mark 22	
No. relays	440	1,400	1,425	9,000+
Word length	2 to 5 fixed decimal	1 to 6 fixed pt.	1 to 6 fixed pt.	1 to 7 floating pt.
Memory cap.	7 numbers	10	10	30 total
Mult. speed	4 sec.	1 sec.	1 sec.	0.8 sec.
Mult. method	repeated add.	table look-up	table look-up	rep. add.
Cost		$65,000	$65,000	$500,000
Size	2 panels	5 panels	5 panels	27 panels 10 tons

The Model V was a powerful machine. But by the time it was finished in 1946 attention was turning toward the much faster vacuum tube technology. So it represents in many ways the limit to what can be done with relay technology. Because of its flexible programming power and its built-in reliability circuits it was able to keep up with the much faster electronic computers for many applications, but those kinds of features could also be added to future electronic machines, whereas there was no way to increase the intrinsic speed of relay computers much beyond what the Model V's relays had.[42]

The most interesting aspect of the Model V's design was that it had two separate arithmetic units, each capable of operating as an independent computer with its own memory registers and input-output devices. Small-scale problems could be run in pairs on the machine, saving time, while bigger problems could take over both processors. (Some confusion has arisen about the Model V because of this arrangement: each processor was called a "computer" in the literature describing the Model V. Today they would be called "processors.") Associated with each processor (using the modern term) were fifteen memory registers, for a total of thirty for the whole machine. A master control unit directed instructions to one or both processors according to their availability. This control unit was separate from the control units in the processor that directed the sequence of arithmetic, memory, and input/output operations; it controlled the control, so to speak. (Stibitz called it a "superbranching" capability.) Thus in a very real sense the Model V had what is now called an "operating system"—a control unit that supervises and manages the flow of work through a computer. (Operating systems—much more sophisticated, of course—became commonplace in the third generation of large computers, after 1965.)

The flexibility provided by superbranching allowed the Model V to out-perform the much faster electronic computers for certain problems. It obviously added to the machine's cost and complexity. Its successor, the Model VI, designed for Bell Labs' internal use, had only one processor.[43]

RELIABILITY

Besides programming power, the later Bell computers stressed extraordinary reliability. The Model I was checked by running selected problems whose answers were known beforehand at the beginning and end of each day. (That was also done on the Harvard Mark I every few hours.) If the machine gave correct answers to those "diagnostic" problems (which were specially formulated to put all the pieces of the machine through their paces), then its users could be reasonably sure that the answers it gave between those diagnostic sessions also were correct.[44]

But that approach had its obvious drawbacks. Long problems had to be interrupted every so often, intermediate data saved, then a diagnostic run. And if the diagnostic program revealed a mechanical failure, all the work going back to the last diagnostic session had to be discarded, since there was no way of knowing exactly when the failure occurred.

For very fast machines which execute long programs that is a serious drawback. It is even more serious for machines like the Bell computers that used telephone relays. In contrast to mechanical devices or to electronic tubes, relays have a tendency to fail intermittently. Should a piece of dust lodge itself between two relay contacts, that circuit will fail, though the rest of the relay will be fine. After a few cycles, the dust particle may shake itself loose, after which everything will return to normal. Thus an entire computation may be way off without any machine failure showing up during a diagnostic session. By contrast, when a vacuum tube or a mechanical cam fails, it (usually) stays that way, so a failure is more easily isolated and corrected.

Other than that kind of intermittent failure, relays are reliable devices. They are well suited for ordinary telephone circuits, where the loss of a few seconds of a conversation or an occasional bad connection is tolerable. But for a computer that is intolerable. Bell's engineers recognized that a computer system should shut down completely when any of its circuits failed, as that usually meant the machine was delivering wrong answers. (By contrast, telephone users do not like their phone service shut down at all if it can be avoided—even if that means accepting poorer service.)[45]

So a philosophy of reliability emerged at Bell Labs that reflected the difference between computing and telephony. Bell's engineers designed computer circuits that checked themselves at every step of a computation, like policemen looking over everyone's shoulder. The circuits were designed not only to add, subtract, store numbers, and so on; they were also designed to check that they had done those things correctly, and to stop the machine otherwise.

Bell's engineers were also guided by their experience in designing telephone circuits that had to operate long hours unattended in often hostile environments. Those circuits were designed to be repaired by semi-skilled technicians; telephone service would be terribly costly if an engineer had to be called in every time a phone line went down or a customer's phone went dead.

The Bell Labs Models II through VI used a system whereby not four but seven binary relays coded each decimal digit. They were divided into two groups of two and five relays; the decimal code was as follows:

Decimal digit	Relays	
0	01	00001
1	01	00010
2	01	00100
3	01	01000
4	01	10000
5	10	00001
6	10	00010
7	10	00100
8	10	01000
9	10	10000

A special circuit checked to see that two and only two relays were energized for each decimal digit. Another circuit checked that for each group one and only one relay was on—that prevented two separate errors from canceling each other out, although certain unusual combinations of malfunctions could go undetected.

Bell Labs called this system a "bi-quinary" notation, since the relays had a weight of either one or five. Actually, it is not a combination of those number bases; rather, it is a seven-bit, mixed decimal code. All the Bell Labs relay computers worked in decimal arithmetic.[46]

Note the similarity of the bi-quinary code to the weights of the beads on a Chinese abacus: beads above the divider bar have a weight of five, those below a weight of one. (Stibitz has said recently that he first realized that the bi-quinary code was similar to the Chinese abacus only after he had designed the relay codes, when someone else pointed it out to him.)[47]

The bi-quinary system was an empirical way of adding redundancy to a circuit to give it more reliability. It worked well for representing decimal numbers but it could not easily be generalized to other types of machines or to other number bases, including binary. Using Stibitz's work as a starting point, Richard Hamming of Bell Labs generalized the concept of error checking and developed a theory that guided computer designers thereafter. That was the so-called parity-checking scheme, which is valid for any coded information in any number base. Using parity checking, an extra binary element (relay or whatever) is added to each code, and that element is turned on or off to make the total number of binary elements "on" an even or odd number, as specified in advance. A separate circuit checks whether that sum is even or odd, and stops the machine if the sum is wrong.

Hamming went on to show that if more redundancy was added to a number code, it could not only detect errors but also *correct* them as well. He worked out the trade-offs of each redundant bit added, and his work has formed the basis for nearly all computer circuit design ever since. It is so integral to modern computers that "only the old-timers are still conscious that somebody once invented it."[48] (One consequence of parity checking is that commercial computers today cannot, strictly speaking, err. They may malfunction, but they cannot deliver the erroneous result $2 + 2 = 5$ unless programmed to do so. What is so often called "computer error" in the popular press is more correctly the result of human errors of programming or of giving the machine the wrong input data. That misperception is unfortunately too current among the lay public today. Only a few special-purpose or experimental computers, like the ILLIAC IV, do not use parity checking.)

In a discussion of the Model V, Hamming said that it had on the average two to five relay malfunctions per day, or the equivalent of one failure for every two to three million relay cycles. If a failure occurred during the day, when an operator was present, the machine would stop; otherwise it would automatically transfer control to its other processor and take up whatever problem was residing there. Thus there was almost no down-time for the Model V.[49]

POSTWAR ACTIVITIES AT BELL LABS

Bell Labs built the Model VI for its own use after the war. (When it was placed in service at their new headquarters in Murray Hill, New Jersey, in 1949, they dismantled the Model I.) The Model VI used the bi-quinary number code, had full conditional branching and subroutine capability, but lacked the dual processors and superbranching power of the Model V. The Model VI marked the end of Bell's role as a builder of relay computers. By 1950 the trend was clearly toward vacuum tubes for computing elements, and that was a technology less familiar to Bell's engineers. The two Model V's and the Model VI were unmatched for their reliability and flexibility in programming, but their speed was on a plateau at least an order of magnitude below even the slowest electronic computers, and that more than offset their advantages.[50]

A tremendous backlog of domestic telephone orders had built up during the war. It was the time of suburban sprawl, as returning G.I.'s and their families moved into Levittowns and other housing tracts across the country. Those suburbs needed telephone service, and until the early fifties Bell's resources were strained to the utmost in providing it. Stibitz left Bell Labs during the war and did not return. It was not at all clear where digital computers fit into Vail's dictum of "one system, one policy, and universal service." Bell was (and is) a regulated monopoly whose every action was always noticed by the government and by its competitors. Whatever the reason, Bell Labs chose not to go into the business of making and selling electronic digital computers.[51]

But the company was active in other ways, one of which was revolutionary. That was the invention of the transistor in 1948, by William Shockley, John Bardeen, and Walter Brattain. Bell Labs had been working on a solid state amplifier to replace their vacuum tube circuits for a long time. The transistor was the result of that search.

Bell intended to use the transistor as an amplifying device for long-distance lines. But like the tube, it could also be used as a digital switch and thus replace their relays as well. But there was little need for that in 1948.

So while the transistor was successfully employed in telephone amplifiers, it was in the commercial computing industry and not in the Bell System where it first found application as a digital switching device. The first transistors were no more reliable than the tubes or relays they were supposed to replace, but by the late 1950's computer manufacturers adopted them wholeheartedly. They were smaller and less prone to fail than tubes; above all they gave off little heat, and that was a big advantage over tubes. Bell Labs had a lot of capital invested in their relay technology; they embarked on a plan of slow and gradual replacement by transistors as the relay circuits wore out. Relay switching is still common today in the telephone system.

Bell Labs saw the potential advantages of transistors for computers—they built one of the first transistorized computers in the world, the TRADIC, in 1955. But they did not go into the commercial computer business.[52]

In 1949 AT&T began fighting an antitrust suit brought against them by the Justice Department, which sought to allow other equipment manufacturers besides Bell's own Western Electric to supply equipment to the Bell System. AT&T fought the suit vigorously, contending that as a regulated monopoly it was exempt from antitrust laws concerning such tie-in agreements. The suit was settled by a Consent Decree between Bell and the Justice Department in January, 1956, by which the Bell System's monopoly structure, including its ownership of Western Electric, remained intact. In return, Bell agreed to enter into no "business other than the furnishing of common carrier communications services."[53]

Going into the computer business seemed to be just the sort of non-communications activity that they agreed to stay out of—although the boundaries between computing and communications are much less clear today. The Bell System continued to supply telephone service; other, nonregulated companies built and sold computers commercially. As the technologies of both evolved, the two activities grew closer to each other, but Bell found itself restrained from moving aggressively into new areas of telecommunications that ironically it had pioneered. (In 1981 that Consent Decree was overturned; in exchange the Bell System will be broken up. Among other consequences, Bell Labs in now free to design and market commercial computers. Whether they will or not is hardly clear; but they certainly have the technical ability to do so. In fact, they may be the only company today with the financial strength to compete with IBM head-to-head.)

Another provision of the 1956 Consent Decree was that Bell Labs agreed to make its patents on the transistor freely available to companies who wanted to manufacture and sell them. A number of companies responded, and within a short time transistors became widely available, more reliable, and cheaper.[53] The next phase of the computer revolution began—the phase in which computers have become dramatically cheaper, smaller, and more integrated into all parts of modern American life. That phase is still going on apace.

Today's telephone system uses a variety of special-purpose digital computers for things like switching, while for other jobs like billing it uses ordinary commercial computers. AT&T is one of IBM's best customers; it also buys a lot of computers from the other manufacturers as well. Bell Labs designs and builds computer chips for their own use, and for those chips they have developed powerful and sophisticated programming tools (for example, the "C" programming language and the UNIX operating system). Whatever else may be said about Bell Labs' position in the modern computing world, they were involved in computing from the start of the age, they still are involved, and there is little question they will continue to be involved.

In conclusion, the story of Bell Laboratories' role in the invention of the computer is one of significant contributions in many areas. These are:

1) The coding of information as a subject of theoretical interest in itself. From Stibitz and Claude Shannon came a notion of information as a quantity that can be treated like any other abstract quantity, as it is processed, transmitted, and coded in machinery.

2) The binary-coded-decimal system of coding numbers, still widely used where information is input or output frequently by a machine.
3) The design philosophy of incorporating redundancy in a computer code to ensure error-free operation, thus relieving the user of the burden of testing the integrity of the system's hardware.

At the same time it is clear that Bell Labs stands outside of the direct ancestral line that leads to the modern computer. In part that is because they were a regulated monopoly, in part because the relay technology they knew best was seen as unsuitable for computers after 1950. But they were, and are, pioneers just the same.

NOTES

1. Gerald Brock, *The Telecommunications Industry: The Dynamics of Market Structure* (Cambridge, Mass.: Harvard, 1981), chapter 4; John Brooks, *Telephone: The First Hundred Years* (New York: Harper & Row, 1976), pp. 138-139.
2. Lillian Hoddeson, "The Emergence of Basic Research in the Bell Telephone System," *Technology and Culture*, 22 (1981), 512-544.
3. A few phone systems around the country still have no dial of any type: the user must turn a crank which signals an operator at a central switchboard. Those few that survive may ironically be preserved as living museum pieces; see "Save Crank Phones? Mainers Split at Hearing," *Boston Globe*, February 12, 1982, pp. 15, 17.
4. Melvin Kranzberg and Carroll Pursell, eds., *Technology in Western Civilization*, vol. 1 (New York: Oxford, 1967), pp. 644-645; Brooks, *Telephone*, pp. 100-101.
5. E. G. Andrews, "Telephone Switching and the Early Bell Laboratories Computers," *Bell System Technical Journal*, 42 (1963), 341-353.
6. Hoddeson, "Basic Research," p. 530; Brock, *Telecommunications*, p. 102.
7. E. G. Andrews, "Telephone Switching," p. 343.
8. Jagit Singh, *Great Ideas of Modern Mathematics* (New York: Dover, 1959), pp. 12-13.
9. Norbert Wiener, *I Am a Mathematician* (Cambridge, Mass.: MIT, 1956), p. 75; David E. Smith, *History of Mathematics*, vol. 2 (New York: Dover, 1958), pp. 261-268.
10. Wiener, *Mathematician*, p. 247; Andrews, "Telephone Switching," p. 343; George Stibitz, memo of August 19, 1938, Box 1, Stibitz Papers, Baker Library, Hanover, N. H.
11. George Stibitz, memo of August 26, 1938, Stibitz Papers, Box 1.
12. "An Inventory of the Papers of George Robert Stibitz, Concerning the Invention and Development of the Digital Computer" (Hanover, N. H.: Dartmouth College, 1973; Henry Tropp, "The Effervescent Years: A Retrospective," *IEEE Spectrum*, 11 (February, 1974), 70-81.
13. Published in part as "Potentials in Curved Surfaces," *Philosophical Magazine*, 7th ser., 25 (1938), 783-785.
14. Tropp, "Effervescent Years," p. 71; Konrad Zuse, *Der Computer, Mein Lebenswerk* (Munich: 1970), pp. 52-53.
15. George Stibitz, letter to the author, December 12, 1978.
16. See, for example, A. Weygandt, "Die Elektromechanische Determinantenmaschine," *Zeitschrift für Instrumentenkunde*, 53 (1933), 114-121.

17. G. R. Stibitz and Evelyn Loveday, "The Relay Computers at Bell Labs," *Datamation* 13 (April, 1967), 35-44; 14 (May 1967), 45-49.

18. Konrad Zuse, "Method for Automatic Execution of Calculations with the Aid of Computers," German Patent Application Z-23139 IX/42m, 1939, translated and reprinted in Brian Randell, ed., *The Origins of Digital Computers: Selected Papers*, 2nd ed. (New York: Springer, 1975), pp. 159-166.

19. Stibitz, memo of March 28, 1938, Stibitz Papers, Box 1; E. G. Andrews, "Telephone Switching," pp. 342-344.

20. Stibitz, memo of March 28, 1938, Stibitz Papers, Box 1.

21. Andrews, "Telephone Switching," pp. 342-344.

22. Anton Glaser, *History of Binary and Other Non-decimal Numeration* (Southhampton, Pa.: privately printed, 1971), pp. 135-140.

23. Stibitz and Loveday, "Relay Computers," p. 35; Glaser, *History of Binary*, pp. 129-153; Evelyn Loveday, "George Stibitz and the Bell Labs Relay Computers," *Datamation*, 24 (September, 1977), 80-85.

24. Andrews, "Telephone Switching."

25. Claude Shannon, "A Symbolic Analysis of Switching Circuits," *Transactions AIEE*, 57 (1938), 713; Hidetosi Takahasi, "Some Important Computers of Japanese Design," *Proceedings, First USA-Japan Computer Conference*, October 3-5, 1972, Tokyo, pp. 692-697.

26. Andrews, "Telephone Switching," p. 344; Malcolm Stevenson, "Bell Labs: A Pioneer in Computing Technology," *Bell Labs Record*, 51 (1973), 344-351.

27. Stibitz and Loveday, "Relay Computers," pp. 45-48.

28. Ibid., p. 41; Stibitz, memo of August 19, 1940, Box 1, Stibitz Papers.

29. Stevenson, "Bell Labs," pp. 345-346.

30. Glaser, *History of Binary*, p. 132.

31. Stibitz, memo of November 1, 1939, Box 1, Stibitz Papers.

32. Stevenson, "Bell Labs," p. 346.

33. "Electric Calculating Machine Devised for Complex Problems," *Science News Letter*, September 14, 1940, p. 163.

34. Stibitz and Loveday, "Relay Computers," pp. 39, 43.

35. There are at least five separate drafts of the Hanover paper in Box 1 of the Stibitz Papers, each with a slightly different description of what was to be demonstrated. One draft has been published in Brian Randell, *Origins of Digital Computers*, pp. 241-246.

36. Wiener, *Mathematician*, pp. 229; T. R. Hollcroft, "The Summer Meeting in Hanover," *Bulletin, American Mathematical Society*, 46 (1940), 861; Andrews, "Telephone Switching," p. 353.

37. Wiener, *Mathematician*, pp. 229-240. Wiener gives the date of the meeting as August, 1940, which is incorrect.

38. Stibitz, memo of August 19, 1940, Box 1, Stibitz Papers; Stibitz and Loveday, "Relay Computers," p. 44; Andrews, "Telephone Switching," pp. 347-348.

39. Charles and Ray Eames, *A Computer Perspective* (Cambridge, Mass.: Harvard, 1973), p. 128.

40. George Stibitz and Jules A. Larrivee, *Mathematics and Computers* (New York: McGraw Hill), pp. 138-139; Randell, *Origins*, p. 239.

41. E. G. Andrews, "A Review of Bell Laboratories Digital Computer Developments," *Review of Electronic Digital Computers*, Joint AIEE-IRE Computer Conference, December 10-12, 1951, Philadelphia, pp. 101-132.

42. Franz Alt, *Electronic Digital Computers* (New York: Academic Press, 1958), pp. 63ff.

43. Andrews, "A Review," pp. 103-104; Andrews, "Telephone Switching," p. 348; Stibitz and Larrivee, *Mathematics and Computers*, p. 148.

44. Stibitz, text of speech delivered at Hanover, dated September 11, 1940, Stibitz Papers, Box 1.

45. This theme is discussed at length in Brock, *Telecommunications Industry*.

46. Edmund Berkeley, *Giant Brains, or Machines that Think* (New York: Wiley, 1949), pp. 132-133.

47. Stibitz, letter to the author, August, 1979.

48. Martin Mayer, "Computers on the Brain," *Esquire*, January, 1969, p. 102.

49. R. W. Hamming, "Error Detecting and Error Correcting Codes," *Bell System Technical Journal*, 26 (1950), 147-160.

50. E. G. Andrews, "A Review," p. 103; Andrews, "The Bell Computer, Model VI," *Annals* of the Harvard Computation Laboratory, 26 (1949), 20-31.

51. Berkeley, *Giant Brains*, p. 143.

52. Brock, *Telecommunications Industry*, pp. 191-192.

53. Ibid., pp. 187-194.

5
Faster, Faster: The ENIAC

> In 1746...I met a Dr. Spence, who was lately arrived from Scotland, and who show'd me some electric experiments. They were imperfectly perform'd, as he was not very expert, but being on a subject quite new to me, they equally surpris'd and pleased me. Soon after my return to Philadelphia, our library company receiv'd from Mr. P. Collinson, Fellow of the Royal Society of London, a present of a glass tube, with some account of the use of it in making such experiments.
>
> —Benjamin Franklin, *Autobiography*

People often speak of computers as belonging to one of several "generations"—beginning not with the machines discussed in this book but rather with the first commercial computers. That term implies a linear evolution of machines and technology. But it is a misleading analogy: the computer did not descend from one or two ancestors. The first ones incorporated bits and pieces from this and that machine: punched tape from telegraphs, relays from telephones, punched cards from accounting machines, vacuum tubes from radios. And so it goes today. Living creatures do not evolve that way. (Mythical creatures like the Centaur combined the best qualities of the man and the horse; but among living animals maybe only the Missouri mule is close to illustrating how machines evolve.)

But if there is a "granddaddy" of all the generations of digital computers, it would have to be the ENIAC, the first working electronic numeric digital computer. It was not a "first generation" computer, since it was not used commercially. Perhaps it belongs to the "zero" generation, since nearly every computer built thereafter owes something to it. What they owe is the subject of this chapter.

The ENIAC was an electronic computer: it was the only early computer except for the British Colossus that computed at electronic speeds. But like all the machines of its day it was a transitional device. It had some relay circuits. It was programmed like an IBM accounting machine. It was a computer, a powerful and fast computer at that, but its design and programming did not become the basis for any computers thereafter. Nothing quite like it was ever built again. Like the Harvard Mark I, the most important thing about the ENIAC was that it existed: it proved to the world that computing at electronic speeds was indeed possible, just as Howard Aiken had proved that Babbage's dream was more than just a dream. In 1945, when the ENIAC ran its first programs, that was important.

What is so important about computing at electronic speeds? The ENIAC computed about 500 times faster than any of the electromechanical computers, a difference of scale that made it an entirely different type of machine. With a relay machine it was always possible to measure computing power in terms of the number of human beings it could replace—that was the measure used in the published accounts of the Bell Labs machines and the Mark I. But the ENIAC was built precisely to tackle a job that by nature was beyond the capabilities of human—or electromechanical—computers.

That was not the first time the pace of technology outran its conceptual understanding. The first steam engines were measured by their "horsepower" —how many horses they could replace for a given task. Matthew Boulton and James Watt charged for their machines accordingly. But a modern diesel locomotive, developing hundreds of horsepower, could never be replaced by an equivalent number of horses. (The problem is not getting all those horses hitched together; it is getting them all to pull in the same direction: to coordinate each horse's power in a meaningful way.) The same is true regarding the ENIAC: it broke through the limits of human computing power, power limited by the fact that if a computing team was too large, its work could not effectively be coordinated. (Incidentally, although little information about the British Colossus has been made public, it is clear that its designers also recognized the absolute importance of electronic speeds for the job of breaking the German codes the British had intercepted. No electromechanical machine could have done it.)[1]

By 1943 Helmut Schreyer in Germany and engineers at IBM and RCA had designed electronic calculating circuits. National Cash Register was looking into the possibility of using vacuum tubes in its machines. There were no doubt many other examples from that time which have not yet come to light; using electronic circuits for all-or-nothing switching was fast becoming an accepted idea.[2]

In the late 1930's, Professor John V. Atanasoff of the physics department of Iowa State College (now Iowa State University) conceived of the idea of using vacuum tube computing circuits to solve systems of linear equations. He got pretty far with that idea—farther than Schreyer, to be sure—but the machine was stalled in its final stage of construction and never did any useful work. Around the same time, at Ursinus College in Collegeville, Pennsylvania (near Philadelphia), Professor John Mauchly was also thinking about computing with electronic elements. He built a few test circuits, and after meeting Atanasoff in 1940 at a meeting of the American Association for the Advancement of Science, he stepped up his efforts to build a digital computer.

Mauchly moved from Ursinus to the Moore School of Electrical Engineering (part of the University of Pennsylvania), at first to learn more about electronics, then staying on as an instructor. There he teamed up with J. Presper Eckert, who had been one of his instructors. From that point the story is not clear, but it seems that Atanasoff's machine was the spark—a small one, but a spark nonetheless—that ignited Mauchly's enthusiasm about electronic digital computers. He and Eckert transformed that enthusiasm into a working computer: the ENIAC. And from the ENIAC came almost everything else.[3]

Well, not quite. That progression from Atanasoff to the ENIAC to the modern computer is not untrue, but the story is hardly so neat and tidy as it implies. An elaborate genealogical chart of the evolution of the computer, full of begettings like the Book of Genesis, obscures the tortuous paths that were really taken.

The question of just who really invented the ENIAC (and by implication, who invented the electronic computer) is fraught with controversy; it has even been the subject of a lawsuit. (The lawsuit has been settled, but the controversy remains.) But there is no doubt as to *why* the ENIAC was invented: it was designed for one specific wartime problem: the preparation and printing of firing tables. Had there not been such a need for those tables, the ENIAC would not have been built. Eventually of course someone would have built an electronic digital computer, but it would not have been the ENIAC.[4] (Computer designers today often do not care about what their creations are used for; they build a machine that can execute certain general "benchmark" programs that test the machine's overall abilities. But that was certainly not true in the 1940's.)

FIRING TABLES

The heavy artillery used in World War Two had remarkable range: some guns could fire a shell twenty miles and more. But that range was useless if the shell could not hit its target. At short ranges the gunner can see the target and make adjustments on the spot; at longer ranges he can station a forward observer to radio back some of that information. But even in those cases he needs a firing table: a table of numbers telling him how to set the firing angle to give him the range he needs. A firing table is simply a table of angle settings and the corresponding ranges they give for a given piece of artillery. The table also gives the velocity of the projectile at impact (needed if it is to pierce an armored target) and perhaps also the angle of fall at impact (needed if the projectile is to clear a rampart or other obstruction).[5]

An analysis of the trajectory of a shell quickly leads to higher-order differential equations, as is so common in describing physical phenomena. The basic physical law is of course Isaac Newton's: an object in the earth's gravitational field falls with a constant acceleration. Acceleration is the rate of change in the velocity of an object; the velocity is the rate of change of the object's position. To find the position of a shell at the end of its trajectory thus requires the solution of a second-order differential equation; to find its terminal velocity requires solving a first-order equation.

That relationship is only a starting point for the preparation of a firing table. The most important additional factor is the resistance of the air. It in turn varies according to the temperature, humidity, and altitude through which the projectile travels; it also varies according to the shape of the projectile. But in the main the air resistance is a function of the velocity of the projectile: the greater the velocity the greater the resistance. So an analysis of the air resistance also leads to a differential equation.

The gunnery officer in the field could not be expected to do the math required to compute a trajectory. Instead he consulted a table for the type of gun and shell he was using. That table could not be so complicated as to be unreadable under battle conditions. Firing tables usually listed just the range and velocity for a given firing angle, with supplemental tables of correction factors for things like crosswinds, other weather conditions, even for drift caused by the rotation of the earth.

What all that meant was that a lot of computation was required for the preparation of even one firing table, and for the many types of guns and projectiles being developed for the war, a lot of tables were needed. The differential equations derived for a trajectory were of the type that could only be solved numerically: that is, it was not possible to find analytic solutions that yielded the trajectory of the shell directly. As with the equations faced by Howard Aiken, trajectories were computed by combinations of elementary operations of arithmetic together with temporary storage of intermediate results and the consulting of tables of mathematical data.[6] The computations were long, tedious, and prone to error, even when done with the aid of desk calculators.

In the 1930's, Vannevar Bush had built an analog computer that could solve differential equations, using a mechanical integrator similar to the familiar device that computes a household electric bill. The basic computing element of his "Differential Analyzer" was a rotating disk, upon which rested another smaller disk whose rotation corresponded to the integral of the desired function. (The watt-hour meter measures the integral of the power a household consumes with respect to time. The power is the product of the voltage, which is a constant 110 volts in America, times the current, which varies from moment to moment depending on what electrical appliances the customer is using. The meter performs that integration by translating those functions into analogous motions of the rotating disk, thereby computing the kilowatt-hours for which the customer is charged. Bush's Differential Analyzer used a more primitive mechanical version of that disk integrator.)[7]

It was an enormously complex machine. By 1942 Bush's Analyzer had been rebuilt and fitted with a number of improvements that gave it more speed and power. Eventually its size and cost put it on a par with the first digital computers such as the Harvard Mark I, although it worked on entirely different principles.

The Differential Analyzer was faster than teams of human computers using desk calculators, but it was still not fast enough. The Moore School of Electrical Engineering at the University of Pennsylvania built a copy of one, and used both it and human computers (mostly recent graduates from women's colleges up and down the Eastern Seaboard) to compute trajectories. Humans took at least several hours to compute a trajectory. The Differential Analyzer could compute one in about twenty minutes. But it was a complicated, unique piece of machinery, and setting it up to compute a specific trajectory took time, during which the machine could do no work. By mid-1942 Ballistic Research Laboratory (BRL) officers realized that neither method could keep up with the ever-increasing demand for firing tables.

So it was against that background in 1942 that John W. Mauchly of the Moore School wrote a memorandum entitled "The Use of Vacuum Tube Devices for Calculating," in which he proposed that an electronic computing device be built to solve differential equations, not by the analog method of the Differential Analyzer, but by the numerical methods used by the teams of human beings with their desk calculators. The difference would be that electronic, not mechanical, devices would perform those calculations, and electronic circuits would furthermore coordinate the elementary arithmetic operations and transfer and store intermediate results automatically. With that approach, Mauchly said, the time needed to compute a trajectory would drop to a minute or two.[8]

In April, 1943, that memorandum grew into a formal proposal by Mauchly, J. Presper Eckert, and John Grist Brainerd for a machine which would retain the automatic operation of the Differential Analyzer, yet use the numerical method that humans used, and do the job much faster than both. They called the machine an "Electronic Diff.* Analyzer," with a footnote referring to the abbreviation "Diff." as meaning not "differential" *á la* Bush's analog computer, but rather "difference," as in the use of finite differences manipulated by ordinary arithmetic. (The term "digital" had not yet come into common use, but that is clearly what they meant.) Soon after the project received funding, Colonel Paul Gillon of the BRL gave it the name ENIAC, for "Electronic Numerical Integrator and Computer."[9]

The idea of building the digital electronic computer was Mauchly's. He was an instructor at the Moore School, but his primary interest was not electronics but meteorology. From 1933 to 1940, while he taught physics at Ursinus College (he was a one-man physics department), he recognized the need to automate the process of computation to advance the art of weather prediction. Weather prediction was at that time just getting a theoretical foundation that showed great promise. Led by Lewis F. Richardson in England, meteorologists had developed sets of equations that, while only a crude approximation of the immensely complex patterns of the weather, nevertheless offered a chance of making reasonably accurate predictions. But their advances required large numbers of computations, and their work was held up in the 1930s's by a lack of computing power.[10]

Mauchly explored the familiar computing techniques of his day: mechanical calculators, punched card equipment, and electronic circuits, both digital and analog. To learn more about electronics he enrolled in a special course at the

Moore School designed to acquaint people with that fast-developing technology, and ended up staying on. J. Presper Eckert was a graduate student at the Moore School who was an instructor in that course. He had been working on various war-related projects, including work on the copy of the Differential Analyzer the Moore School had. Eckert had helped convert some of the machine's units from mechanical to electronic operation, but other than that he had not done much work in computing. But Mauchly's enthusiasm was enough to convince him; his facility with electronics was the perfect complement to Mauchly's vision of high-speed computing machinery.

In December, 1940, Mauchly met John V. Atanasoff and learned that the physics professor from Iowa State had already gone a long way toward building an electronic digital computer. Atanasoff was building a machine that could solve systems of simultaneous linear equations—the same sort of problem that Konrad Zuse was tackling in Germany. But Atanasoff had proposed doing it with electronic circuits, not relays. What was more, Atanasoff had quickly seen the advantages of a digital machine—that is, one that would solve those equations by numerical processes, not by representing the quantities by electrical analogs of voltage or current levels. Other physicists had developed special-purpose machines that could solve systems of linear equations. But Atanasoff's was far more advanced than any of them, both by his use of high-speed electronic circuits, and by his adoption of digital methods of solution.[11]

By the time Mauchly learned of Atanasoff's project, a prototype model had been completed and was almost completely functional. It could handle equations having up to thirty variables, and performed arithmetic on all the variables in an equation simultaneously (reminiscent of punched-card methods). The machine represented numbers in the binary system, with a word length of fifty binary digits, corresponding to about fifteen decimal digits. It did not use floating point. Atanasoff has said recently that he had known of the binary system ever since grade school; in any case, he chose the binary scale for his machine after carefully considering several number bases from the standpoint of maximum theoretical efficiency.

The only part of the machine not working was the input/output device, which was to have coded and read binary digits on cards at very high speed, much faster than commercial punched-card machines could. Mauchly saw that prototype on a visit to Ames, Iowa, in 1940, after meeting Atanasoff in Philadelphia.

Did John V. Atanasoff invent the electronic digital computer? That was the decision of Judge Earl Larson, whose 1974 judgement in a suit against Sperry Univac Corporation declared Eckert and Mauchly's ENIAC patent (which Sperry Univac had acquired) invalid for just that reason.[12]

Atanasoff's machine had two features absolutely central to any modern conception of a computer: high-speed digital electronic circuits, and the binary system. We have already seen why electronic speeds are important. And while it is certainly possible to build a computer using the base ten (or any other base, for that matter), the advantages of the binary scale are overwhelming, especially so at electronic speeds. (The binary system is central to modern computer science; for freshmen computer science students binary arithmetic is the first thing they learn: it is the portal through which all must pass.) Konrad Zuse certainly recognized the practical advantages of the binary system. Atanasoff chose it after proving that it was the best system in theory as well.

Mauchly examined Atanasoff's machine carefully during his visit to Ames, and from his correspondence with the Iowa physics professor there is little doubt that he was impressed by what he saw. Mauchly was thinking about building an electronic computer, but it was only after seeing Atanasoff's machine (and after collaborating with Eckert) that his ideas crystallized into a practical proposal.

The ENIAC grew out of the proposal for an electronic "difference" analyzer. It was a digital machine, and it computed with electronic circuits. It did not use the binary system but rather used electronic versions of the familiar decimal wheels of punched card equipment. In that last regard it was far behind Atanasoff's concept (and Zuse's, and Schreyer's).

But unlike Atanasoff's machine, the ENIAC was programmable. It could compute firing tables, as it was designed to do, but it could also do a lot more—including solving systems of linear equations. Atanasoff stressed the fact that many problems of physics could be cast in the form of systems of simultaneous linear equations, and thus be solved with his machine, but there was no way that he could alter the sequence of operations that it went through. If in fact Mauchly derived his ideas for the ENIAC from Atanasoff, as Judge Earl Larson concluded, then he took an important step forward in proposing a machine whose sequence of operations could be altered by plugboards. But at the same time he and Eckert took a step backward in rejecting Atanasoff's decision to use the binary system.

But there is one final aspect to the story that clinches the argument. The ENIAC worked. Atanasoff's computer was never reliable enough to be put into routine use solving practical problems. If Howard Aiken's Mark I put Babbage's ghost to rest, then the ENIAC, which not only worked but worked well, silenced the many skeptics who said that no computer using vacuum tubes could ever be made to work reliably. Atanasoff's computer, had it been better publicized at the time, might only have added fuel to the skeptics' arguments. And in the 1940's, those arguments were taken very seriously. Charles Babbage first conceived of the idea of an automatic digital computer. John V. Atanasoff, together with Helmut Schreyer and perhaps others, first conceived of an electronic digital computer. John Mauchly and J. Presper Eckert, as leaders of a skilled team at the Moore School, invented the first working electronic numeric digital computer.

BUILDING THE ENIAC

On April 9, 1943, Mauchly, Eckert (whose twenty-fourth birthday it was), and John Grist Brainerd submitted their proposal to the Army; it was approved not long afterward. Their first priority was to design the machine's accumulators—

the devices that would both add and store numbers like those in the Harvard Mark I, only at electronic speeds. They had to be designed before any other parts of the computer. Eckert was already familiar with high-speed electronic counting circuits, which by the 1940's were coming into wide use for counting cosmic rays and nuclear particles emitted from radioactive materials. In both cases the counter must run fast enough to keep up with the events it is counting. At the same time, because they counted large aggregates of events, accuracy was not too critical: it did not matter if they missed a particle now and then. (Absolute accuracy is generally not required in counters. Who cares if an automobile odometer is off by a mile or two?)

Most of the discussion about electronic counting circuits appeared in experimental physics journals, which discussed counting cosmic rays or other nuclear events. (Mauchly especially remembered many articles on counting devices that appeared between 1935 and 1941 in the *Review of Scientific Instruments*.) Those counters either used a gas-filled vacuum tube called a thyratron or else they were descendants of the so-called Eccles-Jordan "flip-flop," first published in 1919. That circuit contained a pair of "triodes"—three-element vacuum tubes—only one of which conducted current at any one time. When the circuit was triggered by an external pulse of current, each tube in it "flipped" into its opposite state: conducting or nonconducting. (H. J. Reich of the University of Illinois called the Eccles-Jordan circuit a "trigger" circuit in his writings, which were widely read. The IBM engineers working on electronic calculators in the 1940's remember the circuit by Reich's name; after the war the term *flip-flop* came into common use.)[13]

The flip-flop was thus fundamentally a binary device, but it worked on different principles from the bi-stable circuit that Helmut Schreyer developed for his doctoral thesis. Schreyer's device used a neon lamp instead of two triodes to maintain the state of the circuit. The Eccles-Jordan device was considerably faster. (Incidentally, Mauchly also investigated neon tube circuits while he was at Ursinus.)

The problem became one of choosing a counting circuit, of which there were plenty of examples described in the technical literature, and making it absolutely reliable. Remember that in a digital computer the loss of even one digit can spoil the results of a computation.[14] The counters then in existence used a variety of number bases. Some counted cosmic rays in the binary system; others used rings of tubes that counted decimally by groups of four binary flip-flops, like George Stibitz's binary-coded-decimal circuits in the Complex Number Computer. Other counters used the bi-quinary system, like the later Bell Labs relay computers, using a total of seven tubes to count a decimal digit.

The circuit Eckert and Mauchly chose for the ENIAC's accumulators coded a decimal number by ten flip-flops, one for each decimal digit. So it took twenty triodes to represent a single decimal number. Those ten flip-flops formed a ring that recorded a number just like the engraved wheels of a mechanical adding machine did. An adding machine's wheel indicated a number by whatever digit was visible through a window. The ENIAC's ring counters indicated their digits by whichever of the ten flip-flops had a different state than the other nine. When a pulse was sent to the ring, it turned off that flip-flop and turned on the one next to it. And when the ring received a series of pulses, they triggered a succession of flip-flops corresponding to an addition of that number. If, say, the fifth flip-flop was "on," and the ring received a train of three pulses, the ring would move from state 5 to states 6 and 7, and finally come to rest with the eighth flip-flop on, representing the sum of five and three. If a train of pulses passed through the nine's position, a carry pulse would be sent to the neighboring ring counter as well.[15] The ENIAC's ring counter worked like the accumulators of Howard Aiken's Mark I, using tubes instead of wheels. (Eckert and Mauchly knew of the Bell Labs computers but not of the Mark I when they began designing the ENIAC.)

Writing a few years after the machine's completion, Eckert said that he rejected the binary and binary-coded-decimal systems because he felt they could not be made reliable enough.[16] The biquinary code was rejected because "it required stable resistors, which were then much more expensive than they are now." More recently, he and Mauchly have given other reasons.[17] The price they paid for their code was that to count a decimal number required many more tubes than, say, Atanasoff's or Schreyer's circuits needed. No other electronic computer after the ENIAC used that coding scheme. Many have represented numbers in base ten, but they usually have used a binary-coded-decimal circuit that requires far fewer flip-flops.

A bank of ten such ring counters (called *decade counters*) could store and add ten-digit decimal numbers. They were called, appropriately, *accumulators*, and they formed the backbone of the computer. Like the Harvard Mark I, the ENIAC's arithmetic was distributed throughout the machine: the accumulators did the addition and subtraction; a separate unit did multiplication, division, and extraction of square roots.

The 1943 proposal called for a machine with ten accumulators, but once preliminary work showed the design was feasible, the BRL asked for a machine with twenty. Each accumulator could store and add ten-digit numbers plus their signs. They were mounted in a series of panels arranged in a long U-shaped configuration which, together with the other parts of the machine, filled a large room (Figures 5.1, 5.2).

In the accumulators, the two triodes of each flip-flop were enclosed in the single tube 6SN7, so there were at least ten such tubes for each ring, 100 for an accumulator. Besides those, there were others needed to ensure that the ring functioned correctly. In fact, each accumulator had 550 tubes, for a total of 550 × 20 or 11,000 tubes for the accumulators alone. The original plans called for the ENIAC to contain 5,000 tubes; as finished it had over 18,000.[18] Recall that in Germany at that time Helmut Schreyer was proposing a computer that would use about 2,000 tubes, a proposal rejected as being too ambitious. The British Colossus, the electronic code-breaking computer completed in 1943, also had

THE ENIAC   113

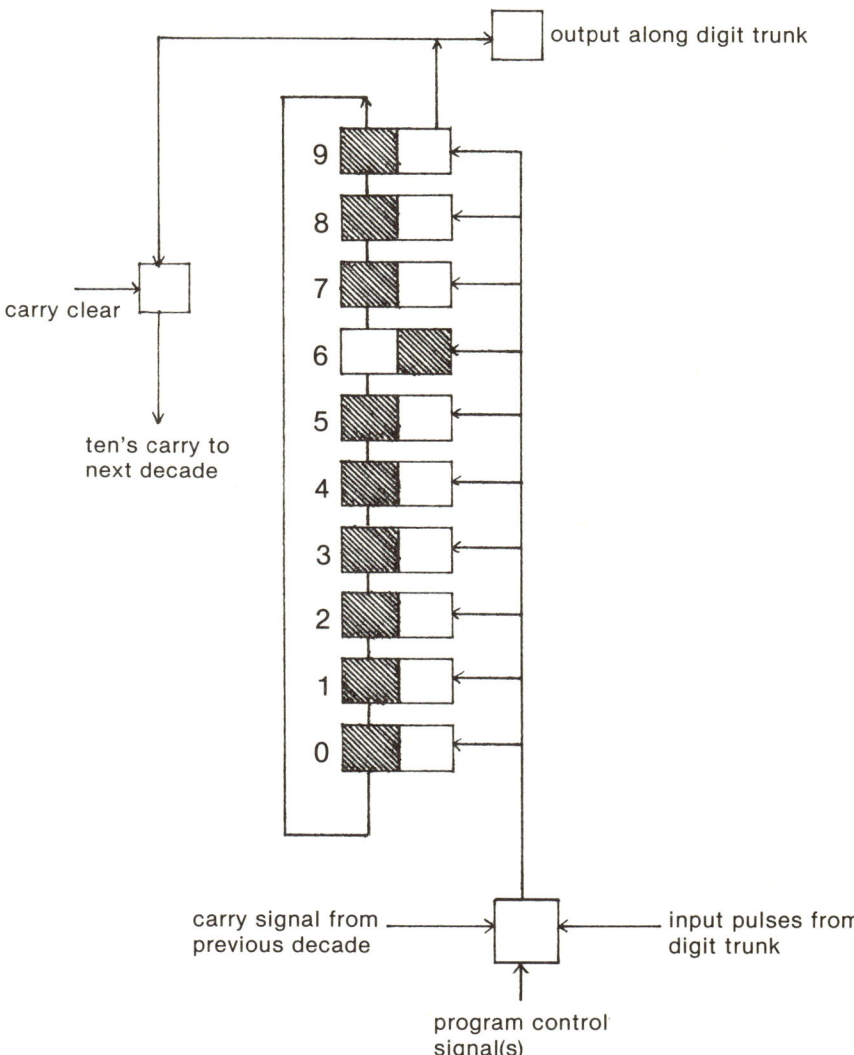

Figure 5.1. Sketch of a Decade Counter

2,000 tubes. By the end of the war ten versions of the Colossus had been built. The ENIAC was by far the most complex piece of electronic equipment built up to that time. Probably no other machine with that many tubes in it has ever been built since, or ever will be built, either. Nowadays all that computing is done with solid-state flip-flops crammed onto chips the size of a fingernail. Tubes still have their place, but not in computers. The circuits of the ENIAC appear more

The ENIAC.
Smithsonian Institution Photo No. 53192.

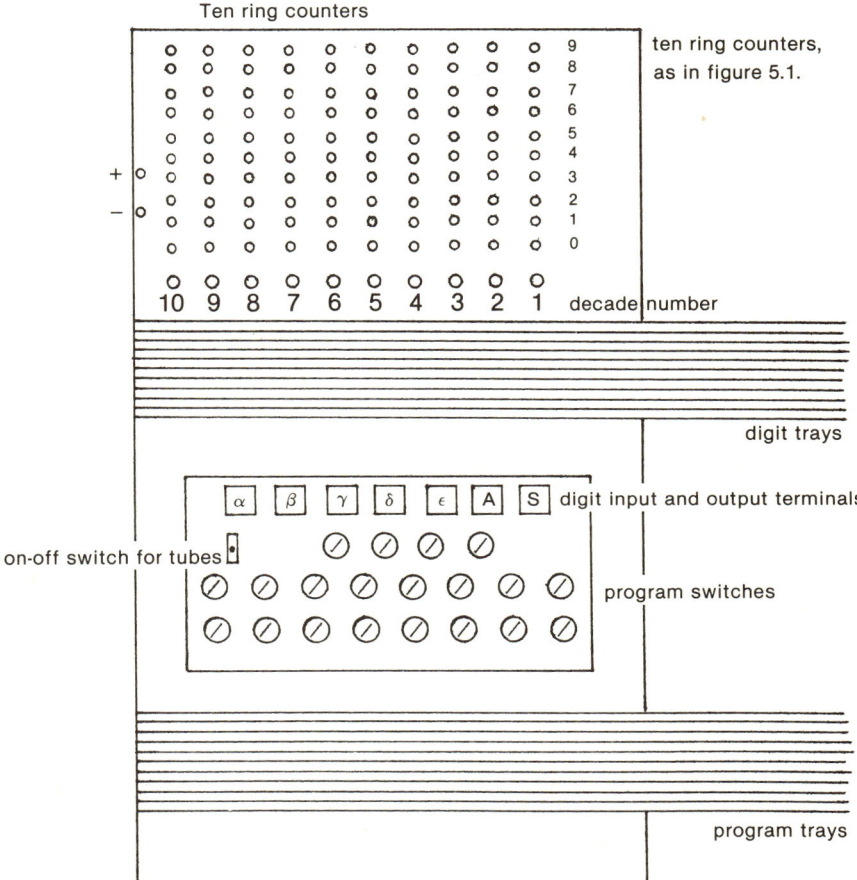

Figure 5.2. One of the ENIAC's Accumulators

and more arcane with the passage of years, although its logical structure can still be deciphered with little difficulty.

STRUCTURE OF THE ENIAC

Besides the twenty accumulators, the ENIAC had a cycling unit, programming units, constant transmitters for the values of functions like the drag function of a projectile, and input/output facilities. In one respect the ENIAC was very different from any of the electromechanical computers. Its program, the sequence of elementary instructions that it was to carry out, was not supplied by punched cards or tape or filmstrip. The reason is clear: the ENIAC's circuits did arithmetic at electronic speeds. That speed would be wasted if the machine had to wait for instructions that were being supplied at mechanical speeds. If a paper tape supplied its programs or function data, as in the Mark I, the ENIAC's accumulators would spend a lot of their time idly waiting to be told what to do next. (The only other electronic computer from that era, the British Colossus, did use paper tape for the input of alphabetic data. Those tapes were mounted on specially designed transport mechanisms that moved with incredible speed. Accounts of the Colossus in action describe tapes flying through the machine, feeding in up to five thousand characters per second. The tape itself quickly wore grooves in the steel guide pins, and since no take-up reel could handle that kind of speed, the tape simply was allowed to pile up at the side of the machine, describing eerie rainbow arcs in the air before settling to the ground in a heap.)[19]

So the ENIAC's instructions were wired into the machine by cables that connected its various parts to one another. Programs were changed by plugging in the cables in a different configuration. I shall have more to say on its programming later.

The ENIAC was a synchronous machine: that is, a central clock coordinated all its actions. Times for all elementary operations were precisely specified as a number of pulses sent out by the cycling unit. At each basic cycle, the cycling unit sent out a set of pulses, each of which had a specific role in controlling the computer. All numbers, algebraic signs, instructions, etc., originated as combinations of pulses from the cycling unit. That is, if the number 5 was to be sent from one accumulator to another, the first accumulator would *not* transmit five pulses to the other one, but it would rather open a "gate" at the second accumulator long enough for five pulses originating at the cycling unit to be passed through. The reason is that pulses lose their shape and intensity quickly. If a pulse that originated at one accumulator traveled through various other parts of the machine, it would soon be so weak that it could not do its job. Therefore all information in the ENIAC was transferred by sets of pulses freshly generated 5,000 times a second by the cycling unit. Even with that arrangement, the accumulators also had "pulse-reshaping" circuits that restored the strength of signals as they arrived.

The basic cycle was 200 microseconds, one addition time. During a cycle ten parallel pulse trains went out. Each had a specific role in controlling the machine. The first, for example, consisted of one pulse 2 microseconds long that came near the end of the 200 microsecond cycle. Its job was to advance the programming units of the computer to their next program step, as specified by the setting of program switches and the plugging of program cables. The second of the ten trains consisted of ten 2-microsecond pulses that came at the beginning of the cycle. Its job was to cycle a ring counter whenever a number was to be read. In this way the contents of an accumulator could be read out by cycling the counters one full revolution, after which each would have returned to its original position.

The next eight trains had similar roles. All but one of them consisted of strings of pulses that were 2 microseconds long, separated from each other by a space of

8 microseconds. Thus the shortest sub-cycle of the ENIAC was 10 microseconds, or a clock frequency of 100 khz (that is, 100,000 cycles per second). For diagnostic purposes it was possible to slow the machine down so that it executed just one of those pulses at a time, or one full addition cycle (twenty pulses long) at a time.

One of the pulses, the "carry-clear" pulse, was 70 microseconds instead of 2 microseconds long, as were the other nine. The reason for that was that during an addition, all ten digits of a number were transmitted simultaneously. Should one of those transfers cause a carry of ten to the next ring counter, that carry had to be held until the next counter was finished with *its* addition; otherwise it would be receiving two pulses at once and would not know how to sort them out. Recall that the ten-pulse mentioned above came at the beginning of an addition cycle. Once all the digit pulses were sent, the carry-clear pulse opened up a gate and held it open long enough for any carries to take place. In the extreme case where a carry propagated itself through all ten decimal places (for example, 1 + 9,999,999,999), that could take up to 25 microseconds, as determined by experiment. So the carry-clear pulse held the gate open long enough to make sure that all the carries got through. An addition therefore took ten short pulse-times to cycle the ring counters, one 70-microsecond pulse-time for the carries, and three short pulse-times for complementing, resetting, and control, for a total of 200 microseconds that made one addition cycle (Figure 5.3). The ENIAC could add 5,000 numbers per second.[20]

A computation proceeded by gating appropriate pulses from the cycling unit around the various arithmetic units of the machine, ending at an accumulator connected to a printer or other output device. So the basic flow was clockwise around the U-shaped configuration, but for all but the most trivial problems there would be multiple paths of number-routing, looping of operations, and branching back to a previous sequence of operations. All that was controlled by the programming units, described next.

The solution of, say, a differential equation implied a combination of elementary arithmetic operations, storage and retrieval of intermediate results, and consulting tables of functions or other data. Machines like the Z3 supplied those operations in a linear sequence, coded into perforated film that passed through a reading device. The ENIAC's program was supplied by rewiring the machine for each specific problem, then directing a programming unit to step through those operations in the proper order.

One implication of that scheme is that there is no reason why the steps have to be executed one at a time in a sequence. The programming unit could send out a pulse to several accumulators at once, directing one to perform an addition, another to read a value from a function table, a third to transmit results to a printer, and so on. Of course those operations could not be ones that needed results of any other operations being performed at the same time, but except for that, the ENIAC could telescope a long sequence of operations into a more compact form, if programmed carefully to do so. In that regard it was like the

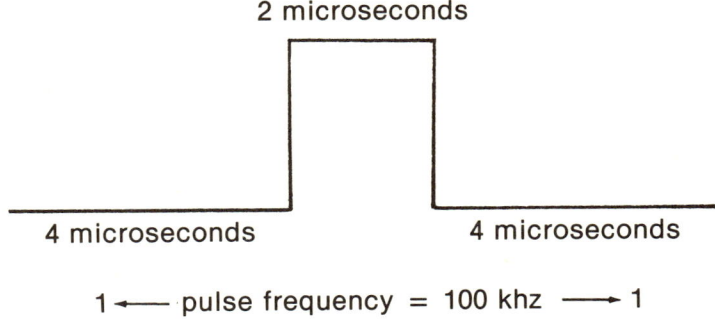

The cycling unit delivered the following trains of pulses:
1) program pulse (1 pulse at the 17th cycle)
2) ten-pulse (10 pulses at the first 10 cycles, shifted a half-cycle in phase)
3) nine-pulse (9 pulses at the first 9 cycles)
4) one-pulse (1 pulse at the first cycle)
5) two-pulse (2 pulses, at the 2nd and 3rd cycles)
6) two'-pulse (2 pulses, at the 4th and 5th cycles)
7) four-pulse (at the 6th, 7th, 8th, and 9th cycles)
8) complement pulse (one pulse at the 10th cycle)
9) carry-clear pulse (one long pulse from the 11th to the 17th cycle)
10) reset-pulse (2 pulses, one at the 13th and one at the 19th cycle).

Figure 5.3. Timing Pulses in the ENIAC

Complex Number Computer, which had a permanently wired program that computed the real and the imaginary parts of a complex product in parallel. (Recall that the Automatic Sequence Controlled Calculator also had a limited parallel capability: to interleave additions between the steps of a multiplication. But it was basically a sequential calculator, as its name implied.)

The team at the Moore School always referred to the ENIAC as a "parallel" machine, for another reason besides its programming. Whenever a number was transferred in or out of the accumulators, all ten digits plus the sign were transferred at once, in parallel, by an eleven-wire "trunk" cable. That was no different from the early electromechanical computers examined thus far: the Mark I, the Bell Labs machines, and the Zuse computers. In its initial configuration, the ENIAC was also capable of parallel program execution as well, within the limits of the problem being solved. But the machine's parallel design was stressed in the initial reports because as the ENIAC neared completion, Eckert and Mauchly were already looking ahead to a new, more powerful computer, eventually called the EDVAC, that would have far fewer tubes than the ENIAC. It would have fewer tubes by doing all its arithmetic serially, that is, numbers would be transmitted one digit at a time, not all at once. At the same time it would execute program steps sequentially, not in parallel, as well, but that was not the major issue facing the computer's designers at the time.

Programming the ENIAC to execute a number of program steps in parallel proved to be exceedingly difficult and time-consuming, although it made the machine very fast. After it was moved from Philadelphia to the Ballistic Research Lab at Aberdeen, Maryland, it was modified so that it could be programmed by setting switches on a function table instead of by plugging in a configuration of cables. That modification made programming a lot easier, but it forever ended the ENIAC's parallel operating capability, a loss lamented by some.[21] So the descriptions of the ENIAC as a "parallel" machine refer to its parallel transfer of numbers. The concept of parallel program execution has reappeared in modern "supercomputers," which are optimized to do the same kinds of complex numerical problems involving differential equations that the ENIAC was built for. Functionally, supercomputers like the ILLIAC IV are the true descendants of the ENIAC.

Programming devices were attached to each accumulator and to the other units of the machine. Program pulses travelled from one to the other along program trunks located just below the trunks carrying numbers. The program trunk contained eleven independent program lines; each line could carry a separate programming signal. The program trunk was a mirror image of the digit trunks, which also had eleven lines for the ten digits plus the sign of a single number. As with the digit signals, all program pulses originated from the cycling unit.

The program device associated with each accumulator or other unit was called a "transceiver" (transmitter-receiver). If, for example, the program called for the contents of accumulator 10 to be added to the contents of accumulator 11, and at the same time be sent to the multiplier unit, the programmer would set switches on accumulator 10 to transmit its contents out on to the digit trunks upon the receipt of a program pulse. Digit trunks to the other accumulator and to the multiplier would be plugged in manually, like a telephone switchboard. Switches on the other units would be set to accept numbers from the digit trunks upon the receipt of a program pulse. There were five possible input paths (labeled with Greek letters in Figure 5.1), and two output paths (labeled "*A*" and "*S*," for the number or for its complement if a subtraction was needed).

The transceiver switches could be set to repeat the above operation, if desired, up to nine times, after which it would send out a program pulse to initiate the next set of operations. In this way short loops of instructions were possible by using these so-called stepper switches. The stepper of one accumulator could be connected to the stepper of another, as well. The 1945 report on the ENIAC describes these subsequences as "sub-routines," possibly the first use of that term; it was a feature that gave the ENIAC far greater programming flexibility than the electromechanical computers which, if they had subroutines at all, had to add them by endless loops of tape or film that were separate from the main sequence tape. It was just not practical to have loops of sequences when the program was fed into the machine by a single long strip of tape.

It is clear that using transceivers to set up sequences at each accumulator made parallel execution possible, provided the programmer kept track of the times required for all the sequences. But the limited number of switch settings (perhaps 300 at most) meant that long sequences were not possible.[22]

A separate unit called the Master Programmer, located next to the cycling unit, solved that problem. The Master Programmer also contained steppers, which in turn could direct the steppers on the individual transceivers throughout the computer. It also contained other switches that could alter the entire path of the program depending on the results of a previous calculation. All these switches were electronic, and so operated at the same speed as the arithmetic units.

Thus the ENIAC had full conditional branching capability as well as a flexible programming scheme. It truly was a general-purpose numeric computer, not restricted to any one mathematical problem. The way it was programmed made it unlikely that it would be used for short problems, since for every new problem someone had to unplug and replug a tangled nest of cables and reset banks of switches. But it certainly could solve short problems if someone wanted it to.

Programming it hardly seemed like programming at all in the usual sense of the word; indeed, the people at the Moore School called it "setting up" the machine for a problem, using a term borrowed from the operation of the Differential Analyzer. Setting up the ENIAC meant a literal rewiring of the computer—creating a special-purpose machine—to solve a given problem. Compare that with the Bell Labs Complex Number Computer: a special-purpose machine that was "hard-wired" to do complex arithmetic, and nothing more. Each time the ENIAC was set up, it transformed itself into something like that, only its wires were not soldered in but could be unplugged and rewired for a new problem.

All computer programming is a reconfiguration of the circuits to turn the machine into a special-purpose device that solves the specific problem at hand. For the ENIAC, that wiring was literally done by plugboards (and setting switches); computers programmed by paper tapes do the same thing, only the rewiring is abstracted by one level: the code on the tape represents the internal rewiring of the computer in such a way as to solve a given problem.

Setting up the ENIAC was a slow and tedious process, taking at least a day for a typical problem. It meant that the computer was best suited for long problems requiring lots of runs using different input data. Setting up a short sequence took almost as long, during which time the machine could do no work, so those kinds of problems were seldom done. This certainly put the ENIAC at a disadvantage compared to the other electromechanical computers, such as the Bell Labs Model V, also built to do ballistics work.[23]

Eckert and Mauchly recognized this drawback. In their plans for the EDVAC, the successor to the ENIAC, they considered the idea of storing the computer's program internally in a high-speed magnetic drum or disk memory, so that the set-up could be rapidly changed, while still allowing instructions to be supplied to the arithmetic units as fast as the data. That was the genesis of the stored-program principle, which is absolutely central to any modern concept of a digital computer. "Calculations can be performed at high speed only if instructions are supplied at high speed," Mauchly said.[24] Supplying the program by a paper tape could not achieve that speed. (Modern computers are often programmed by paper tape, but the instructions on that tape are not directly executed as they pass through the machine, as was the case with the pre-1945 machines. Instead the program is read from the tape into an internal memory, from which it is then executed by the machine at electronic speeds.)

The ENIAC did not store program instructions in its memory, but the effect of plugging in its cables and of setting its switches was the same. Its "program" was integral to the computer; it did not exist as an entity outside of it somehow. From the machine's point of view, the next instruction was always right "there," whenever it was needed.

The ENIAC stayed at the Moore School through 1946; then it was moved to the Ballistic Research Lab at Aberdeen. The people who used it there, many having had no contact with the Moore School, modified its programming method to make setting up problems much easier.

Recall that digit trunks had eleven wires for the ten decimal digits plus their sign, while program trunks also had eleven wires for eleven separate program channels. Both program pulses and digit pulses came from the same initiating and cycling units, and were of similar shape and intensity. In the ENIAC, a pulse was a pulse: all circuits handled pulses of the same shape and intensity. That philosophy reflected the ENIAC's debt to cosmic ray and other pulse-counting devices.

At Aberdeen R. H. Clippinger modified the ENIAC so that numerical data stored on one of the functions tables were routed along the program trunks, thus allowing the machine to be programmed much faster. One person could be setting up a program on a function table not connected to the computer, while the computer was executing another program. That made programming much faster and easier. Eckert has said recently that he and Mauchly provided for that modification in the initial design of the ENIAC; the fact that the program trunks were mirror images of the digit trunks seems to suggest that. But while the ENIAC was in Philadelphia it was always programmed by the method of plugging cables and setting switches. After 1948 that programming method was abandoned. This meant that parallel execution of program steps was no longer possible, since the machine could execute only one coded instruction from the function table at a time. That slowed down the machine quite a bit, but it reduced set-up time from a whole day to a few hours.[25]

OTHER UNITS: THE MULTIPLIER

Since the ENIAC was a decimal machine, its designers had to decide whether to implement multiplication by either repeated addition or table look-up. Although electronic speeds would have made the former method quite fast, they rejected it. While there were twenty places in the ENIAC where addition and subtraction could take place, there was only one multiplier. The multiplier had to handle every multiplication in a problem, so it had to be as fast as possible. And given the types of problems the computer was designed for, multiplications could appear as frequently as additions in the problem set-up.

The ENIAC's multiplier consisted of several panels, and with it were associated six of the accumulators: two for storing the operands, two for the partial products, and two for the final product. The product contained up to twenty digits, from which the operator could select ten for further computation.

A matrix of resistors formed the multiplier's times table. When that matrix received pulses corresponding to two decimal digits, it returned two pulses that represented the product of those two digits. (Many products do not contain two digits, for example, $2 \times 3 = 6$, but the matrix always returned two, in that case $2 \times 3 = 06$.) One accumulator received the units part of a product; another received the tens part. When all digits had been multiplied, those partial products were summed up to give the answer. That method of splitting each product into its units and tens parts was inspired by the IBM's 601 electromechanical multiplier, which also was the basis for the multiplier in the Harvard Mark I (see Chapter 3).

The entire process of multiplying two ten-digit numbers together took fourteen addition cycles, or 2.8 milliseconds. The ENIAC could therefore multiply 357 numbers per second, often reported in the popular press as 360 per second. It was hundreds of times faster than any other computer of its day.

THE FUNCTION TABLES AND OTHER UNITS

Like the multiplier, a grid of resistors also made up the function tables, but their values could be changed by setting dial switches. These tables were vital to the ENIAC's overall design, as in numerical integration the values of a function being integrated have to be supplied at high speed. Each table stored up to 100 values, for arguments ranging from -2 to 101. (The "extra" values at each end allowed the function to be interpolated throughout its range.) Three tables were built, but only one could be attached to the computer at any one time. While the machine was solving a problem, an operator could set up the other tables for the next problem—it was a tedious and error-prone job, so having extra tables kept idle time to a minimum. That was even more the case after one of the tables was used to store coded instructions. For some frequently used functions, pre-wired assemblies replaced a few banks of switches. Each function value could have up to twelve digits of accuracy, or the whole table could be split up to give 200 function values at six-digit precision.[26]

The input/output facilities were standard IBM card readers and punches modified to accept program pulses from the cycling unit. Their speeds were grossly out of balance with those of the rest of the machine, but early in the project it had been decided that the risks of developing faster devices from scratch were too great. Recall that a high-speed input/output device was the only part of Atanasoff's computer that did not work. The ENIAC's users had to program around that speed imbalance by carefully interleaving printing and card reading with other operations. In that way, the computer's electronic units would not lie idle waiting for the electromechanical units to finish printing or reading in data.

Obviously that required that the accumulators not be tied up holding a number while it was being printed. So a "buffer" register built of telephone relays took the number from the accumulator for delivery to the printer, leaving the electronic units free to go on with other business. That buffer was built by Sam Williams, the same man who collaborated with George Stibitz on the Bell Labs series of relay computers. So both IBM and Bell Labs, besides having their own large-scale electromechanical computing projects during the war, also were involved with the ENIAC, but only "peripherally."

The buffer relays did perform one calculation. A negative number was represented in the accumulators by its tens-complement form, but IBM equipment printed a negative number by its absolute value preceded by a minus sign. The buffer relays performed that conversion. That was the only piece of computing on the ENIAC not done electronically. Table 5.1 lists the full specifications for the machine as it existed in 1946.

Table 5.1. THE ENIAC

Builders:	J. Presper Eckert, John W. Mauchly. Also Arthur Burks, Kite Sharpless, John Davis, Robert Shaw, and others
Place:	Moore School of Electrical Engineering, University of Pennsylvania, Philadelphia. Later moved to the Ballistic Research Laboratory, Aberdeen, Maryland.
Dates:	Proposed April, 1943; authorized June, 1943; completed by November, 1945; first problem run December, 1945. Dedicated February 16, 1946; moved to Aberdeen November, 1946; dismantled October 2, 1955. Parts now in various museums, including the Smithsonian, Washington, D.C., and the Science Museum, London.
Cost:	$500,000 (exactly $486,804.22, according to Goldstine), funded by the Army.
Technology:	Vacuum tubes for computing; electromechanical input and output: card readers, card punches, printers; telephone relay buffer store.
Physical specifications:	40 panels, each 9' x 2' x 1', arranged in a U-shape; other units on casters could be positioned at various places. 18,000 tubes, 1,500 relays. 80 different DC voltages, ranging from -920 to +550 volts; main power 240 volts, 60 Hz. Power consumption: 150 kW, 80 kW for tube heaters, 45 kW for other electronic circuits, 5 kW for input/output devices, 20 kW for ventilating and cooling.
Architecture:	Word length: 10 decimal digits plus sign; ten's complement for negative numbers and subtraction; fixed decimal point—switch-selected; multi-

Table 5.1 *Continued*

	plication by table look-up. Addition and subtraction done in accumulators; separate unit for multiplication, division, and square-rooting. Other units for cycling (timing), pulse generation, and programming.
Memory:	20 numbers in the accumulators: 100 read-only numbers in a function table; other storage by punched cards; also twenty 10-digit constant switches.
Speed:	Pulse frequency, 100 kHz, or one pulse every 10 microseconds. Basic cycle was one addition time, 20 pulses, or 200 microseconds (5,000 additions/second).
	Multiplication time, 14 addition times, or 2,800 microseconds (357 multiplications/second). Division time varied, up to 38 divisions/second. The ENIAC could be run at slower speeds, including a single pulse at a time, or a single cycle at a time, for diagnostic purposes.
Programming:	Plugboards and switch settings. Full conditional branching and subroutine capability; also the ability to perform parallel sequences of operations. Slow to set up: a day or two for each new problem.
Input:	80-channel IBM punched-card reader; could read 2 numbers/second.
Output:	Standard IBM printer. Each accumulator also had a bank of neon lights showing its contents; at normal speeds these were of course illegible, but at diagnostic speeds they could be read.
Miscellaneous:	Much of the metalwork and other physical construction done by Livingston & Conway, Inc., a Philadelphia construction firm. Cooling system designed and built by Eggly Engineers, also of Philadelphia. RCA of Camden, New Jersey, supplied the tubes.

EVALUATION OF THE ENIAC

The ENIAC was a pioneering machine. But it had an inelegant design, was hard to program, had a limited memory capacity, and had slow input/output facilities. That much was frankly acknowledged by its builders in their reports on the machine written in 1945 as the machine was being completed.[27]

Those reports devote much space to the ENIAC's successor, the EDVAC, in which Eckert and Mauchly hoped to overcome most of the ENIAC's deficiencies. The EDVAC (Electronic Discrete VAriable Computer) would use binary arithmetic, would have a high-speed read-write memory of large capacity, and would execute programs that were internally stored in its memory.

In the EDVAC there would also be a separation of memory functions and arithmetic. It needed a fast and large memory, which would be much more difficult to achieve if each memory cell also had to be capable of performing addition, as the ENIAC's accumulators did. Thus its designers returned to the overall structure for a computer that Charles Babbage had decided upon a hundred years earlier for his Analytical Engine (and which Konrad Zuse independently rediscovered in the late 1930's).

Aside from those design shortcomings, the ENIAC's biggest drawback was that it had far too many tubes. That was the chief reason why some government and military officials, including George Stibitz, were reluctant to fund the project at all. No one was sure that the ENIAC would run long enough between tube failures to do any useful work.[28] Tubes are inherently less reliable than other electronic components; that is why they are not soldered into a circuit the way resistors or capacitors are, but are rather mounted in sockets for easy replacement. Even after the ENIAC was unveiled to the public and demonstrated its reliability, other computer designers (including Zuse and Aiken) continued to use the slower relay technology.

But the ENIAC was actually quite reliable in absolute terms, and much more reliable than the relay computers when its speed is taken into account. If the ENIAC could be made to run without a tube failure for only one hour, it could in that hour do more computing than the Bell Labs Model V could do in fifteen *days* of round-the-clock operation, based on their relative multiplication speeds. The claim that the relay computers could, and often were, operated unattended through the night (something the ENIAC never could do) must be tempered by that fact.

A graph of failure rates of electronic components looks like the letter *U*. Failure are high when the components are new, then follows a long period of trouble-free operation, followed by a gradual increase in failures as the components age. Whenever the ENIAC was turned on it would usually blow a tube. When a tube is cold, its filament has a different resistance and physical shape than when it is hot, so it is more likely to burn out when it is first turned on.[29] So the ENIAC was hardly ever turned off. Surprisingly few cases of wiring mistakes turned up, and there were a few malfunctions due to "cold-soldered" connections, where the solder did not receive enough heat to form a good electrical bond. But those were quickly located and fixed.

After the tubes were left on all the time, the ENIAC could run about twenty hours between tube failures—a remarkably good record, due mainly to the conservative ratings at which the tubes and all other components in the computer were run. After it was moved from Philadelphia to Aberdeen, failures were more frequent, but eventually there, too, a good in-service record was established.

Besides the oft-mentioned fact that all the components were run well below their rated capacity, the design of the ENIAC was such that when a failure did occur, it could be isolated and repaired quickly. Indeed, at no time while it was in Philadelphia was the ENIAC ever shut down for more than a few days. The increased complexity of its design actually made it more reliable: by having a complicated power supply delivering many different voltages to the circuits, the machine could be run at slower speeds, down to one pulse at a time, to track down a problem. Neon bulbs revealed the contents of the accumulators; normally they blinked too fast to be readable but at single-step speeds they were.[30]

The ENIAC's ring counters were designed to be unplugged as a unit. If one malfunctioned, an identical spare, known to be in good working order, could be plugged in, while the defective one was brought to a bench where it could be repaired without tying up the whole computer. This sort of "modular" approach to systems reliability is taken for granted in the computer industry today, but it was hardly known at that time.

There was no provision for the kind of elaborate internal checking pioneered by Bell Labs in their relay computers. Before working on a problem, at intervals during the solution, and after running the problem, its programmers ran special diagnostic programs to test the circuits.[31]

But it was still clear that the ENIAC had too many tubes. Eckert and Mauchly stressed that in the EDVAC they would have the same computing power with one-sixth the number of tubes. They had made the ENIAC a reliable computer, but just barely. In a sense the skeptics were right in being pessimistic about vacuum tubes. The reliability problem was always a serious one until tubes were replaced by transistors after 1960—thereby lifting the whole question of computer engineering, and with it reliability, to a new level of sophistication.

HOW THE MACHINE WAS USED

The acronym *ENIAC* stood for Electronic Numeric Integrator and Computer, and that is a good description of what kind of work it did. If Bessel functions were the Mark I's bread and butter, then the solution of differential equations by numeric methods was the ENIAC's. Its original goal was to compute and tabulate firing tables, and that goal remained central throughout its design, development, and construction. But the way it was built meant that it could do much more than that. By the time the computer was ready for testing late in 1945, the war was over, and the need for firing tables had lost some of its urgency; but that did not really matter. Differential equations of the kind encountered in ballistics are also found throughout physics, and if the ENIAC could be programmed to solve them, it would be kept busy.

The first problem it attacked linked the ENIAC with that other great project of the Second World War, the Manhattan Project. In July of 1945 the world's first atomic bomb exploded over the forbidding deserts of New Mexico. Building that bomb required, among many other things, a lot of computation. Its fissionable material was ignited by an implosion of a carefully shaped and timed firing of TNT, and the scientists who designed it had to calculate the geometry of the shock wave to an exacting tolerance. Most of the computing at Los Alamos was done by mechanical desk calculators and IBM punched card equipment.

But even as the atomic explosions at Hiroshima and Nagasaki hastened the end of the war, the scientists at Los Alamos were looking toward the hydrogen bomb, the "Super," which would have a much higher yield than the fission bomb. Designing it required even more calculations, far too many to be done manually or even with an electromechanical computer. Right then along came news of the ENIAC's nearing completion. Nicholas Metropolis and Stanley Frankel went to

Philadelphia late in 1945 and arranged that the first problem the ENIAC would run would be a classified problem to test the feasibility of the Super's design.[32] Few people at the Moore School, including Eckert and Mauchly, could even be told of the nature of the problem, but of course they were given the mathematical equations the ENIAC was to solve. It was a very large partial differential equation whose set-up required a million punched cards for input and transfer of numeric data. The problem overwhelmed the ENIAC's internal memory, so it was divided into sections, with intermediate results punched onto cards and reentered into the machine.

The ENIAC solved the problem—without ever having the chance to go through any shakedown or test phase. Actually, the Super computation *was* the shakedown cruise for the ENIAC. Right from the beginning it proved itself to be a fine machine indeed.[33] The problem itself remains classified to this day, but it is known that the answer computed by the ENIAC showed that the Super would not work as designed. It was a design based on freezing the heavier isotopes of hydrogen and detonating them by the compression from a fission bomb. Even after the negative results of the ENIAC's computation, a test of the so-called wet bomb design was conducted at Eniwetok in the Pacific in 1951. In that test, fusions of hydrogen nuclei did take place, but there was no thermonuclear explosion. (Early in 1951, Stanislaw Ulam and Edward Teller conceived of a different approach, one using not the blast wave but rather the x-ray emission of the fission bomb to fuse the hydrogen. That approach led to America's first hydrogen bomb shortly thereafter.)

The ENIAC proved its worth so quickly that it was busy from that moment on. There never was any time for testing or "running in" the machine. Its move to Aberdeen was postponed until late 1946 because of the urgency of the first problems it solved. When it finally was moved, it was turned off in November, 1946, and not started up again until late summer, 1947. So for most of the year 1947 the world had to get along once again without any electronic numeric computers.

Questions of whether or not the ENIAC was truly a general-purpose numeric computer are best answered by looking at some of the problems it did in that first year. Herman Goldstine, who with his wife Adele did much of the programming of the ENIAC, has documented problems in computing tables of trigonometric series, another simulation of a nuclear reaction, problems concerning the propagation of shock waves in compressible fluids, and even a problem in number theory submitted by D. H. Lehmer. The ENIAC also tackled a problem in weather forecasting—Mauchly's old dream—though it was not Mauchly but John von Neumann who submitted it.

The British physicist D. R. Hartree used the ENIAC between April and July, 1946, for a problem involving the flow of a compressible fluid over a surface, such as air over the surface of a wing travelling faster than the speed of sound. Hartree had already used the Differential Analyzer for that problem. He found the ENIAC's memory too limited for its solution by an iterative method, but he tried a different approach more suitable for the ENIAC's structure, and it worked well. He divided the area to be computed into 250 intervals, and the machine computed and punched answers to seven-place decimal accuracy.

Hartree's work is especially interesting because it was a full-scale problem that taxed the ENIAC's full capabilities, but it was not a ballistics calculation. Although it involved the numerical solution of an ordinary differential equation, its set-up was very different from the kinds of set-ups Eckert and Mauchly had envisioned for computing firing tables. So from the very beginning, the ENIAC showed that it had a broad range of applicability.[34] Another consequence of Hartree's work was that he published an account of it in a series of notes in the British journal *Nature*, in 1946, as well as in a longer paper in the *Philosophical Transactions* of the Royal Society in 1948. Those articles helped publicize the speed and power of the new invention. In general, the ENIAC never strayed far from numerical integration of differential equations. That was what it did best. But at least it could do other things, easily enough for some persons to make the attempt. After it was installed at Aberdeen, it finally got a chance to compute firing tables, which it did reliably and well for many years.

By the end of 1945 the new computer had scarcely begun running, yet it was already clear that the whole project was going to be a success. The war was over, and those who had been working so hard on the computer wanted to share their excitement with others. A public dedication was held in February, 1946, during which the machine demonstrated its ability to sum and multiply numbers at speeds few people could adequately comprehend. Representatives of the press watched as the machine computed a full trajectory in twenty seconds—faster than the shell itself travelled from the gun to its target. That seems like a silly comparison by today's standards of measuring computer speeds, but it was enough to convince the more skeptical members of the audience.

With the lifting of wartime secrecy the development of the digital computer entered a new phase. Communication barriers were not lifted entirely or immediately, but the published descriptions of the various projects meant that subsequent computer projects would proceed more along common lines. The "pre-historic" age ended, and there followed a more direct line of descent to the present day. From 1945 to 1950 a consensus emerged: the computer's future lay in machines that were electronic, not electromechanical, and digital, not analog. They would compute in the binary scale, and they would have as much high-speed read-write memory as possible. The memory would be restricted to storage and retrieval of data; all arithmetic would be concentrated in a separate unit specially built for that purpose. Most important, future computers would store not only numerical data but also their own programs in that same internal high-speed memory. How those concepts, especially the last one, emerged, will be discussed next.

NOTES

1. I. J. Good, "Early Work on Computers at Bletchly," *Cryptologiia*, 3 (1979), 65-77; Simon Lavington, *Early British Computers* (Bedford, Mass.: Digital Press, 1980), Chapters 1, 2.

2. Cuthbert Hurd, "Early IBM Computers: Edited Testimony," *Annals of the History of Computing*, 3 (1981), 163-182.

3. Herman H. Goldstine, *The Computer from Pascal to von Neumann* (Princeton: Princeton University Press, 1972), Part Two; Nancy Stern, *From ENIAC to UNIVAC* (Bedford, Mass: Digital Press, 1981); Arthur Burks, "The ENIAC: First General-Purpose Electronic Computer," *Annals of the History of Computing*, 3 (1981), 310-389.

4. John Brainerd, "Genesis of the ENIAC," *Technology and Culture*, 17 (1976), 482-488; Goldstine, *Computer*, pp. 127-139.

5. Gilbert A. Bliss, *Mathematics for Exterior Ballistics* (New York, 1944); Edward McShane, John Kelley, and Franklin Reno, *Exterior Ballistics* (Denver: University of Denver Press, 1953), especially the Appendix on its history, pp. 742-799; Forest Moulton, *New Methods in Exterior Ballistics* (Chicago: University of Chicago Press, 1926); Thomas J. Hayes, *Exterior Ballistics* (New York: Wiley, 1938).

6. Goldstine, *Computer*, pp. 146, 137-138.

7. Burks, "The ENIAC."

8. John Mauchly, "The ENIAC," in N. Metropolis, J. Howlett, and G. -C. Rota, eds., *A History of Computing in the Twentieth Century* (New York: Academic Press, 1980), pp. 541-550.

9. Nancy Stern, "From ENIAC to UNIVAC: A Case Study in the History of Technology," Dissertation, SUNY, Stony Brook, New York, 1978, pp. 41-48; Goldstine, *Computer*, p. 150.

10. Nancy Stern, "John W. Mauchly: 1907-1980," *Annals of the History of Computing*, 2 (1980), 100-103; Lewis F. Richardson, *Weather Prediction by Numerical Methods* (Cambridge, England, 1922).

11. Burks, "The ENIAC"; letter from John V. Atanasoff to the author, May 25, 1980; for an example of a special-purpose mechanical device that solved systems of linear equations, see the description of the "Wilbur Equation-solver" in Charles and Ray Eames, *A Computer Perspective* (Cambridge, Mass.: Harvard), p. 113.

12. *The Industrial Reorganization Act*: Hearings Before the Subcommittee of the Judiciary, U.S. Senate, 93rd Congress, Part 7: The Computer Industry, July 23-26, 1974; Earl R. Larson, *Findings of Fact, Conclusions of Law and Order for Judgement*, File No. 4-67 Civ. 138, Honeywell, Inc., vs. Sperry Rand Corporation and Illinois Scientific Developments, Inc., U.S. District Court, District of Minnesota, Fourth Division, October 19, 1973.

13. H. J. Reich, "Trigger Circuits," *Electronics*, August, 1939, pp. 14-17; Hurd, "IBM Computers"; W. H. Eccles and F. W. Jordan, "A Trigger Relay Utilising Three-Element Thermionic Vacuum Tubes," *The Radio Review*, 1 (1919), 143-146.

14. J. Presper Eckert, "The ENIAC," in Metropolis, Howlett, and Rota, *A History of Computing*, pp. 525-539; Mauchly, "The ENIAC," in Metropolis, Howlett, and Rota, pp. 541-550; J. Presper Eckert, "A Survey of Digital Computer Memory Systems," *Proceedings, IRE*, 41 (1953), 1393-1406.

15. Arthur Burks, "Computing Circuits of the ENIAC," *Proceedings, IRE*, 35 (1947), 756-767.

16. Eckert, "Survey of Memory Systems."

17. Eckert, "Survey of Memory Systems"; Mauchly, "The ENIAC."

18. Burks, "Computing Circuits of the ENIAC"; Burks, "The ENIAC."

19. For a popular account of the Colossus, based on interviews with some of the participants, see Christopher Evans, *The Micro Millennium* (New York, 1980), pp. 34-36. Evans's interviews are available as the "Pioneers of Computing" series from the Science Museum, London.

20. Burks, "Computing Circuits"; J. G. Brainerd and T. K. Sharpless, "The ENIAC," *Electrical Engineering* (February, 1948), pp. 163-172; J. P. Eckert, et al., "Electronic Numerical Integrator and Computer," U.S. Patent No. 3,120,606 (June 26, 1947); Herman Goldstine and Adele Goldstine, "The Electronic Numerical Integrator and Computer," *Mathematical Tables and Other Aids to Computation*, 2 (1946), 97-110.

21. D. H. Lehmer, "A History of the Sieve Process," in *A History of Computing in the Twentieth Century*, N. Metropolis, J. Howlett, and G. -C. Rota, eds. (New York: Academic Press, 1980), pp. 445-456.

22. U.S. National Defense Research Committee, Applied Mathematics Panel, "Description of the ENIAC and Comments on Electronic Computing Machines," Report 171.2R, November 30, 1945.

23. Franz Alt, "A Bell Laboratories Computing Machine, Part II," in Brian Randell, ed., *Origins of Digital Computers*, p. 527.

24. John Mauchly, "Preparation of Problems for EDVAC-type Machines," in Randell, *Origins*, p. 366.

25. Burks, "Computing Circuits of the ENIAC"; National Defense Research Committee, "Description of the ENIAC," p. 3/9; N. Metropolis and W. J. Worlton, "A Trilogy on Errors in the History of Computing," *First USA-Japan Computer Conference*, October 3-5, 1972 (Tokyo), pp. 683-691; J. P. Eckert, "ENIAC," in Metropolis, Howlett, and Rota, *History of Computing*.

26. For this and the following descriptions of the ENIAC's structure I have relied mostly on Burks, "The ENIAC," cited above.

27. National Defense Research Committee, "Description of the ENIAC," pp. 2/4-2/5, also section 4.

28. J. Presper Eckert, "Thoughts on the History of Computing," *Computer* (December, 1976), pp. 58-65.

29. Goldstine, *The Computer*, p. 145; Brainerd and Sharpless, "The ENIAC," pp. 168-169.

30. *Industrial Reorganization Act*, p. 5810; Eckert, "Survey of Digital Memory," p. 1394.

31. Brainerd and Sharpless, "The ENIAC," p. 169.

32. Burks, "The ENIAC."

33. Nancy Stern, *ENIAC to UNIVAC*, pp. 62-63; Goldstine, *The Computer*, p. 234.

34. Hartree published several accounts of his experience with the ENIAC: "The ENIAC: An Electronic Computing Machine," *Nature*, 157 (April 20, 1946), p. 527; and 158 (October 12, 1946), pp. 500-506; a description of the problem he ran on it appears in *Calculating Instruments and Machines* (Urbana: University of Illinois Press, 1949).

6
To the First Generation

> The unexpected results would then enable machine owners to say with something akin to parental pride, "My machine (instead of 'my little boy') said such a funny thing this morning!"
> —Sarah Turing, quoting her son Alan M. Turing, c. 1950

At the end of the Second World War computing machines abounded in an astonishing variety. There were network analyzers, differential analyzers, analog computers for directing gunfire; cross-footing punches, punched-card readers, tabulators, sorters, collaters, and multipliers. There were key-driven adding machines, and mechanical calculators: hand-cranked, lever-actuated, and electrically driven; also slide rules, planimeters, and other analog instruments. There were machines that solved certain differential equations, and machines that solved simultaneous equations: some analog, others digital. And there were automatic digital computers: Zuse's Z4, the Harvard Mark I, the Bell Labs Relay Computers.

Finally there was the ENIAC: an electronic, programmable digital computer. In some ways it was like the other computers. It cost as much as the Mark I; it was as complex as the Differential Analyzer; it computed with electronic circuits like the IBM 603 Multiplier. But its combination of features made it unique. And in Britain there was a corresponding electronic computer, the Colossus (actually, ten copies were built by 1946). It did not do arithmetic, but used vacuum tube circuits to help break the codes of intercepted German radio messages. (Only a handful of persons knew of its existence; not until 1970 was it first publicly mentioned in a paper by I. J. Good.) Like the ENIAC the Colossus was to be an influential machine, but for most in Britain the first news of an electronic digital computer was Hartree's note on the ENIAC in *Nature* in 1946.[1]

Besides those computers, there were others in 1946 still in the planning stage or under construction: the IBM SSEC, the Bell Labs Model VI, the EDVAC from the Moore School, and the Mark II from Howard Aiken's lab at Harvard. The end of the war lifted a lot of pressure to get the machines running quickly, so some of those projects dragged on through the end of the decade. The result was that the ENIAC was the only large-scale electronic computer in service in America for a few years, while in Germany the Z4 was the only digital computer in continental Europe until 1950, and even it was only marginally operational. The Colossus computers were probably also kept in service, even if there were no more German codes to break. They were just too important to send to the scrap-heap.

If computer construction slowed down right after the war, it was not for a lack of interest. Conferences were held at both the Moore School and Harvard where interested persons from all over were able to compare their individual projects, as well as get a close-up view of two of the biggest computers of them all. Those conferences were a forum where the many different theoretical approaches to computing could be criticized, and where a consensus about what computers *ought* to look like first took form. The proceedings of those conferences were published later in the decade and were widely read throughout America and Europe. They serve as a bench mark to fix the state of the art of machine computation as it stood in the immediate postwar years.[2]

In both the Moore School Lectures and the Harvard Symposium on Large-Scale Calculating Machinery the number of persons wanting to attend far exceeded expectations. Herman Goldstine saw that as a sign that "it was obvious to everyone that there was an extremely large but latent worldwide need for computers."[3] Of course, he wrote those words twenty-five years after the events, at a time when computers had become cheap, small, and almost ubiquitous. The excitement of those conferences was genuine; it reflected the discovery by many computing pioneers that they were not alone.

Except for the Colossus, the computers from that era were all numerical processing machines. They tackled problems by doing a lot of arithmetic on arrays of input data, boiling the numbers down to a determinant, an integral, or the range of a shell's trajectory. The end of the war signaled an end to the pressure to do those calculations, and there was an opportunity to think about just what problems a computer should be designed to solve. Emphasis continued on numerical capabilities, but from 1946 on there was a gradual understanding that the computer is a machine capable of processing any data that could be put into coded form—and that encompassed a lot more than numerical data.

That shift was not at all obvious in 1946. (Konrad Zuse had defined "reckoning" that way, but he did not participate in these postwar conferences.) An understanding of the true nature of computing emerged from discussions among the computer pioneers about their machines, and especially about a feature they were considering for future computers. That feature was of course the stored-program concept, which, when finally understood, revealed the logical basis of what they had just invented.

THE STORED-PROGRAM CONCEPT

A modern digital computer stores its instructions and data in the same physical memory units. Any memory register can store either a program's instructions or the data on which it acts. One reason for that is speed—as Eckert and Mauchly recognized in their thoughts on the ENIAC's successor, an electronic computer must have its instructions as well as its data supplied at speeds comparable to that of its electronic processing units.

But why should both be stored in the same way in the same registers? Instructions do not look anything like numbers: they are usually much shorter, and they do not otherwise seem to have much in common with numbers.

One practical reason is that every problem has a different mix of instructions and data; furthermore bulk memory devices are not cheap. Therefore in the interests of economy it pays to pack everything onto the same physical devices, rather than have separate memories for instructions and data, with wasted space in one or both units.

But that is only part of the answer. The reason a computer stores them identically is that fundamentally they *are* identical—they are equivalent to each other. That means, among other things, that each can be converted to the other. There is simply no good reason for not keeping them together, especially for the kinds of problems computers have been doing since the war—problems not characterized as long sequences of numerical calculations. (Indeed, a machine that does only numerical calculations may store data and program instructions separately, so long as both are in a high-speed memory. Modern programmable calculators have such a structure, and thereby take advantage of the relatively shorter length of calculator instructions.) The stored program principle, when recognized and implemented, was the key to the power of the electronic digital computer; it gave the world since 1945 the "computer revolution."

Decimal multiplication illustrates that equivalence. Recall that a calculator designer has two choices: the machine can multiply either by repeated addition or by looking up products in a times table. The two methods are equivalent in that each calculates the same answer But they proceed in different ways. The former consists of a lot of detailed instructions: add two numbers, shift a radix point to the left or right, add again, etc. The latter consists of fewer instructions, but requires looking up partial products in a data table. A designer can trade off one for the other, thereby giving the computer the desired speed, ease of construction, and cost. The example on page 134 shows that equivalence. Machine multiplication is perhaps a trivial example, but the principle it illustrates holds true for more complicated computer operations as well.

Another way of stating the relationship is to say that a computer program causes the machine to perform actions that rearrange its input data into a structure different from what it was when those data were fed into it. The (dynamic) action of a computer is thus described by the (static) structure of the data it contains at the end of a computation.

For practical purposes there is no good reason to draw a distinction which for many problems might turn out to be artificial and restrictive. So besides the advantage of high speed and efficient use of memory space, a computer will store its program internally in the same memory units as its data. Beyond a reasonable

MULTIPLICATION OF 355 × 4

By Repeated Addition		By Table Look-up	
355		355	
× 4		× 4	
355		200	units part of product
+355		+122	tens part ("carry")
			obtained from a table
710	add 355 to	1420	
+355	itself four		
1065			
+355	times		
1420			

limit, the designer or programmer has a lot of leeway in choosing how the computer will do its business. He or she can choose to replace instructions by sets of data, "hardware" by "software," or vice versa. (The limits are theoretically very small: a machine having a repertoire of only a few simple operations, and enough memory space, can do any computation that any computer, no matter how sophisticated, can do.)

That relationship is like the equivalence of mass and energy in relativistic physics, or like the relation between position and momentum in quantum mechanics. At the smallest level of observation they cannot be distinguished (cf. Heisenberg's Uncertainty Principle). By analogy, at the level of an individual yes-or-no binary digit (bit), one cannot say whether it signifies an action as part of a program or whether it is part of the data on which the program acts.[4]

But the concept is of more than just theoretical interest. A machine which stores its data and instructions together can take advantage of that fact. What's more, for certain types of problems the advantages of *not* separating them become significant. Those problems are precisely the ones that involve a lot of logical switching and branching of instructions, mixed in with numerical processing.

THE STORED PROGRAM: ALAN M. TURING

In 1936, a decade before the first real computing machines were built, the British mathematician Alan Turing wrote a paper concerning the concept of computing, in which he suggested the equivalence of data and instructions.[5] Alan Turing's contribution to the history of computing is difficult to measure. In the postwar conferences on the design of computers he was almost never cited; few persons attending them even knew who he was. Even in the development of British computers there is little agreement as to what he contributed. He was a member of the team at Bletchley Park that designed and built the Colossus. But just what he did there is still classified information, although it is known that he made absolutely crucial contributions to their cracking of the coded messages sent by the Germans' "Enigma" and *Geheimschreiber* ("secret writer") machines. After the war Turing was involved with two important British computing projects, the Automatic Computing Engine (ACE) at the National Physical Laboratory in Teddington, and later the computing projects at the University of Manchester. But his contribution to those projects is by no means as clear as, say, Eckert's to the ENIAC or Stibitz's to the Complex Number Computer. (He died in 1954 before it occurred to anyone to ask him those questions. So we may never know.)

Yet he has a central place in the history of computing for that 1936 paper alone. It was there that he answered the question "What does a computer do when it computes?" adequately for the first time—yielding among other things the relationship between a machine's operations and its data just described.[6]

No stored-program digital computers existed in 1936, but there were of course human computers as well as computing installations where people manipulated numerical data with electromechanical or punched card machinery. And a century earlier Charles Babbage had a clear idea of what his Analytical Engine was supposed to do. But that empirical understanding was inadequate for mathematicians concerned with the question of whether one may decide in advance whether one may or may not compute the answer to a mathematical problem, by whatever means. That question was called the "Entscheidungsproblem," German for "decision problem." The Göttingen mathematician David Hilbert first posed it in the 1920s. For a problem like:

$$4x^2 + 2x - 3 = 0$$

there is no trouble, but what about lengthier problems, especially ones involving not ordinary algebra but statements of symbolic logic and their rules of combination? Was there an effective procedure for testing such a problem and finding out whether a solution to such a problem exists?

Turing proved that there is no such procedure; he proved it by giving for the first time a logically rigorous definition of what it means to compute a solution to a problem by some definite process. That definition had to be good enough to convince the mathematical logicians, who were a skeptical lot to begin with. It did not really have to convince those who worked with computing machines: they went merrily on with their computing, oblivious to the debate over the logical fundamentals. But as stored-program electronic computers with enormous power and speed appeared after the war, such a definition was needed. Turing's has served that need ever since.

Alan Turing was born in 1912 and according to his mother was "a scholar born." He showed a precocious talent for mathematics, and entered King's College, Cambridge, in 1931, where he excelled—passing Part II of the Tripos with distinction in 1934 ("He came out a Wrangler with a B star"), being elected to a fellowship at King's in 1935, and winning the Smith's Prize in 1936 for his thesis on "The Gaussian Error Function."[7]

That same year (1936) he submitted his paper "On Computable Numbers, with an Application to the Entscheidungsproblem" to the *Proceedings* of the London Mathematical Society, where it appeared early the next year. Mathematical logicians quickly recognized it as a fundamental contribution to their field, and Turing as a brilliant and wholly original thinker.

The "computing machine" he constructed to test the decision-problem was a paper abstraction of the activity a human being goes through when computing a number. A human computer would presumably have at his or her disposal enough sheets of paper, a pencil or other instrument to make marks on that paper (and an eraser to erase marks from that paper). Turing gave his "machine" not sheets but a long strip of paper, of which only one space at a time was accessible for writing or erasing. But his machine could advance or back up along that strip, and the strip was considered to be of indefinite length, so it was effectively the same as ordinary sheets of paper. Likewise his machine had a restricted set of symbols that could be marked on the strip: the binary digits 1 and 0, plus a few more; but that, too, was only an abstraction of the presumably richer repertoire of symbols that humans use when they do arithmetic.

The most interesting part of his "machine" was the way it acted depending on what symbol it saw on the tape at any moment. Turing's machine was capable of assuming a finite number of states (which he called "configurations"); its action at any moment depended on the combination of the state it was in and the symbol it scanned on the tape. It could write a new symbol on the tape, erase whatever symbol was there, move the tape a space to the left or right, or stop the machine completely.

The closest human analogy to this idea is to think of a person doing a computation who is constantly being interrupted as he works: the telephone rings, someone comes to the door, etc. Each time that happens he has to stop what he is doing and make a note telling himself where he left off, so that he can resume the calculation later on. So he writes a description of the "state" of the computation, writing it down somewhere on the same sheets of paper, using the same symbols as those used for the computation itself.

Now imagine that he is interrupted at *every* little step of the computation. His sheets of paper will then contain not only the computation itself but also a complete description of the steps necessary to proceed with it.

It is not difficult to conceive of a machine endowed with those capabilities of scanning a tape, writing or erasing a symbol on that tape, moving the tape backwards or forwards a square at a time, and halting. Such a primitive machine could compute the answer to any problem whose description was supplied to it by a sequence of symbols on a paper tape; it could do that as well as any other machine, however sophisticated. (By showing that there were problems for which his machine would never halt, Turing proved that the decision-problem could have no solution.)

From the standpoint of actual computers like the kinds built after 1940, Turing's machine has several interesting aspects. First, unlike, say, Zuse's Z3, whose program takes the form of a linear list of instructions, Turing's machine jumps around at every step, depending on the results of its last action. *Every* step a Turing machine makes is a "conditional branch"—this in spite of the fact that it has only a linear tape on which to operate. Second, the actions specified by the machine's internal table and by the sequence of symbols on the tape are so intertwined with the data on the tape or in the machine that it is impossible to say which is which. The machine's configurations represent both its internally stored data and its program. Thus in 1936 Turing first described the stored program principle.

Finally, he showed that his machine could not only compute numbers, but that it could also compute a set of symbols, which when fed into another Turing machine, would make it act like the first. In other words, a computer can produce programs as well as data as output. Furthermore, any general-purpose computer can be programmed to simulate the behavior of any other special-purpose computer. Turing proved, mathematically, what the ENIAC's programmers knew they were doing each time they rewired their computer for a new job.

How influential was that paper on the development of digital computers (that is, aside from its well-documented influence on mathematical logic)? It must have played a role in the design of the British code-breaking machines built at Bletchley Park, including the electronic Colossus. Turing was not ignorant of electrical engineering, and even in 1936 he had talked of the possibility of building an actual machine that did what his paper machine could do.[8]

In 1945 he wrote a report on the design of a full-scale general-purpose digital computer along the lines of the American EDVAC, then being planned by the ENIAC team. That report describes a computer much influenced by the Americans' ideas but at the same time reveals that Turing had a different understanding of the nature of a computer. In particular, he proposed a machine that would not only store its program internally, but in contrast to the EDVAC design, would not necessarily store its instructions as a linear list in the tradition of the paper tape machines. Instead it would have a program decoder that would allow instructions to be placed anywhere in the computer's memory, in any order. The Automatic Computing Engine, or ACE, was to be very much in the spirit of Turing's theoretical work of the previous decade. Turing left the ACE project in 1947, and the machines that the National Physical Laboratory eventually built (the Pilot ACE in 1950, and the ACE in 1959) did not conform to his ideas that strongly. But his influence was there nonetheless.

THE STORED PROGRAM: JOHN VON NEUMANN

The central figure in the transition of computing from machines like the ENIAC to the modern stored-program computer is John von Neumann (1903-1957), the Hungarian-born mathematician whose contributions to that "queen of sciences" ranged wide and deep.

Von Neumann came to America in 1930, and with the onset of the Second World War he willingly offered his services to the Allied cause. He managed somehow to involve himself with half a dozen wartime projects simultaneously. Among them was the Manhattan Project, where he concentrated his mathematical genius on the complex problem of designing the explosive lenses for the first atomic bomb.

Indeed it is surprising that computing machinery was something he was not involved with at the beginning of the war. That changed in the summer of 1944, when by chance he learned of the ENIAC (then still under construction) while waiting for a train at the Aberdeen, Maryland, station.

Not long after, von Neumann joined the ENIAC team. (It welcomed him at first although later on that team broke up, in part because of resentment by some of the other members of his activities.) By late 1944 the design of the ENIAC was already frozen, but Eckert and Mauchly had begun designing its successor, the EDVAC. The central feature of the EDVAC would be its far larger high-speed memory—on the order of a thousand numbers instead of the ENIAC's twenty. In 1944 Eckert was thinking of using a magnetic drum or disk to store those numbers, but later he adopted as a storage medium a tube of mercury in which digits would be stored by acoustic pulses. (Since the speed of sound in mercury is much lower than the speed of electrical pulses in wires, trains of pulses could be recycled through the mercury column and periodically refreshed by electrical circuits, thereby storing a good number of digits.)

Eckert had further recognized as early as January, 1944, that the memory units should store the program as well as the data. Even though the ENIAC was not finished yet, he recognized that programming it was going to be tough. The next computer would be much easier to program by virtue of its internal read/write program storage.[9]

Into that state of affairs stepped von Neumann. He joined the discussions regarding the EDVAC—and he grasped its principles almost immediately. By the middle of 1945, those principles included the following:

First, it would have as much high-speed memory as possible, using the mercury delay lines. That implied that the memory unit would only store numbers; to have it perform addition as well would make it complicated and expensive. The EDVAC would have storage registers, in contrast to the ENIAC's accumulators.

Second, the EDVAC would have a central arithmetic unit which performed all arithmetic, including addition. There would be only one such arithmetic unit, through which all computations would flow. That meant that the EDVAC would have fewer tubes than the ENIAC (despite the EDVAC's larger memory). It also meant that its programs would consist of a sequential list of instructions, performed one at a time. The EDVAC could not execute several program steps simultaneously, as the Harvard Mark I or the ENIAC could. Whatever time was lost they felt would be more than made up by the ability to set it up for a new problem more quickly.

Third, the EDVAC would not only execute programs sequentially: it would also handle the numbers themselves sequentially—that is, a digit at a time—instead of in parallel. That followed mainly from the nature of the storage medium. The mercury delay lines stored numbers as trains of acoustic pulses, so it was natural that operations such as addition would be performed digit by digit as each emerged from the mercury tank.

Finally, the EDVAC would use the binary system of numeration throughout. Separate program routines converted those numbers to and from decimal at the beginning and end of a computation.

In all but the serial method of doing arithmetic, the EDVAC's "architecture" most resembled the Zuse relay computers, of all the pre-1945 machines. That overall design reflected the optimum balance between complexity, power, and speed, both for Zuse's relay implementation and for the Moore School's electronic approach.

Von Neumann contributed to the EDVAC's design, although it is hard to say in what specific ways. He summarized its features in a document called "First Draft of a Report on the EDVAC," written in the spring of 1945. It was not published in full until 1981, but when it first appeared it was widely circulated and read in typescript. The report was enormously influential. In it he described the logical design of the EDVAC, with its high-speed memory and overall architecture. He also described its use of the binary system, and its ability to store programs internally. Electronic computers have pretty nearly all looked that way ever since.[10]

The report also stressed the EDVAC's sequential processing of both program instructions and individual digits of numbers. But even as that design was taking form at the Moore School, von Neumann broke with Eckert and Mauchly and went to the Institute for Advanced Study in Princeton, where he initiated a project for a new computer, similar to the EDVAC but having a memory device that could deliver all the digits of a number in parallel, as the ENIAC's accumulators or the Zuse computers did. Descriptions of that "IAS" computer appeared in 1946, in papers coauthored by von Neumann, Arthur Burks, and Herman H. Goldstine. (Burks and Goldstine had also left the Moore School when von Neumann did. Von Neumann's dissatisfaction with his role on the EDVAC team may be inferred from the fact that the IAS had a policy of not doing experimental work. Von Neumann used his considerable powers of persuasion to get them to make an exception in his case.)[11]

The machine described in those reports would not be completed until 1952, but the reports themselves established a design philosophy for computers that has persisted to the present day, despite the amazing shrinkage of the electronic components that go into them.

To sum up, the design (which has come to be called the "von Neumann architecture") resembles the EDVAC's except that all digits of numbers in the machine are manipulated in parallel, to increase speed. (Program steps are still executed sequentially.) The memory unit of the computer is further designed to be random-access, with any item as quickly accessible as any other. Memory is organized into several hierarchical levels, with slow, high-capacity memory units, such as magnetic tape or punched card readers, serving as a back-up to the fast, but expensive and smaller main memory.

Finally, the IAS machine was to have a simple, basic set of a few instructions, out of which all the computer's actions would be formed. With each instruction (there were about two dozen) there would be only one address, giving the memory location of one operand on which it would act. The other operand, if there was one, was assumed to be already in one of the arithmetic unit's registers; the result would likewise remain in the arithmetic unit, to be used for the next step if desired. The address of the next instruction was likewise not given; it was assumed to be in the memory location right next to the instruction just executed. Thus although the IAS machine was a stored-program computer, it normally executed instructions in a steady linear stream coming from the memory, just as if they were coming off a tape. The difference of course was that among the instructions were special "branch" commands that directed the program to jump to a different memory location for the next instruction, and since the computer had a random-access memory, those jumps were just as fast as any other sequence.

With some modifications the IAS design has survived as the paradigm of modern computer architectures. But other types have found a place as well. For example, pocket calculators process numbers one digit at a time (serially), like the EDVAC, not because they use a cyclic memory device, but because that design requires fewer interconnections from one part of the calculator to another. Fewer connections mean fewer wires—hence the calculator can fit nicely in a shirt pocket. (It is also slower, but for most calculator applications that is not a problem.) Probably the most radical deviation from the von Neumann type of architecture appears in so-called supercomputers which process several streams of data in parallel, like the ENIAC. There are some experimental computer designs that mix storage and arithmetic, like the accumulators of the Harvard Mark I and the ENIAC. But for the most part the only difference between the IAS and modern computers is that the latter have many more instructions than the dozen or two the EDVAC or the IAS had. The von Neumann architecture is not without its flaws, but any reports of its demise are exaggerated. It hangs on tenaciously through successive generations of hardware and programming innovations.

Table 6.1 summarizes the design philosophies of those early computers, with a few modern examples thrown in for comparison.

PROGRAMMING: ZUSE

Von Neumann's "First Draft on the EDVAC" said little about how one actually coded a stored-program computer to solve problems. He wrote out a possible code for sorting data on the EDVAC, but it was not included in that draft.[12] In 1945, Konrad Zuse was also thinking about how to write programs for his

Table 6.1 TYPES OF COMPUTER ARCHITECTURES

Method of Executing Program Instructions	Handling of Numbers to and from Memory Registers	
	Serially	In Parallel
SERIALLY	EDVAC-type (cyclic memory) EDSAC (1949) UNIVAC (1951) Pocket calculators	von Neumann-type (random-access memory) Z3, Z4 (1941, 1945) ENIAC after 1948 Most modern computers
IN PARALLEL	Atanasoff-Berry Computer (1939) STARAN (Goodyear Aerospace Co., 1974) Other modern experimental designs	ENIAC before 1948 ILLIAC IV (1976) Other modern super-computers

computer, the Z4. He was living in a Bavarian village, where everyone's first priority was getting enough food each day. His Z4 had just barely survived, and he had managed to get it running intermittently. Zuse did not have a chance to participate in the immediate postwar computing conferences centered in the United States. So he found himself with some time to think about just what he had invented. Independently he began developing ideas about how to program digital computers to take the fullest advantage of their powers.

Like his earlier work, Zuse's development of a theory of programming paralleled the Anglo-Americans' in many ways, yet because of his isolation it looked different in its details. We are fortunate to have it because it lay completely outside of the mainstream. It shows us how different things might have been, how what we have today is not necessarily the best of all possible worlds.

Most of the wartime computers were designed as sequential number processors. They were built to follow a strict plan for every set of inputs, but gradually their designers recognized that the machine itself could perform the logical operations of choosing the plan of calculation for those numbers, and of automatically switching plans depending on the results of a previous operation. Those logical abilities assumed greater and greater importance in computer design, so that by 1945 it was recognized that it was best to treat logical and numeric operations identically in the internal workings of the computer.

That transition required a rethinking of the ways to describe computer programs. To code a computer to evaluate an expression like

$$F(x) = x^3 + 4x^2 + 3$$

for successive values of x from 1 to 10 is easy: the programmer simply specifies the sequence of arithmetic for that formula and arranges to have it accept the successive values of x as input.

But where there are not one but many algebraic sequences, each invoked depending on the results of a previous calculation, that scheme breaks down. A familiar example is computing an employee's weekly payroll check: the formula that computes his pay depends on whether he worked overtime or not, what kinds of insurance plan he has, tax deductions, etc.: all logical decisions that usually mean a different formula for each and every employee. Computer programming thus has a dynamic aspect to it that the conventions of ordinary algebraic notation cannot adequately describe. John Mauchly recognized that in a discussion of programming the EDVAC: "Thus is created a new set of operations which might be said to form a calculus of instructions."[13] Independently of Mauchly, Konrad Zuse was developing such a calculus, which he called the "Plan Calculus" (*Plankalkül*). It was a first step toward what we know today as a "programming language."[14]

Whatever form the Plan Calculus took, it had an ultimate requirement that a machine had to take its statements and translate them into the correct actions. In other words, questions like whether a person worked overtime or not (thereby determining which formula to use to compute his wages) ultimately had to be cast in terms of yes-no values represented by physical devices within the computer. Another requirement came from the sequential way digital computers operated: any program had to be of the form of a long linear list of symbols, even if the actions it described may have originally been concurrent.

The Plan Calculus, as Zuse first sketched it in 1945, did not satisfy the second requirement. Its notation was two-dimensional, designed to be read both across and down at the same time (reminiscent of Zuse's first thoughts on computing in graphical terms). It would have been easy enough to convert it into linear strings of symbols, however, but he never got that far with it.

It was not directly readable by machine, either, but at least in the Plan Calculus every statement revealed the bit structure implied by its action—that was why it was a two-dimensional notation. That is the Plan Calculus's most distinctive feature. Modern programming practice dictates the opposite: a programmer should know only what he absolutely has to about the computer's inner workings. The rationale for that philosophy is that those details would only be confusing and do not contribute anything to the writing of better programs. The Plan Calculus has never been implemented on a digital computer, although in recent years Zuse has reworked it and cleared up some of its original inconsistencies. Recently there has been a renewed interest in the design of programming languages, and the design philosophy of the Plan Calculus could certainly contribute to the current debate. But it is likely to remain only an historical artifact.

The following example shows how the Plan Calculus would describe a test to see whether or not a worker is eligible for overtime pay as part of his payroll computation:

	V ≥	V $\xrightarrow{}$	V
V	0	1	2
K	n.6		
S	1.6	1.6	1

In that statement the variables are $V0$, $V1$, and $V2$. Note that the subscripts are directly below the letter; the label "V" in the far left column indicates that the numbers in the second row are in fact the subscripts of the variable (V = "Variable-index").

The first variable $V0$ is a number which represents *all* the information about a specific employee. From that number the program selects those digits which tell how many hours he worked the previous week: that information is contained in the six binary digits which appear in the nth place. The third row, labelled "K" for "Komponent-index," does that. The last row, labelled "S" for "Structur-index," indicates that the information thus selected is of the form of a one-by-six array of binary digits. In that way the program reveals what is happening to individual binary values within the computer, if the programmer wants to know that.

The next variable, $V1$, is the value above which overtime wages are paid. It is also a simple list of six binary digits, and presumably has already been specified elsewhere in the program. The symbol $\xrightarrow{}$ is similar to the conditional statement of symbolic logic, and states that if the expression on the left is true (that is, if the employee worked more than the specified number of hours), then assign the value "1" to the variable $V2$. Thus $V2$ takes on the value 1 or 0, for each employee, depending on how many hours he worked.

Aside from the subscripts running below each variable in columns, this notation is not all that different from modern programming languages. (One difference is that it assigns values from left to right, as the machine itself operates. Nearly all modern programming languages place the variable being assigned at the left. That difference reflects Zuse's background as an engineer, while other languages reveal their debt to the mathematician's notion of a function.)

He worked out the details of coding complex problems using the Plan Calculus, even showing how it could be used to describe how a computer might play chess. But in the long run programming languages developed along different lines—from more conventional notations of ordinary algebra. It would be many years before computers would be playing chess—and when they finally did, they would be programmed in algebraic languages not really suitable for that kind of problem.

In 1944 Zuse envisioned a separate machine that would accept formulas written in an algebraic notation (or possibly a version of the Plan Calculus) and produce as output a string of binary digits that his Z4 computer would accept as a program. He called it a "Plan Preparation Machine" (*Planfertigungsgeräte*); later he called it a *"Programmator."* The machine would keep track of expressions in parentheses, and would test for errors such as an unequal number of left and right parentheses, or more than one equals sign in an expression. It would further be able to shift between a main sequence and subroutines automatically.[15]

He never built the Plan Preparation Machine. By the time the Z4 was installed and running at the Federal Technical Institute in Zürich, it had become clear that a general-purpose computer could do both jobs: translate a program from an algebraic to a binary machine code, and then execute the new program. Heinz Rutishauser was the person at Zürich who recognized this ability. It was a startling idea at the time but seems obvious after the fact.

Rutishauser independently rediscovered the concept of a universal machine that Turing described in 1936: a computer's output may not only consist of "answers" to numerical problems; it may also be another program. (The program which does that is called a "compiler.") In that way persons need not be conversant in machine code, which after all consists of only zeros and ones, to be able to write programs. Once again the key to a computer's ability to do that translation is the stored program principle. Ironically, though, Rutishauser developed his notion of a compiler after working with the Z4, which did not store its program internally.

IMPLICATIONS OF THE STORED PROGRAM PRINCIPLE

Compiler programs did not appear until the 1950s. The immediate impact of the stored program principle was to increase the range of problems a computer could solve. Computers before 1945 were best suited to numerical problems coded as long sequences of arithmetic operations. Conditional branches were rare, if they appeared at all. The early machines like the Bell Labs Model V, which had conditional branch facilities in the form of separate loops of tapes, constrained the programmer to use it only in cases that were well known in advance. He or she had to know just where in the execution of a problem a branch to a subroutine tape would occur, roughly how often that would occur, and so on.

But with a stored-program computer the conditional branch facility becomes an integral part of the programming process. The programmer may specify loops to be performed over and over until some limit is reached, as before, but his program need only sketch out the general flow of instructions. He need not know the particulars of just where and when those loops enter into a program—the computer itself can keep track of that. By having the computer modify the program, a short piece of code can express a much longer sequence of machine instructions. To a computer, a terse string of a few program statements is like a sonnet: it evokes a much more complex mix of machine actions and states. That in turn reduces the length of the code that has to be stored internally, reducing the computer's memory requirements to the point where they become technically feasible.

The ability of a stored-program computer to generate its own sequence of actions from a brief sketch supplied by its programmer implies a redefinition of the nature of computing which is still poorly understood. One of the first clear statements about a computer's power came from Ada Augusta, Countess of Lovelace, in a note describing Babbage's Analytical Engine. It is all the more remarkable considering that she wrote it in 1842, for a machine that had not been built (and probably may never be built). In her notes to F. L. Menabrea's description of the Analytical Engine, she said:

The Analytical Engine has no pretensions whatever to *originate* anything. It can do whatever we know *how to order it* to perform. It can *follow* analysis; but it has no power of *anticipating* any analytical relations or truths. Its province is to assist us in making *available* what we are already acquainted with.[16]

A corollary to her statement is that a computer is incapable of "surprising" its operator by behaving in some unanticipated way.

It is true that a computer can do only what it is programmed to do. It is also true that it has the ability to choose between alternate courses of action, depending on the value of a previously computed sequence. Whatever action it may take must, however, be fully specified in advance by the programmer, even though he or she may not know how the computation might proceed for a given input datum.

It is therefore possible for the human operator to chart out in advance all the possible paths of a computation, so indeed the machine could not originate an unanticipated action. There are, however, two qualifications to that attribute which alter the picture, and which have the combined result of endowing a computer with precisely those abilities to surprise, originate, and anticipate.

The first qualification is the high speed of electronic components. An electronic computer can make so many decisions and branch to so many different sequences in an hour's time that it would take a human being a lifetime to trace all of them out for even one piece of input data. In principle it is still possible, but in practice a human cannot simulate the activity of an electronic computer. That was why electronic computers were built in the first place.

The second qualification is a direct consequence of the stored program principle: the fact that a computer may treat its instructions as data and perform operations on them, thereby forming an entirely new set of operations which it may then execute. Not only can the machine choose among sequences depending on the result of a previous operation: it can also modify its future response to those results—in short, it can "learn" from its past experience, in the same sense as that word applies to human behavior. Note that we are still within the bounds of Countess Lovelace's statement that a computer can do only what it has been told to do. It is still possible to specify in advance all the potential ways a computer might act, given a specific input datum. A computer has a finite number of elements; if it has n binary devices (memory places, flip-flops, gates, etc.), then it can assume one of 2^n states. But that is only the number of possible states for one unit of time. For the next step in a program it again has that range of possible states, and so on. The number of possible states grows astronomically very fast. (Consider for example a rudimentary "computer" having a memory of only seven binary digits, and an arithmetic unit of only three digits. Thus $n = 10$, so it is capable of $2^{10} = 1,024$ different states. If we restrict that machine to programs of only ten steps each, there are already $(2^{10})^{10}$ possible programs (over 10^{30}). Even if 99.999 percent of those programs were meaningless, that still leaves quite a few. It is true that modern programming wisdom states that one should never write a program that modifies itself in the way just described. Doing that makes the program almost impossible to understand; it also means that the program cannot be put into a read-only-memory. But that does not alter the essential fact: the number of states a stored-program computer can assume grows exponentially as the number of program steps increases.)

Although in all cases there is only a finite number of possibilities, the explosive combinatorial growth of complexity precludes any possibility that a human can follow a computer's activities by hand calculations. Therefore computers can, indeed, surprise, originate, create—one might say they can "think"—if programmed to do so. Computers programmed to play chess routinely defeat those who programmed them. Of course if that upsets the programmer he or she may decide to reprogram the machine so that it does not play such a good game. That is the meaning of the popular phrase stating that computers will never take over because one can always "pull out the plug." In that sense the human being retains control over the machine, as Countess Lovelace said. But only in that sense.

Talking about computers playing chess, thinking, and otherwise acting intelligently seemed a bit preposterous in the late 1940's, when it was a struggle just to get a machine running at all. Alan Turing was especially fond of such talk. He could always respond to those who were skeptical about the power of a computer with a *mot juste* guaranteed to infuriate and disarm them. Even today the idea of a machine acting that way is unsettling, no less so now that hobby shops sell pocket-size chess-playing computers that can checkmate most of us—and then tell us so in a synthesized voice.

All that activity, and with it the debate over machine vs. human intelligence, is the consequence of the stored program principle, coupled with the high switching speeds of electronic circuits. The more immediate consequence was the rapid development of programming languages, letting persons from all walks of life avail themselves of the new invention. Those languages include familiar ones like BASIC, routinely taught to school children, and even "menu"-type languages like those found at automatic bank tellers, which allow just about anyone (even the barely literate) to program the bank's computer in a rudimentary way. The study of programming languages has paralleled the development of algebra from the time of Viète and Descartes, when it was first realized that one could manipulate expressions such as

$$3(x + y) - 4(x - y),$$

transforming that into

$$3x + 3y - 4x + 4y,$$

or

$$7y - x,$$

without having to worry about what x or y stood for.

The theoretical study of the nature of computing has taken us far from the discussions of pieces of hardware that so much dominated the history of computers before 1945. Nevertheless it was against the background of those early machines that the theory first took form. By 1950 a few stored-program machines were completed and running, so the theory of computing had a chance to merge with its practice. In 1951 commercial computers appeared for the first time—the UNIVAC in America, the Ferranti Mark I and the LEO in Britain. UNIVACs were built in a production run (of a dozen or so total), and with the installation of the first at the U.S Bureau of the Census in the spring of that year, the computer age entered "the first generation."

NOTES

1. I. J. Good, "Some Future Social Repercussions of Computers, *International Journal of Environmental Studies*, 1 (1970), 67-79; for a sampling of the variety of machines in use at the time, see Charles and Ray Eames, *A Computer Perspective* (Cambridge, Mass.: Harvard, 1973); D. R. Hartree, *Calculating Instruments and Machines* (Urbana: University of Illinois Press, 1949).

2. Published as *Symposium on Large Scale Calculating Machinery* (Cambridge, Mass.: Harvard, 1947); the Moore School Lectures appeared as *Theory and Techniques for Design of Digital Computers* (Philadelphia: Moore School of Electrical Engineering, 1947).

3. Herman Goldstine, *The Computer from Pascal to von Neumann* (Princeton: Princeton University Press, 1972), p. 246.

4. Dr. K. Brünnstein, private communication.

5. A. M. Turing, "On Computable Numbers, with an Application to the Entscheidungsproblem," *Proceedings*, London Mathematical Society, 2nd series, 42 (1936), 230-267.

6. Eames, *Computer Perspective*, pp. 124-125; Sara Turing, *Alan M. Turing* (Cambridge, England: W. Heffer and Sons, 1959), pp. 41-50.

7. Sara Turing, p. 47.

8. Ibid., p. 49.

9. J. Presper Eckert, "A Survey of Digital Memory Systems," *Proceedings IRE*, 41 (1953), 1393-1406; N. Metropolis and J. Worlton, "A Trilogy on Errors in the History of Computing," *First USA-Japan Computer Conference, Proceedings*, Tokyo, 1972, pp. 683-691.

10. John von Neumann, "First Draft of a Report on the EDVAC," published in Nancy Stern, *From ENIAC to UNIVAC* (Bedford, Mass.: Digital Press, 1981), pp. 177-246.

11. Arthur Burks, Herman Goldstine, and John von Neumann, "Preliminary Discussion of the Logical Design of an Electronic Computing Instrument," Part I (Princeton, N.J., 1946); that and later reports have been reprinted in John von Neumann, *Collected Works*, vol. 5 (New York: Pergamon, 1963), pp. 34ff.

12. Donald Knuth, "Von Neumann's First Computer Program," *Computing Surveys*, 2 (1970), 247-260.

13. John Mauchly, "Preparation of Problems for EDVAC-type Machines," *Symposium on Large Scale Digital Calculating Machinery*, pp. 203-207.

14. Konrad Zuse, "Der Plankalkül," privately printed, 244 pp., 1967; Konrad Zuse, *Beschreibung des Plankalküls* (Munich, 1977); Joachim Hohmann, *Eine Untersuchung des Plankalküls, im Vergleich mit algorithmischen Sprachen* (Bonn: Gesellschaft für Mathematik und Datenverarbeitung, Report No. 104, 1975); F. L. Bauer, "The Plankalkül of Konrad Zuse: A Forerunner of Today's Programming Languages," *Communications ACM*, 15 (1972), 678-685.

15. Konrad Zuse, "Planfertigungsgeräte," MS 010/024, Zuse Archive (Gesellschaft für Mathematik und Datenverarbeitung, Bonn); Konrad Zuse, "Der Programmator," *Zeitschrift für Angewandte Mathematik und Mechanik*, 32 (1952), 246.

16. Philip and Emily Morrison, eds., *Charles Babbage and his Calculating Machines* (New York: Dover, 1961), p. 285.

7
The Revolution?

> The Revolution is over.
>
> —attributed to Robespierre in 1791

DIRECTIONS FOR USING:

For THINKING:—Wind the Clock-work Man under his left arm, (marked No. 1.)

For SPEAKING:—Wind the Clock-work Man under his right arm, (marked No. 2.)

For WALKING
and ACTION:—Wind Clock-work in the middle of his back, (marked No. 3.)

—from L. Frank Baum, *Ozma of Oz* (1907)

Someone could have built a working computer long before 1935—Babbage almost did. The components (relays, vacuum tubes, teletypes, etc.) had all been around for quite a while. But the burst of activity after 1935 shows that only then were social and economic conditions really favorable for the computer's invention. The demands of business, government, and science had built up to a point where it is not surprising that the idea of an automatic computer occurred simultaneously to a number of inventors at that time. The Second World War was the catalyst that brought those demands together, while providing the necessary technical and (at least in America) financial support. There would have been computers had the war never taken place, but those computers would not look the way they do today, nor is it likely that there would be a computer impact as revolutionary as it is today. From the writings of the computer pioneers in the late 1930's one sees a modest vision: a few computers in the universities, some in government, modest-sized computers for industrial use, but not much more. They hardly foresaw the giant scale of the first computers, nor did they see the impact of their creation on everyday life. In America today, large and complex computer systems are an important part of industrial production, payroll and accounting, taxation, telephone and television service, transportation, and military defense.

Yet the computer's impact, like that of any pervasive technology, cannot be easily judged. Certainly for the roomsful of clerks who labored over adding machines life has changed, as it has for the scientist who no longer has to struggle with doing matrix calculations by hand. That is really just a small segment of society that has felt the impact of the computer. One easily forgets that the pioneers in computing did not envision their machines as doing much more.

Nowhere is that better illustrated than by the frequent statements made in the early days that only four or five computers of the speed and power of the ENIAC would be needed to satisfy all the computing requirements of the United States. (It was felt that three would satisfy England's requirements—with perhaps one more for the Scots!) It is hard to pin down just who made those estimates, but such a vision of the future was common in the early days.[1] Obviously they were wrong—they looked at the computer only in terms of the human beings it was replacing, as the automobile was first called the "horseless carriage," or the radio the "wireless." In terms of what the computer replaced they were correct: five computers like the ENIAC could do as much work as 400,000 human beings equipped with desk calculators, considering their respective multiplication speeds and the fact that a computer can work around the clock.

What they did not foresee was that the computer would soon be doing work of a very different kind, work that no human beings could do. With the adoption of the stored program principle, it became possible to program computers to sort and otherwise keep track of vast quantities of information, a task that human beings simply cannot do above a small threshold, and for which manual aids like file cards are likewise inadequate. The other unforeseen development was the adoption of high-level languages in lieu of arcane binary codes to get a computer to do its work. That innovation, also a consequence of the stored program principle, meant that a trained mathematician does not have to accompany every computer to its every job. And finally there has been the revolution in electronics technology that reduced the size and electric power requirements for computers—who could have foreseen that?

Some of the skewed perception of the computer's potential was due to the military's influence. The American armed forces supported computing projects because they faced problems so complex (for instance, firing tables) that existing means for their solution were felt to be totally inadequate. The immediate onset of the Cold War in 1945, especially with its focus on nuclear weapons, continued that atmosphere. As late as 1950 only one large-scale computing machine (the IBM SSEC) was not under military control in America.[2]

Among other things that meant that computers would be geared toward number processing, and they would tend to be as large and fast as technically feasible. If anyone had an idea of building a modest-sized computer for small businesses, for libraries, or even for game-playing, he or she would not have found much support. But today the most exciting part of the computer business is at the small end—in computers for small businesses and the home. (Konrad Zuse was alone among the computer pioneers in wanting to sell small computers at first, slowly graduating to bigger machines as one gained more experience. It is no coincidence that he was working in postwar Germany, where he did not have the financial support of the military that John von Neumann had in America.)

But has there really been a computer "revolution" after all? Some have argued that its invention has not fundamentally altered social or economic patterns of American life; if anything, the computer has made it easier for the patterns existing before 1945 to persist.[3] But "revolution" is an appropriate word aside from the question of the computer's impact on society. Its invention has triggered a revolution in thinking, in our understanding of our place in the universe, much as Copernicus's *On the Revolution of the Heavenly Orbs* did after A.D. 1600.

For one thing, it changed the whole concept of a "machine." By the classical definition, a machine is an assemblage of stiff elements, so arranged as to perform one specific motion. Any other motions are defined as "play," of which a good machine has little.[4] By that definition a computer is hardly a machine, since it is certainly not restricted to one specific "motion." A computer is a universal machine; it can do "anything"—that is, whatever we can program it to do. And we continue to be startled at the ingenuity of human beings in dreaming up new applications for the computer. Once programmed it begins to look more like a classical machine, doing one specific thing, but whatever that thing is can neither be specified nor foreseen by the computer manufacturer as it is sent out the factory door. That quality is a natural consequence of the fact that even when programmed, it is not possible to determine the actions of a computer in advance.

Computer pioneers used a biological analogy is sketching out their thoughts on building their machinery—for example, they called the storage unit a "memory," the programming code a "language." Von Neumann even based his description of the EDVAC on a neural notation, referring to the computer's various "organs." Those terms have probably caused more confusion than anything else. But they have won out over more prosaic terms like *store* or *programming plan*.

But the analogy works the other way, too: the structure and function of the computer provides human beings with a powerful model to aid our understanding of human thought. Mechanical analogies are certainly nothing new (Thomas Hobbes's introduction to his *Leviathan* being a famous example) but the analogy of the computer to the brain is much more powerful precisely because it is not a simple machine in the classical sense. The rich and complex behavior of a computer, set in motion by its executing an internally stored program of modest length, is an appropriate model for biological systems, in which an organism's characteristics represent an "expression" of information coded in its DNA. Modern computers contain read-only-memories (ROMs) which, like an organism's DNA, cannot be altered. They also contain random-access memories (RAMs) whose contents can be changed at will; these information stores also have their biological counterparts in those parts of the brain that can remember experiences and alter their future behavior based on what they have learned.

All that reasoning by analogy has its limits, of course: the brain is not a computer, nor is human or animal behavior the expression of "programs." But there is enough in common in that both represent complex systems. Mathematical theories of such systems have proven useful to our understanding of both.[5]

Some of those ideas were on the minds of the builders of the first computing machines as they struggled with their arrangements of levers, pins, relays, tubes, wires, and paper tapes. The gulf between "reckoning" and "thinking" could at times appear narrow enough to suggest that one day an arithmetic machine might become a thinking machine. But on the whole their story has been one of perseverance, attention to details, and just plain hard work. The pioneers had a vision of creating something new and perhaps revolutionary. Precisely because they were facing unknown areas of inquiry and experience, what they said and did in response can be useful to us today, as it was remarkably free from a narrowness of vision that today's "mature" science of computing suffers from. Yes, we should understand computers and how they affect our lives today. If for no other reason, it might be a good way to help us understand ourselves.

NOTES

1. John Wells, "The Origins of the Computer Industry: A Case Study in Radical Technological Change," Dissertation, Yale University, 1978, p. 96; Robert Noyce, "Microelectronics," *Scientific American*, 237 (September, 1977), 64; Edmund Berkeley, "Sense and Nonsense about Computers and their Applications," World Computer Pioneer Conference, Proceedings (Lladudno, Wales, 1970), p. 2/5; and most recently Philip J. Davis and Reuben Hersh, *The Mathematical Experience* (New York: Houghton Mifflin, 1981), p. 14; the estimate for England and Scotland is quoted in Simon Lavington, *Early British Computers* (Bedford, Mass.: Digital Press, 1980), p. 104.

2. "The Thinking Machine," *Time*, January 23, 1950, cover and pp. 54-60.

3. Joseph Weizenbaum, *Computer Power and Human Reason* (San Francisco: Freeman, 1975).

4. Abbott Payson Usher, *A History of Mechanical Inventions*, revised edition (Cambridge, Mass.: Harvard, 1954), pp. 116-118.

5. See, for example, Douglas R. Hofstadter, *Gödel, Escher, Bach: An Eternal Golden Braid* (New York: Random House, 1979); also John Holland, *Adaptation in Natural and Artificial Systems: An Introductory Analysis with Application to Biology, Control, and Artificial Intelligence* (Ann Arbor: University of Michigan Press, 1975).

GLOSSARY A
Translations and Equivalents of German Terms

The terminology used throughout computer science today comes from the English language. Those terms gradually assumed their meanings after 1950, when commercial installations of computers began. Inasmuch as Konrad Zuse was working independently and without much contact with Anglo-American computing activities before and after the Second World War, he developed an independent terminology, which is nonetheless equivalent to the more familiar words in use today. The following table lists first Zuse's term plus any related German terms, followed by a literal English translation, and finally the modern English term I feel comes closest to describing what Zuse intended. I caution the reader, however, that the modern terms are not exact equivalents, but are intended only to suggest a similar concept.

Zuse's Term	Literal Translation	Modern Equivalent
Bedingungskombinatorik (Aussagenkalkül)	conditional combinatoric	predicate calculus, symbolic logic
"Ergibt"; =>	results in, produces	assignment, "let"
halblogarithmisches Form (gleitendes Komma)	semi-logarithmic form	floating point, scientific notation
Ja-Nein Wert (Dual-Ziffer)	yes-no value	binary digit, bit
Kalkül	calculus	language
Leitwerk	control unit	control
Logistic (Informatik)	logistic	computer science
Plan (Rechenplan)	plan	program, algorithm
Planfertigung	plan-preparation	compiler, interpreter
Plankalkül	plan-calculus	programming language
Rechenanlage	calculating installation	computer
Rechenmaschine	calculating machine	calculator
Rechenwerk	calculating unit	central processor
Rechnen	reckon, figure	compute
Sekundal (Dual System)	secondary	binary system

Zuse's Term	Literal Translation	Modern Equivalent
Speicherwerk	storage unit	memory unit
Vorschrift	prescription	algorithm
Wahlwerke, Wahlpyramid	choice unit	decision tree, memory addressing
Zell	cell	word, address, register

GLOSSARY B
Technical Terms Used in the Text

The following glossary gives a brief description of some of the technical terms discussed in the text. During the early history of computing, few of these terms had a fixed meaning. Some, like *computer* itself, changed their meanings several times from 1935 to the present. Others, like *accumulator*, had well-defined meanings but various individuals interpreted them differently. In all cases I have attempted to provide a definition of a term as it might have been defined in the period from 1935 to 1945. Where this definition is at variance with the modern one, I give that too.

Accumulator. A mechanical or electrical device which is capable of both storing a number and adding another number to it. Contrast with *register* (q.v.), which can store but not add. The main difference between the two is that an accumulator's digit elements are linked to one another so that a carry may take place. See also *counter*.

Addressing. The method by which a computer stores and retrieves data from its memory cells. Typically each cell is given a numerical address, and appropriate circuits direct the computer to connect a cell with a given address to its central arithmetic unit.

Algorithm. One of the most fundamental concepts in computing. "A finite set of rules which gives a sequence of operations for solving a specific type of problem," according to Donald E. Knuth (*The Art of Computer Programming*, vol. 1 [Reading, Mass., 1969], p. 4). A precise and unambiguous recipe which is sure to lead to an answer to a problem.

Arithmetic. The four fundamental operations of addition, subtraction, multiplication, and division. Sometimes the operation of taking the square root is included. The arithmetic unit of a computer is usually fitted with the capability of performing only those operations. All other "computing" must be built up of combinations of them, plus storing and retrieving numbers from the memory.

Binary. Any representation of numbers or logical values by a system in which only two possible states are allowed. A simple switch, a two-position lever, a relay, or a flip-flop are all binary devices. Binary numbers are usually written as combinations of the two binary digits 1 and 0; binary logic is usually expressed as combinations of true and false values. Konrad Zuse used the letters L and O for both, and in a computer it is common to mix both logical and numerical values.

Calculator. A machine which manipulates primarily numerical data. Before 1935: usually a desk-sized machine that performed the four operations of arithmetic. 1935-1945:

sometimes used synonymously with *computer*. Today: a computing device which operates in the (binary coded) decimal system and which is optimized for numerical calculations. If such a device is programmable, the program is usually stored in a memory kept separate from the data memory.

Calculus. Latin word for *pebble*—a stone used as an aid to counting. Modern colloquial meaning refers to the method of differentiating and integrating functions, as simultaneously discovered by Isaac Newton and G. W. Leibniz in the 17th century. Its general meaning (as, say, Konrad Zuse used it) is the expression of mathematical concepts by a system of well-defined symbols.

Compiler. A computer program whose output is another program—one which can then be directly executed by the circuits of the machine. Compilers allow one to write programs using a richer and more familiar notation than long strings of binary digits.

Complement. The complement of a number is the difference between that number and 10000...(to as many zeros as the original number has). In the decimal system, the complement of 354 is 1,000 - 354, or 646. (Binary numbers have corresponding complements as well.) Computers usually subtract by adding the complement of a number, for example, 421 - 354 is computed as 421 + 646, or 1,067. If the machine's registers have only three places, the "1" at the left drops out, giving the true difference 67. A variation of this scheme is to take the difference between each digit and 9, giving the so-called nines complement, instead of the "tens complement" just described. That has the advantage of not requiring any borrowing of digits to form the complement, but a 1 must be added (the so-called end-around carry) to give the correct answer for subtraction.

Computer. Before 1945: a person who did calculations. After 1945: a machine capable of the four operations of arithmetic, automatic storage and retrieval of intermediate results, and automatic input and output, all directed by a control unit. The modern definition is a machine which can manipulate symbolic information in any combination or way one desires, and which contains an internally stored program, which the machine may also manipulate if desired.

Control. That part of a computer that routes numbers to and from other sections of the machine: memory, input/output, arithmetic. Usually directed by a program.

Counter. A physical device that represents a number and which can also add quantities, but only by *one* unit at a time. If an accumulator contains the number 354, one can change its contents to 454 simply by adding the digit "1" to the third decimal place. (Old, full-keyboard adding machines had this ability.) But for a counter to go from representing 354 to 454, it would have to go through all the states in between: 354, 355, 356,..., 452, 453, 454. An automobile odometer is a counter: it counts the miles one at a time (unless someone tampers with it). Modern computers have at least one counter that steps through the program stored in successive memory locations. It normally increments itself by one unit at each program cycle, but there are provisions to have it make longer jumps as well. A much older definition is a table where business transactions were carried out with the help of pebbles, an abacus, or a counting board. Hence the phrases "over the counter transactions," and the like.

Data. Latin "things which are given" (singular *datum*). Generally, the material put into a computer in coded form and then acted upon by the machine. It usually refers to numerical inputs as opposed to the program which is also fed in.

Electromechanical. Electrical circuits in which mechanical parts do the actual switching, as in a relay, a household light switch, push buttons, etc. Electromechanical calculators work just like mechanical ones, except that the power is supplied by an electric motor instead of by human muscles pulling a lever or turning a crank.

Electronic. Circuits in which all switching is done by the electrons themselves, as in a vacuum tube or transistor. Because the mass of an electron is so small, electronic switches are much faster than electromechanical ones.

Floating point. Also called "scientific notation." Representing a quantity by two numbers: one showing the digits of the number, the other its magnitude. The second number tells where the decimal point is to be placed in the first number (binary point if using base two).

Large-scale. Does not refer to the physical size of the machinery, even though nearly all the early large-scale computers were also physically very big. It refers rather to the fact that it can solve problems whose scale would severely tax human computers. Solving a system of forty simultaneous equations would be such a problem; it would be almost impossible to solve without an automatic computer.

Memory. Any physical device which is capable of holding the representation of a number for later retrieval and use. A memory is said to be *random-access* (RAM) if the time it takes to get one number from it is the same as the time to get any other number. *Cyclic* or *serial* memories (for example, magnetic tape units) require more time to get some contents than others. Some memories cannot be altered once their contents are fixed; they are called *read-only* memories (ROM).

Parallel. Doing more than one thing at a time. In computing, there are two contexts. A parallel data structure means that when a number is manipulated in the computer, all of its digits are handled at once. (Once again, mechanical adding machines work this way.) A parallel program structure means that more than one program step is carried out at once (cf. the ENIAC). Contrast with *serial* or *sequential*.

Program. A list of instructions which is supplied to a computer in coded form, and which causes the computer to carry out an algorithm (q.v.) that will solve a problem. Strictly speaking, a program must be of the form that a machine can "understand" —an algorithm need not be. Neither may contain any ambiguities in its expression.

Programming language. The set of symbols, plus the associated rules for combining those symbols, with which a computer program is written. Only in that abstract sense do programming languages resemble human languages. A computer "understands" a programming language when it acts the way we want it to after being programmed in that language.

Register. A physical device which accepts and stores data. In contrast to an accumulator (q.v.), when a new number is sent to a register it overwrites whatever number is already there. The word *register* also loosely applies to units in the central processor of a computer in which arithmetic and temporary storage are both performed.

Sequential. Doing one arithmetic operation at a time. The classic von Neumann architecture specifies a computer that transfers numbers in parallel but which executes program steps sequentially.

Serial. Handling numbers one digit at a time. Examples are the way most humans do arithmetic using a pencil and paper, or the way a seven-digit telephone number is dialed one digit at a time.

Symbolic logic. A set of symbols and rules for their manipulation, which treat logical rather than numeric values. The most common form of symbolic logic handles only the two values "true" and "false," thereby enabling it to mesh nicely with binary arithmetic, which is also two-valued. The "logic" of a computer refers informally to its internal electronic circuits. Also called *Boolean algebra*.

Synchronous. Operation of the computer is controlled by a central clock. A synchronous computer works like a symphony orchestra, in which the conductor coordinates all the activities of the players. All actions of the computer are done with reference to its clock cycle. By contrast, a human being does each step in solving a problem as soon as he has finished the preceding step; he does not have to wait for a specific clock cycle. The Bell Labs Model I was an asynchronous computer, but most others were (and are) synchronous.

Word. A block of physical elements in which numbers or other data are manipulated as a group. A "word-length" of ten decimal digits means that numbers of up to that many digits (to a maximum value of 9,999,999,999) can be handled as a block. Some computers have the ability to split a word in half, thereby doubling the number of storage cells in the computer, while halving their individual digit capacity. Where it is necessary to handle numbers of greater digit length than the word length, two adjacent cells may be joined together, for so-called double-precision.

APPENDIX
Program Listings

Following are listings of original program codes written for the Z3 and ASCC. Each is then translated into a program for an HP 41C pocket calculator. While this calculator employs a logic quite different from the Zuse and Aiken machines, I have written the programs for it to conform as closely as possible to the logical flow of the originals.

I also include a 41C program that "emulates" the operation of the Bell Labs Model I as it performed complex division. This program requires a printer connected to the 41C.

(1) EVALUATING A 3 × 3 DETERMINANT ON THE Z3

Matrix:

$$\begin{pmatrix} V1 & V2 & V3 \\ V4 & V5 & V6 \\ V7 & V8 & V9 \end{pmatrix}$$

Sequence of evaluation:

V1 × V5 × V9, store as V10
V2 × V6 × V7, store as V11
V3 × V4 × V8, store as V12
V1 × V6 × V8, store as V13
V2 × V4 × V9, store as V14
V3 × V5 × V7, store as V15
Add the first three products (V10, V11, V12), then subtract the last three (V13, V14, V15). Display the result and halt the machine.

STEP	OPERATION	ADDRESS	STEP	OPERATION	ADDRESS
1	Store	1	31	Read	8
2	Store	2	32	Multiply	
3	Store	3	33	Store	13
4	Store	4	34	Read	2
5	Store	5	35	Read	4
6	Store	6	36	Multiply	
7	Store	7	37	Read	9
8	Store	8	38	Multiply	
9	Store	9	39	Store	14
10	Read	1	40	Read	3
11	Read	5	41	Read	5
12	Multiply		42	Multiply	
13	Read	9	43	Read	7
14	Multiply		44	Multiply	
15	Store	10	45	Store	15
16	Read	2	46	Read	10
17	Read	6	47	Read	11
18	Multiply		48	Add	
19	Read	7	49	Read	12
20	Multiply		50	Add	
21	Store	11	51	Read	13
22	Read	3	52	Subtract	
23	Read	4	53	Read	14
24	Multiply		54	Subtract	
25	Read	8	55	Read	15
26	Multiply		56	Subtract	
27	Store	12	57	Stop and display	
28	Read	1			
29	Read	6			
30	Multiply				

LISTING OF A CORRESPONDING PROGRAM FOR THE HP 41C CALCULATOR

STEP	OPERATION		STEP	OPERATION
01	Lbl "Z3"		34	RCL 08
02	STO 01		35	*
03	R/S		36	STO 12
04	STO 02		37	RCL 01
05	R/S		38	RCL 06
06	STO 03		39	*
07	R/S		40	RCL 08
08	STO 04		41	*
09	R/S		42	STO 13
10	STO 05		43	RCL 02
11	R/S		44	RCL 04
12	STO 06		45	*
13	R/S		46	RCL 09
14	STO 07		47	*
15	R/S		48	STO 14
16	STO 08		49	RCL 03
17	R/S		50	RCL 05
18	STO 09		51	*
19	RCL 01		52	RCL 07
20	RCL 05		53	*
21	*		54	STO 15
22	RCL 09		55	RCL 10
23	*		56	RCL 11
24	STO 10		57	+
25	RCL 02		58	RCL 12
26	RCL 06		59	+
27	*		60	RCL 13
28	RCL 07		61	-
29	*		62	RCL 14
30	STO 11		63	-
31	RCL 03		64	RCL 15
32	RCL 04		65	-
33	*		66	.END.

Instructions: 1) Key in program.
2) Size 016 or greater.
3) Key in V1, XEQ "Z3"; key in V2 through V9 and R/S after each entry. After last entry calculator computes the determinant.

Examples: $\begin{vmatrix} 5 & 3 & 4 \\ 7 & 4 & 7 \\ 1 & 2 & 1 \end{vmatrix} = -10$ $\begin{vmatrix} 2 & 5 & 4 \\ 5 & 7 & 7 \\ 3 & 1 & 1 \end{vmatrix} = 16$

(2) EVALUATION OF THE POLYNOMIAL

$$F(x) = x^4 + 3x^3 - 3x^2/4 - 22x + 3$$

rewritten as:

$$F(x) = (((x+3)x - 3/4)x - 22)x + 3$$

for

$$5 \le x \le 10, \ x \text{ incremented by } 0.01$$

as coded on the Harvard Mark I.

line #	out 00000000 87654321	in 00000000 87654321	miscellaneous 00000000 87654321	comments
Starting tape				
1	1	1	7	clear Register 1
2	7 5 1	1	7	x from switch 9
3	2	2	7	clear Register 2
4	7 5 2	2	7	add 3 to x in R2
5	7	7	7	clear Register 64
6	7 5 21	7	7	x from R11 to R64
Main control tape				
1	7 4 1	1	7	Δx from Sw1 to R1
2	7 4 2	7	7	Δx from Sw2 to R64
3	7 4 1	2	7	Δx from Sw1 to R2
--- 4	2	76 1	7	----rerun line-----
5			7	
6				
7	1		7	x_n from R1 to
8			7	multiplier
9			7	
10	21	21	7	clear R3
11	7 43 1	21	32	-.75 from Sw5 to R3
12		21	7	(x+3)x to R3
13	21	76 1	7	(x+3)x-.75 to
14			7	multiplier
15			7	
16	1		7	x_n from R1 to
17			7	multiplier
18			7	
19	3	3	7	clear R4
20	7 432	3	32	-22 from Sw6 to R4
21		3	7	((x+3)x-.75)x to R4
22	3	76 1	7	((x+3)x-.75)x-22
23			7	from R4 to mult.
24				
25	1		7	x_n from R1 to
26			7	multiplier
27			7	
28	3 1	3 1	7	clear R5
29	7 4321	3 1	7	3 from Sw7 to R5
30		3 1	7	(((x+3)x-.75)x-22)x
31	3 1	7 5 3		to R5
32			5 1	
33	7	7 5 3		punch results
34	7 43	7 5 3		
35			7 5	
36			87	

The operator would first set numerical constants on the switches, plug the necessary cables to set the decimal point and the printing unit, then run the starting tape to initialize the machine. He or she would then run the routine tape once for each value of x, from 5.00 to 9.99. The routine tape could be spliced into a loop, or it could be mechanically backed up for each run.

For each run, the calculator would punch successive values of x and $F(x)$, until the final punch card for $x = 9.99$ was read. The operator would then manually stop the machine.

The operator adjusted the position of the decimal point by plugging a cable on the multiplying unit. He also plugged a printer or other output mechanism to the output register whose value is coded as line "_7_5_3_ _" on line 31.

HP 41C CALCULATOR PROGRAM FOR THE SAME PROBLEM

HP 41C CALCULATOR PROGRAM FOR THE SAME PROBLEM.

STEP	OPERATION	COMMENTS	STEP	OPERATION	COMMENTS
01	LBL "ASCC"		31	*	
02	RCL 09		32	RCL 05	
03	ST + 01	Initialize	33	ST - 05	
04	RCL 02		34	RCL 03	
05	ST - 02		35	ST + 05	
06	RCL 03		36	RDN	
07	ST + 02	(x+3) in R2	37	RDN	
08	RCL 01		38	ST + 05	F(x)
09	ST + 02		39	RCL 01	in R5
10	RCL 02		40	PSE	
11	*	(x+3)x	41	RCL 05	
12	RCL 07		42	PSE	
13	ST - 07		43	FS? 55	
14	RCL 04		44	XEQ "Print"	
15	ST - 07		45	RDN	
16	RDN		46	10	test
17	RDN		47	x=y?	for
18	ST + 07		48	RTN	end
19	RCL 07		49	GTO "ASCC"	
20	RCL 01		50	LBL "Print"	
21	*	((x+3)x-.75)x	51	FIX 2	
22	RCL 00		52	CLA	print
23	ST - 00		53	ARCL Y	x,
24	RCL 06		54	" ⊢ "	F(x)
25	ST - 00		55	FIX 9	
26	RDN		56	ARCL X	
27	RDN		57	PRA	
28	ST + 00		58	AOFF	
29	RCL 00		59	RTN	
30	RCL 01		60	.END	

To run: 1) Key in program.
      2) Size > 10
      3) Initialize: 0.01   STO 09
                     4.99   STO 01
                     3.00   STO 03
                     0.75   STO 04
                   22.00   STO 06
      4) XEQ "ASCC"

Program displays x, then $F(x)$ at pause, prints both values if a printer is attached. Takes approx 5 sec./iteration, or about an hour for the entire range of x from 5 to 10 in increments of .01.

Sample output:

```
         5.00       874.2500000
         5.01       881.2244480
         5.02       888.2378842
         5.03       895.2904468
           .            .
           .            .
           .            .
         9.97      12,562.72916
         9.98      12,611.01536
         9.99      12,659.43888
        10.00      12,708.00000
```

PROGRAM LISTINGS

(3) HP 41C LISTING TO DIVIDE TWO COMPLEX NUMBERS

Numbers are entered in reverse order, divisor first, like the Bell Labs Complex Number Computer. Program requires a 41C printer.

STEP	OPERATION	COMMENTS		STEP	OPERATION	COMMENTS
01	LBL "Complex"			36	ARCL 04	
02	FIX 8			37	" | - "	(space)
03	SF 27			38	ARCL 05	
04	ADV			39	" | -="	
05	CLA			40	PRA	
06	"c ?"			41	RCL 04	
07	PROMPT			42	RCL 00	
08	STO 00	input		43	*	
09	CLA	denominator		44	RCL 05	
10	"d ?"			45	RCL 01	compute
11	PROMPT			46	*	complex
12	STO 01			47	+	quotient
13	RCL 00			48	RCL 03	
14	x^2			49	/	
15	RCL 01			50	RCL 05	
16	x^2	compute		51	RCL 00	
17	+	"r"		52	*	
18	STO 03			53	RCL 04	
19	CLA			54	RCL 01	
20	"a ?"			55	*	
21	PROMPT			56	-	
22	STO 04			57	RCL 03	
23	CLA	input		58	/	
24	"b ?"	numerator		59	CLA	
25	PROMPT			60	ARCL Y	print
26	STO 05			61	" | - "	output,
27	CLA			62	ACA	including
28	ARCL 00			63	105	special
29	" | - "			64	ACCHR	character
30	ARCL 01	print input,		65	RDN	for "i."
31	ACA	including		66	CLA	
32	92	special		67	ARCL X	
33	ACCHR	character		68	ACA	
34	PRBUF	for reversed		69	PRBUF	
35	CLA	division		70	.END.	

Key in Program, XEQ "Complex." Key in c, d, a, and b at prompts, followed by R/S. Calculator prints inputs as soon as all are keyed in (following the reversed order); then the quotient.

Sample output:

```
        0.45632450  0.45367899  \
        0.31612848  0.20028853  =
        0.56785431  i-0.12564533
```

Selected Bibliography

The following bibliography lists only works that are especially relevant to computing's pioneering years, 1935-1945. The reader should consult the journal *Annals of the History of Computing*, especially the extensive bibliography by Brian Randell in vol. 1, no. 2 (October, 1979) of that journal, for a more comprehensive list of references.

Abramowitz, Milton, et al., eds. *Handbook of Mathematical Functions, with Formulas, Graphs, and Mathematical Tables*. National Bureau of Standards, Applied Mathematics Series, 55 (June, 1964), 355-494.

Aiken, Howard H. "Proposed Automatic Calculating Machine." *IEEE Spectrum*, 1 (August, 1964), 62-69.

Aiken, Howard H., and Hopper, Grace M. "The Automatic Sequence Controlled Calculator." *Electrical Engineering*, 65 (1946), 384-391, 449-454, 522-528.

Aiken, Howard H., and Staff of the Harvard Computation Laboratory. *A Manual of Operation for the Automatic Sequence Controlled Calculator*. Annals of the Harvard Computation Laboratory, vol. 1. Cambridge, Mass.: Harvard University Press, 1946.

Alt, Franz L. 1948. "A Bell Telephone Laboratories Computing Machine." *Mathematical Tables and Other Aids to Computation*, 3 (1948), 1-13, 69-84.

———. 1958. *Electronic Digital Computers: Their Use in Science and Engineering*. New York: Academic Press, 1958.

Andrews, E. G. 1949. "The Bell Computer, Model VI." *Proceedings of a Second Symposium on Large-Scale Digital Calculating Machinery*, September 13-16, 1949. Annals of the Harvard Computation Laboratory, vol. 26. Cambridge, Mass.: Harvard University Press, 1951, pp. 20-31.

———.1951. "A Review of the Bell Laboratories' Digital Computer Developments," in *Review of Electronic Digital Computers, Joint AIEE-IRE Computer Conference*, December 10-12, 1951, Philadelphia. New York: AIEE, 1952, pp. 101-105.

———. 1957. "Bell Laboratories Digital Computers." *Bell Labs Record*, 35 (1957), 81-84.

———. 1963. "Telephone Switching and the Early Bell Laboratories Computers." *Bell System Technical Journal*, 42 (1963), 341-353.

Andrews, E. G., and Bode, H. W. "Use of the Relay Digital Computer." *Electrical Engineering*, 69 (1950), 158-163.

Bauer, F. L. "Between Zuse and Rutishauser—The Early Development of Digital Computing in Central Europe." Munich, Technical University, Dept. of Informatics, Report #7629, 1976, 41pp.

———, and Wössner, H. "The 'Plankalkül' of Konrad Zuse: A Forerunner of Today's Programming Languages." *Communications ACM*, 15 (1972), 678-685.

Belden, Thomas G., and Belden, Marva R. *The Lengthening Shadow: The Life of Thomas J. Watson*. Boston: Little, Brown, 1962.

Bergstein, Harold. "An Interview with Eckert and Mauchly." *Datamation*, 8/4 (April, 1962), 25-30.

Berkeley, Edmund C. *Giant Brains, or Machines that Think*. New York: Wiley, 1949.

Bernstein, Jeremy. *The Analytical Engine: Computers, Past, Present and Future*. New York: Random House, 1964.

Bliss, Gilbert A. *Mathematics for Exterior Ballistics*. New York: Wiley, 1944.

Bloch, Richard M. "Mark I Calculator." *Proceedings of a Symposium on Large-Scale Digital Calculating Machinery*, January, 1947. *Annals of the Harvard Computation Laboratory*, vol. 16, Cambridge, Mass., Harvard University Press, 1948, pp. 23-30.

Bonn, Gesellschaft für Mathematik und Datenverarbeitung (GMD). *Catalog of the Personal Papers of Konrad Zuse*, 1979, 97pp.

Bowden, B. V. *Faster than Thought*. London: Pitman, 1955.

Brainerd, J. G., and Sharpless, T. K. "The ENIAC." *Electrical Engineering*, 67 (1948), 163-172.

Brainerd, John G. "Conference Report—International Research Conference on the History of Computing, Los Alamos, June 10-15, 1976." *Technology and Culture*, 18 (1977), 218-221.

Buchholz, Werner, ed. "The Computer Issue." *Proceedings IRE*, 41/10 (1953).

Burks, Arthur W. 1946. "Super Electronic Computing Machine." *Electronics Industries*, 5 (July, 1946), 62-67, 96.

———. 1947. "Electronic Computing Circuits of the ENIAC." *Proceedings IRE*, 35 (1947), 756-767.

———; Goldstine, Herman; and von Neumann, John. "Preliminary Discussion of the Logical Design of an Electronic Computing Instrument." Princeton, Institute for Advanced Study, 1946. In John von Neumann, *Collected Works*, vol. 5 (Oxford: Pergamon Press, 1963), 34-79.

Computers and Their Future. World Computer Pioneer Conference, Lladudno, 1970. London: Richard Williams and Partners, 1970.

Couffignal, Louis. 1933. *Les Machines à Calculer, leurs principes, leur évolution*. Paris: Gauthier Villian, 1933, 86pp.

———. 1936. "Calcul Mechanique sur l'emploi de la numeration binaire dans les machines à calculer et les instruments nomoméchaniques. *Comptes Rendus*, 202 (1936), 1745-1747, 1970-1972.

Cremer, Hubert, ed. *Probleme der Entwicklung programmgesteuerter Rechengeräte und Integrieranlagen*. Aachen, Technical College, 1953.

Czauderna, Karl-Heinz. *Konrad Zuse—der Weg zu seinem Computer Z3 und dessen Verwircklichung*. Munich: Oldenburg, 1979, 105pp.

Dartmouth College, Baker Library, Hanover, N.H. *An Inventory of the Papers of George Robert Stibitz, Concerning the Development of the Digital Computer*. Hanover, 1973, 127pp.

De Beauclair, Wilfred. *Rechnen mit Maschinen*. Braunschweig: Vieweg, 1968, 313pp.

———, and Schmid, D. "Geschichtliche Entwicklung." *Taschenbuch der Informatik. vol 1*. K. Steinbuch and W. Weber, eds. Berlin, Heidelberg, New York: Springer, 1974, pp. 1-45.

Desmonde, W. H., and Berkling, K. J. "The Zuse Z3." *Datamation*, 12/9 (1966), 30-31.

Dreyer, H. J. "Solution of Systems of Linear Equations by Means of Punched-Card Machines—Auflösung von Systemen linearer Gleichungen mit Lochkarten-Maschinen." U.S. Air Force, Air Material Command, Wright Field, Dayton, Ohio, Translation No. F-TS-1046-RE, December, 1946.

———, and Walther, A. *Entwicklung Mathematischer Instrumente in Deutschland 1939 bis 1945*. Bericht A3, Institut für Praktische Mathematik, Technische Hochschule Darmstadt, August 19, 1946.

Eames, Charles, and Eames, Ray, office of. *A Computer Perspective*. Cambridge, Mass.: Harvard University Press, 1973, 175pp.

Eccles, W. H., and Jordan, F. W. "Trigger Relay." *Science Abstracts*, B22 (1919), 437-438.

Eckert, J. Presper. 1953. "A Survey of Digital Computer Memory Systems." *Proceedings IRE*, 41 (1953), 1393-1406.

———. 1976. "Thoughts on the History of Computing." *Computer* (December, 1976), pp. 58-65.

———, Lukoff, H., and Smoliar, G. "A Dynamically Regenerated Electrostatic Memory System." *Proceedings IRE*, 38 (1950), 498-510.

Eckert, Wallace. *Punched Card Methods in Scientific Computation*. New York: Thomas J. Watson Astronomical Computing Bureau, Columbia University, 1940.

"Electric Calculating Machine Devised for Complex Problems." *Science News Letter* (September 14, 1940), pp. 163-164.

Engineering Research Associates. *High-Speed Computing Devices*. New York: McGraw-Hill, 1950.

Evans, C. *Pioneers of Computing Series* (a series of taped interviews). London, The Science Museum, 1981.

Ganzhorn, Karl, and Walter, Wolfgang. *Die Geschichtliche Entwicklung der Datenverarbeitung*. Rev. ed. Stuttgart: IBM Corp., 1975, 80pp.

Gardner, W. David. "Will the Inventor of the First Digital Computer Please Stand Up?" *Datamation*, 20/2 (February, 1974), 84, 88-90.

"Giant New Calculator." *Science News Letter*, 46 (August 12, 1944), p. 111.

Glaser, Anton. *History of Binary and Other Nondecimal Numeration*. Southhampton, Pa.: privately printed, 1971, 196pp.

Goldbach, Wend, and Schneider, Rolf. "Beschreibung der Rechenanlage Z3." *Zuse Forum, 2/4 (September, 1963)*, 19-31.

Goldschneider, Peter, and Zemenek, H. *Computer: Werkzeug der Information*. Berlin: Springer-Verlag, 1971.

Goldstine, Herman H. *The Computer from Pascal to von Neumann*. Princeton: Princeton University Press, 1972, 378pp.

———, and Goldstine, Adele. "The Electronic Numerical Integrator and Computer (ENIAC)." *Mathematical Tables and Other Aids to Computation*, 2 (1946), 97-110.

Good, Irving John. 1970. "Some Future Social Repercussions of Computers." *International Journal of Environmental Studies*, 1 (1970), 67-79.

———. 1979. "Early Work on Computers at Bletchley." *Cryptologiia*, 3 (1979), 65-77.

Graef, Martin, ed. *350 Jahre Rechenmaschinen*. Munich: Hausner, 1973, 124pp.
Great Britain, British Intelligence Objectives Subcommittee. "Organization of Deutsche Versuchsanstalt für Luftfahrt (DVL)." B.I.O.S. Final Report # 200, undated, 3pp.
Great Britain, Field Information Agency, Technical (FIAT). "Applied Mathematics Research in Germany, with Particular Reference to Naval Applications." B.I.O.S. Final Report # 79, undated, 65pp.
―――. "The Development of Theoretical and Applied Mechanics in German Institutions During the War." FIAT Final Report # 1167, May 30, 1947, 3pp.
Hamming, Richard W. 1950a. "Error Detecting and Correcting Codes." *Bell System Technical Journal*, 26 (1950), 147-160.
―――. 1950b. "Error Detecting and Correcting Codes." *Bell Laboratories Record*, 28 (1950), 193-197.
Harmon, Margaret. *Stretching Man's Mind*. New York: Mason/Charter, 1975, 239pp.
Harrison, Joseph O. "The Preparation of Problems for the Mark I Calculator." *Proceedings of a Symposium on Large-Scale Calculating Machinery*. Cambridge, Mass: Harvard University Press, 1948, pp. 208-210.
Hartree, D. R. 1946. "The ENIAC, an Electronic Calculating Machine." *Nature*, 157 (April 20, 1946), 527; 158 (October 12, 1946), 500-506.
―――. 1947. "Recent Developments in Calculating Machines." *Journal of Scientific Instruments*, 24 (1947), 172-176.
―――. 1948. *Calculating Instruments and Machines*. Urbana, Ill.: University of Illinois Press, 1949, 138pp.
Harvard University, Computation Laboratory. 1946. *A Manual of Operation for the Automatic Sequence Controlled Calculator*. Cambridge, Mass.: Harvard University Press, 1946, 562pp.
―――. 1948. *Proceedings of a Symposium on Large-Scale Digital Calculating Machinery*. Cambridge, Mass.: Harvard University Press, 1948.
Hertwig, August. "Die Zahlenrechnungen bei der Lösung zahlreicher linearer Gleichungen." *Jahrbuch der Deutschen Akademie für Luftfahrtforschung* (1943-1944), pp. 221-225.
Hilbert, David, and Ackerman, W. *Grundzüge der theoretischen Logik*. Berlin: Julius Springer Verlag, 1934.
―――, and Bernays, P. *Grundlagen der Mathematik*. Berlin: Julius Springer Verlag, 1934.
Hoffmann, Walter. *Digitale Informationswandler*. Braunschweig: Vieweg, 1962.
Hohmann, Joachim. *Eine Untersuchung des Plankalküls im Vergleich mit algorithmischen Sprachen*. Bonn, GMD, report #104, 1975, 193pp.
Hollcroft, T. R. "The Summer Meeting in Hanover." *Bulletin, American Mathematical Society*, 46 (1940), 859-861.
Hollingdale, S. H., and Toothill, G. C. *Electronic Computers*. Harmondsworth: Penguin Books, 1965, 334pp.
Hughes, Thomas Parke. "ENIAC: Invention of a Computer." *Technikgeschichte*, 42 (1975), 148-165.
Huskey, H. D. "Chronology of Computing Devices." *IEEE Transactions on Computers*, 25 (1976), 1190-1208.
IBM Corporation. 1945. "IBM Automatic Sequence Controlled Calculator." Privately printed, 1945, 6pp.

———. 1954. *Bibliography on the Use of IBM Machines in Science, Statistics, and Education.* New York: Thomas J. Watson Scientific Computing Laboratory, January, 1954.
Knuth, Donald E. *The Art of Computer Programming: Vol. 1: Fundamental Algorithms. Vol. 2: Seminumerical Algorithms.* Reading, Mass.: Addison Wesley, 1969, 1973.
———, and Pardo, L. T. "The Early Development of Programming Languages." Stanford University, Computer Science Dept., Report STAN-CS-76-562, August, 1976.
Küssner, H. G. 1929. "Flügelschwingung an Flugzeugen." *Zeitschrift für Angewandte Mathematik und Mechanik,* 9 (1929), 492-493.
———. 1936. "Zusammenfassender Bericht über den instationären Auftrieb von Flügeln." *Luftfahrtforschung,* 13 (1936), 410-429.
Larson, Judge Earl R. *Findings of Fact, Conclusions of Law and Order for Judgement.* File #4-67, Civ. 138, Honeywell, Inc. vs. Sperry Rand Corp. and Illinois Scientific Developments, Inc., U.S. District Court, District of Minnesota, Fourth Division, October 19, 1973, 319pp.
Lehmer, D. H. "A Photoelectric Number Sieve." *American Mathematical Monthly,* 40 (1933), 401-406.
Leibniz, G. W. *Mathematische Schriften, Vol. 5: Die Mathematische Abhandlungen,* ed. by C. I. Gerhardt. Hildesheim: Georg Olms Verlagsbuchhandlung, 1962.
Loveday, Evelyn. "George Stibitz and the Bell Labs Relay Computers." *Datamation,* September, 1977, pp. 80-85.
Lü [sic]. "Eine programmgesteuerte elektrische Rechenmaschine." *Bulletin, Association Suisse des Electriciens,* 41 (1950), 607-609.
Lyndon, R. C. "The Zuse Computer." *Mathematical Tables and Other Aids to Computation,* 2 (1947), 355-359.
"Mathematical Robot." *Time,* August 14, 1944, p. 72.
Mauchly, John W. "Preparation of Programs for EDVAC-type Machines." *Proceedings of a Symposium on Large-Scale Digital Calculating Machines,* January, 1947, *Annals of the Harvard Computation Laboratory,* vol. 16, Cambridge, Mass: Harvard University Press, 1948, pp. 203-207.
———. "Mauchly on the Trials of Building the ENIAC." *IEEE Spectrum,* 12/4 (1975), 75-76.
Merzbach, Uta. "George Scheutz and the First Printing Calculator." Smithsonian Studies in History and Technology, #36, Washington, D.C., 1977, 74pp.
Meschowski, Herbert, ed. *Grundlagen der modernen Mathematik.* Darmstadt: Wissenschaftliche Buchgesellschaft, 1975.
Metropolis, N., and Worlton, J. "A Trilogy on Errors in the History of Computing." *First USA-Japan Computer Conference, Proceedings.* Tokyo, October 3-5, 1972, pp. 21/1-21/9.
Meyer zur Capellan, W. *Mathematische Instrumente.* 3rd ed. Leipzig: Akademie Verlag, 1949.
Montgomery, G. A. *Digital Calculating Machines.* London: Blackie, 1951.
Morrison, Philip, and Morrison, Emily, eds. *Charles Babbage and his Calculating Engines.* New York: Dover, 1961, 400pp.
Murray, Francis J. *Mathematical Machines, Vol. 1: Digital Computers.* New York: Columbia University Press, 1961.
Newman, James R., ed. "Mathematical Machines: Can a Machine Think?" *The World of*

Mathematics, vol. 4, part 19. New York: Simon and Schuster, 1956, pp. 2070-2133.
Oettinger, Anthony, "Howard Aiken." *Communications ACM*, 5 (1962), 298-299, 359.
Overhoff, Gerhard. "Automatic Calculating Engine." U.S. Air Force, Air Interrogation Unit, Austria. Interrogation Summary, # AIU/IS/33, November 8, 1946, 4pp.
Pennsylvania University, Moore School of Electrical Engineering. 1945. "Description of the ENIAC and Comments on Electronic Digital Computing Machines." U.S. National Defense Research Committee, Applied Mathematics Panel, AMP Report #171.2R, November 30, 1945.
———. 1948. *Theory and Techniques for Design of Electronic Digital Computers, Lectures Given at the Moore School, 8 July-31 August, 1946*. 4 vols. Philadelphia: Moore School of Electrical Engineering, June 30, 1948.
Phelps, Byron E. "The Beginnings of Electronic Computation." IBM Corporation, Systems Development Division, Poughkeepsie, New York, Report TR-OO.2259, December 9, 1971.
Piesch, Hansi. "Begriff der allgemeinen Schaltungstechnik. *Archiv der Elektrotechnik*, 33 (1939), 672-686, 733-746.
Pocock, Rowland F. *German Guided Missiles of the Second World War*. New York: Arco, 1967.
Randell, Brian. 1972. "On Alan Turing and the Origins of Digital Computers." *Machine Intelligence*, 7 (1972), 3-20.
———. 1977. "Colossus: Godfather of the Computer." *New Scientist*, 73/1038 (February 10, 1977), 346-348.
———, ed. 1975. *The Origins of Digital Computers: Selected Papers*. 2nd edition. Berlin, Heidelberg, New York: Springer Verlag, 1975, 464pp.
Reich, H. J. "Trigger Circuits." *Electronics* (August, 1939), pp. 14-17.
Reid, Constance. *Hilbert*. Berlin, Heidelberg, New York: Springer Verlag, 1970, 290pp.
"Relay Computer for the Army." *Bell Laboratories Record*, 26/5 (1948), 208-209.
Rodgers, William. *Think: A Biography of the Watsons and IBM*. New York: Stein and Day, 1969, 311pp.
Rosenberg, Jerry. *The Computer Prophets*. New York: Macmillan, 1969.
Rutishauser, H. 1951. "Erste Erfahrungen mit dem programmgesteuerten Rechengerät Z4 von K. Zuse." *Zeitschrift für Angewandte Mathematik und Mechanik*, 31 (1951), 254.
———. 1952. "Automatische Rechenplanfertigung bei programmgesteuerten Rechenmaschinen." *Mitteilungen aus dem Institut für angewandte Mathematik an der ETH*, Zürich, #3, 1952.
———. 1956. "Massnahmen zur Vereinfachung des Programmieriens (Bericht über die in 5-jahriger Programmierungsarbeit mit der Z4 gewonnen Erfahrungen," *NTF*, 4 (1956), 26-27.
———. 1967. *Description of Algol 60*. Berlin: Springer Verlag, 1967.
———, Speiser, A., Stiefel, E. 1950. "Programmgesteuerte digitale Rechengeräte." *Zeitschrift für angewandte Mathematik und Physik*, 1 (1950), 339-362.
———.1951. "Programmgesteuerte digitale Rechengeräte." *Mitteilung aus dem Institut für angewandte Mathematik an der ETH, Zürich*, #2 (1951).
Sarton, George. *The Study of the History of Mathematics*. New York: Dover, 1957.

Schreyer, Helmut. 1941. "Das Röhrenrelais und seine Schaltungstechnik." Dissertation, Techniche Hochschule, Berlin, August 20, 1941, 56pp.

———. 1977. "Die Entwicklung des Versuchsmodells einer electronischen Rechenmaschine." MS, Mosbach/Baden, August 1, 1977, 14pp.

Shannon, Claude. "A Symbolic Analysis of Switching Circuits." *Transactions AIEE*, 57 (1938), 713.

Smith, Thomas M. "Some Perspectives on the Early History of Computers." *Perspectives on the Computer Revolution*, Z. W. Pylyshyn, ed. Englewood Cliffs, N.J.: Prentice-Hall, 1970, pp. 7-15.

Snyder, Samuel S. "Influence of U.S. Cryptologic Organizations on the Digital Computer Industry." *Journal of Systems and Software*, 1 (1979), 87-102.

Steinbuch, Karl. *Die Informierte Gesellschaft: Geschichte und Zukunft der Nachrichtentechnik*. Stuttgart: Rowohlt, 1966.

Stern, Nancy. *From ENIAC to UNIVAC*. Bedford, Mass.: Digital Press, 1981.

Stevenson, Malcolm G. "Bell Labs: A Pioneer in Computing Technology." *Bell Laboratories Record*, 51 (1973), 334-351; 52 (1974), 12-20, 55-63.

Stibitz, George R. 1938. "Potentials in Curved Surfaces." *Philosophical Magazine, 7th series*, 25 (1938), 783-785.

———. 1945. "Relay Computers." U.S. Office of Scientific Research and Development, Applied Mathematics Panel, Report #171.1R, February, 1945, 83pp.

———. 1946. "Introduction to the Course on Electronic Digital Computers." Pennsylvania University, *Theory and Techniques for Design of Electronic Digital Computers*, vol. 1, pp. 1-19, lecture of July 8, 1946.

———. 1948. "The Organization of Large-Scale Calculating Machinery." *Annals of the Harvard Computation Laboratory*, 16 (1948), 91-100.

———. 1978. "Stored Programs—A Reply." *Byte*, 3 (1978), 142.

———, and Loveday, Evelyn. "The Relay Computers at Bell Labs." *Datamation*, 13 (April, 1967), 35-44; (May, 1967), 45-49.

Stiefel, E. 1953. "La machine à calculer arithmetique Z4 de l'école Polytechnique Federale à Zurich." *Colloque Internationale du C. N. R. S.*, Paris, 8-13 January, 1951, pp. 33-40. Paris: editions du C. N. R. S., 1953.

———. 1955. "Rechenautomat im Dienst der Technik: Erfahrungen mit dem Zusen-Rechenautomaten Z4." *Arbeitsgemeinschaft für Forschung des Landes Nordheim-Westfalen*, 45 (1955), 29-45.

Stolterfoht, O. "Die Vielseitigkeit von Schaltmöglichkeiten." *Zeitschrift für Fernmeldetechnik, Werk, und Gerätebau*, 1/8 (April 20, 1920), 201-208; 2 (1921), 141-166, 185-189.

Stucken, H. "Programmgesteuerte Rechenmaschine in Deutschland." *Physikalische Blätter*, 6 (1950), 166-170.

Swartzlander, Earl. *Computer Design Development: Principal Papers*. Rochelle Park, N.J.: Hayden Books, 1976.

Takahasi, H. "Some Important Computers of Japanese Design." *First USA-Japan Computer Conference, Proceedings*, Tokyo, 1972. Session 21-2, 6pp.

Teichmann, Alfred. "Das Flattern von Trag- und Leitwerken." *Deutsche Akademie der Luftfahrtforschung, Schriften*. 49 (1941), 48pp.

"The Thinking Machine." *Time*, January 23, 1950, cover, pp. 54-60.

"The Thirsk Totalizer." *Electrical Review*, 106 (February 7, 1930), 268-269.

"Torres and his Remarkable Automatic Devices." *Scientific American, Supplement*, 80/2079 (November 6, 1915), 296-298.
Torrey, Volta. "Robot Mathematician Knows All the Answers." *Popular Science Monthly*, 145 (October, 1944), 86-89, 222, 226, 230.
Tropp, Henry. "The Effervescent Years: A Retrospective." *IEEE Spectrum*, 11 (February, 1974), 70-81.
Turck, J.A.V. *Origin of Modern Calculating Machines*. New York, 1921.
Turing, Alan M. 1936. "On Computable Numbers, with an Application to the Entscheidungsproblem." *Proceedings, London Mathematical Society*, series 2, 42 (1936), 230-267.
―――. 1970. "Intelligent Machinery." *Machine Intelligence*, 5 (1970), 1-23.
Turing, Sara. *Alan M. Turing*. Cambridge, England: W. Heffer, 1959.
U.S. Atomic Energy Commission, Brookhaven National Laboratory. *Bibliography on Machine Computation, 1945-1954*. U.S. OTS, 1955, 36pp.
U.S. Office of Naval Research. *A Survey of Automatic Digital Computers*. Washington, D.C., 1953, 109pp.
U.S. Congress. Senate. *The Industrial Reorganization Act. Hearings before the Subcommittee on Antitrust and Monopoly of the Committee on the Judiciary*. 93rd Congress, 2nd Session, on S. 1167, Part 7: The Computer Industry, July 23-26, 1974.
Valtat, Raymond. "Machine à calculer fondeé sur l'emploi de la numeration binaire." *Comptes Rendus*, 202 (1936), 1745-1747.
van Heijenoort, J. *From Frege to Gödel: A Source Book in Mathematical Logic, 1879-1931*. Cambridge, Mass.: Harvard University Press, 1967.
van Wijngaarden, A. "Algemeen Overzicht over moderne Rekenmachines." *Nederlands Tijdschrift voor Natuurkunde*, 15 (1949), 244-254.
von Freytag Löringhoff. "Prof. Schickards Tübinger Rechenmaschine von 1623 im Tübinger Rathaus." *Kleine Tübinger Schriften*, 4 (1973), 16pp.
von Neumann, John. 1955. *Entwicklung und Ausnutzung neuerer mathematischer Maschinen*. Köln & Opladen: Westdeutscher Verlag, 1955.
―――. 1958. *The Computer and the Brain*. New Haven: Yale University Press, 1958.
Walther, A. "Neuzeitliche mathematische Maschinen." *ETZ*, 61 (1940), 33-36.
―――, and Dreyer, H. J. 1946. "Gerate für beliebige Rechenzwecke (Entwickling mathematische Instrumente in Deutschland, 1939-1945)." Darmstadt, Institut für Praktische Mathematik, Bericht A3, August 19, 1946.
―――. 1948. "Mathematische Maschinen und Instrumente; Instrumentelle Verfahren." F.I.A.T. Review of German Science, 1939-1946, Applied Mathematics, Part 1, pp. 129-165 (Wiesbaden: Office of Military Government for Germany, Field Information Agency, Technical, 1948).
―――. 1949. "Die Integrieranlage IPM-Ott fur gewöhnliche Differentialgleichungen." *Naturwissenschaften*, 7 (1949), 199-206.
Wells, John V. "The Origins of the Computer Industry. A Case Study in Radical Technological Change." Dissertation, Yale University, 1978.
Werkmeister, P. "Die Auflösung eines Systems linearer Gleichungen mit Hilfe der Rechenmaschine 'Hamann-Automat'". *Zeitschrift für Instrumentenkunde*, 51 (1931), 490-491.
Weygandt, A. "Die elektromechanische Determinantmaschine." *Zeitschrift für Instrumentenkunde*, 53 (1933), 114-121.

Wiener, Norbert. 1948. *Cybernetics: Or Control and Communication in the Animal and the Machine.* Cambridge, Mass.: MIT Press, 1948, 2nd ed., 1961, 212pp.
———. 1953. *Ex-Prodigy.* Cambridge, Mass: MIT Press, 1953, 309pp.
———. 1956. *I Am a Mathematician.* Cambridge, Mass.: MIT Press, 1956, 380pp.
Wilkes, M. V. "How Babbage's Dream Came True." *Nature*, 257 (1975), 541-544.
Willers, Friedrich A. 1926. *Mathematische Instrumente.* Berlin and Leipzig, 1926.
———. 1951. *Mathematische Maschinen und Instrumente.* Berlin: Akademie Verlag, 1951.
———. 1952-1953. "Aus der Frühzeit der Rechenmaschinen." *Wissenschaftliche Zeitschrift aus der Technische Hochschule Dresden*, 2/2 (1952-1953), 151-158.
Winterbotham, F. W. *The Ultra Secret.* New York: Harper & Row, 1974.
Wynn-Williams, C. E. "A Thyraton 'Scale-of-Two' Counter." *Royal Society of London, Proceedings, A*, 136 (1932), 312-324.
Zacher, Hans J. *Die Hauptschriften der Dyadik von G. W. Leibniz, ein Beitrag zur Geschichte des binären Zahlensystems.* Frankfurt-am-Main: Klostermann, 1973, 384pp.
Zemanek, H. "Geschichte der Automaten." *Elektronische Rechenanlagen*, 5 (1963), 199; 6 (1964), 5-6, 57-58.
Zuse, Konrad. 1948. "Ein Neues Rechengerät für technische und wissenschaftliche Rechnungen." *Wirtschaft Spiegel*, 1 (1948), 55-58.
———. 1948-49. "Über den allgemeinen Plankalkül als Mittel zur Formulierung schematisch-kombinativer Aufgaben." *Archiv der Mathematik*, 1 (1948-49), 441-449.
———. 1949. "Die mathematische Voraussetzungen für die Entwicklung logisch-kombinativer Rechenmaschinen." *Zeitschrift für Angewandte Mathematik und Mechanik*, 29 (1949), 36-37.
———. 1950a. "Programmgesteuerte Rechenmaschinen in Deutschland." *Zeitschrift für Angewandte Mathematik und Mechanik*, 30 (1950), 292-293.
———. 1950b. "Deutsche programmgesteuerte Rechenanlage für wissenschaftliche Berechnungen." *Vermessungstechnische Rundschau*, 12 (1950), 249-253.
———. 1952. "Der Programmator." *Zeitschrift für Angewandte Mathematik und Mechanik*, 32 (1952), 246.
———. 1953. "Über programmgesteuerte Rechenanlage für industrielle Verwendung." H. Cremer, ed., *Probleme der Entwicklung programmgesteuerter Rechengerate und Integrieranlagen* (Aachen, 1953), pp. 55-75.
———. 1956-1957. "Grosse oder kleine programmgesteuerte Rechengeräte?" *Unternehmungsforschung, Operations Research*, 1 (1956-57), 117-122.
———. 1959. "Über den Plankalkül." *Elektronischen Rechenanlagen*, 1 (1959), 68-71.
———. 1962. "Entwicklung einer Rechengerate—Entwicklung von der Mechanik zur Elektronik." Walter Hoffmann, ed., *Digitale Informationswandler* (Braunschweig, 1962), pp. 508-532.
———. 1963. "Ansatze einer Theorie des allgemeinen Rechnens unter besonderer Berüchtsichtigung des Aussagenkalküls und dessen Verwendung auf Relaisschaltungen." Privately printed, 1963, 123pp.
———. 1967. "Zur Forderung der Entwicklung programmgesteuerter Rechengeräte durch die DVL." *DVL Nachrichten*, 34 (1967), 294.
———. 1968. "Gesichtspunkte zur sprachlichen Formulierung in Vielfachzugriffssystems

unter Berüchtsichtigung des 'Plankalküls'". W. Händler, ed., *Teilnehmer Rechensysteme* (Munich: R. Oldenbourg Verlag, 1968), pp. 223-230.

———. 1970. *Der Computer, Mein Lebenswerk*. Munich: Verlag Moderne Industrie, 1970, 221pp.

———. 1972a. "Der Plankalkül," Bonn, GMD, Bericht #63, 1972, 285pp.

———. 1972b. "Rechender Raum." *Nova Acta Leopoldina*, 37/1 (1972), 129-137.

———. 1973. "Die ersten programmgesteuerten Relais-Rechenmaschine." M. Graef, ed., *350 Jahre Rechenmaschinen* (Munich: Hanser, 1973), pp. 51-56.

———. 1975a. "Zur Problematik der Rechenautomaten." H. Meschowski, ed., *Grundlagen der Modernen Mathematik* (Darmstadt, 1975), pp. 253-309.

———. 1975b. "Gesichtspunkte zur Beurteilung algorithmischer Sprachen." Bonn, GMD Bericht #105, 1975, 156pp.

———. 1976a. "The Plankalkuel" (partial translation of "Der Plankalkül"). Bonn, GMD Bericht #106, 1976, 244pp.

———. 1976b. "Some Remarks on the History of Computing in Germany." Paper presented at the International Research Conference on the History of Computing, Los Alamos, June 10-15, 1976. Published in N. Metropolis, J. Howlett, and Gian-Carlo Rota, eds., *A History of Computing in the Twentieth Century*. New York: Academic Press, 1980, pp. 611-627.

———. 1977. *Beschreibung des Plankalküls*. Munich: Oldenburg, 1977, 165pp.

———. 1979. "The Emancipation of Data Processing." Paper presented at the Advanced Course on General Net Theory of Processes and Systems, Hamburg, October 10, 1979.

Index

Abacus, 3, 98
Aberdeen, Md., 95, 121, 127-128, 138. *See also* Ballistic Research Lab
Accumulators, 53, 110-112; on ENIAC, 113-114
ACE (Automatic Computing Engine), 135, 137
Ackermann, W., 24
Ada Augusta, Countess of Lovelace, 56-57, 65, 145-146
Adding machines, 3, 5, 111
Addition, decimal, 52-53. *See also* Arithmetic, decimal
Aerodynamics Research Institute (DVL), 28-29
Aiken, Howard H., xi, 6, 43, 68; and Babbage, 56-57, 62, 64-65; construction of ASCC, 49; education, 44; first thoughts on computing, 45; postwar activities, 68-70
ALGOL (programming language), 23
Analog computing, 73, 107-108
Analytical Engine. *See* Babbage, Charles
APL (programming language), 70
Apollonius, 77
Architecture, computer, 14-15, 96, 139-141
Arithmetic, 4; binary, 17, 21, 47, 87, 109-110; complex, 34, 76-81, 89; decimal, 16, 47, 53, 117, 133-134; floating vs. fixed point, 31, 35, 47; serial vs. parallel, 118-119, 138-139

ASCC (Automatic Sequence Controlled Calculator), xi, 6, 43, 46, 48, 52; construction, 49; cost, 51; description of, 52-58; programming, 56-61; and punched card machines, 51; specifications, 58; use, 65-68
Atanasoff, John V., 105-106, 109-110, 122
AT&T, 74, 92, 100
Atomic bomb, 66, 126-127, 138

Babbage, Charles, 17, 46-48, 56, 62, 64; and Analytical Engine, 14-15, 124-125, 145; and Difference Engine, 62-63, 67
Ballistic Research Lab, 108. *See also* Aberdeen, Md.
Bardeen, John, 92
BASIC (programming language), 147
Bell, Alexander Graham, 73-74
Bell Laboratories, xi, 6, 73-75, 78, 85, 93, 123
Bell Labs Model I. *See* Complex Number Computer
Bell Labs Models II-VI, 89, 94-96; specifications of II-V, 95
Bell Telephone Company. *See* AT&T
Berkeley, Edmund, 73
Berlin, 14, 16, 18-19, 37-38; Technical College of Berlin-Charlottenberg, 10-11, 15; University of Berlin, 18
Bessel functions, 66-67
Binary arithmetic. *See* Arithmetic, binary

Binary-coded decimal (BCD), 81-84, 87, 101. *See also* Arithmetic, binary
Bi-quinary notation, 97-98
Bloch, Richard, 56
Brainerd, John G., 108, 110
Brattain, Walter, 99
Brooks, Fred, 70
Brown, T. H., 48
Bryce, James, 49
Bush, Vannevar, 48, 93, 107
Buttmann, W., 18

Calculators: and computers, 18, 47, 51, 55, 78, 132-133, 150; mechanical, 3, 5, 16, 52-53, 75, 108; pocket programmable, 132, 140
Cambridge, England, 135
Cambridge, Mass. *See* Harvard University; MIT
Clippinger, R. H., 121
Colossus, 104-105, 112-113, 116, 131-132, 135, 137
Compiler programs, 144
Complements, 53, 55, 83-84, 123
Complex Number Computer (Bell Labs Model I), 76, 81-85, 89-91, 118, 120; public demonstration, 92-93; specifications, 86
Computer: analog, 107-108; definition, xi-xii, 4, 5, 7, 92, 128, 132, 135, 145; digital, 53, 108-109; electromechanical, 52; electronic, 105, 109, 112, 145-146; human, xi, 38, 136, 150; prehistory, xi, 3. *See also* Architecture, computer
Comrie, L. J., 68
Conant, James B., 51
Conditional branch capability, 55, 65, 120, 134, 137, 144
Control, devices for, 4, 18, 46-47, 81, 96. *See also* Plugboards
Copernicus, N., 151
Counters, 54, 111

Dartmouth College, 92-93
de Beauclair, W., 34, 37
de Forest, Lee, 74
Descartes, Rene, 147

Determinants, 35-36, 37
Differences, method of finite, 62-64
Differential Analyzer, 48, 107-108, 127
Differential equations, 44, 66, 106-108, 119, 128; numerical solution of, 44, 107, 126-128
Digital vs. analog computation, 53, 73, 108
Dreyer, H. J., 37
Durfee, Benjamin, 49
DVL (Deutsche Versuchsanstalt fur Luftfahrtforschung). *See* Aerodynamics Research Institute

Eccles-Jordan flip-flop. *See* Flip-flop
Eckert, J. Presper, 106, 108, 109, 111, 138
Eckert, Wallace, 48, 51
EDVAC (Electronic Discrete Variable Computer), 118-119, 120, 124, 126, 137-138; design of, 138-139
ENIAC (Electronic Numeric Integrator and Computer), xii, 7, 28, 104-106, 108, 131-133, 138, 150-151; construction, 110; and EDVAC, 138; patent, 109; programming, 115, 116, 117-120, 137; proposal for, 108, 112; specifications, 122-123; use, 126-128
Errors, computer: ASCC, 61-62, 65, 67; Bell Labs Computers, 96-98; ENIAC, 125

Fast, August, 37
Firing tables, 66, 106-107, 128. *See also* Tables, mathematical
Flip-flop, 111-112
Flutter problem, 29, 37
Frankel, S., 126
Franklin, Benjamin, 104
Fry, T. C., 92

Gate, electronic, 116-117
Gauss, Karl F., 77
General Electric Co., 77, 78
German Army Command (OKH), 28
Gillon, Paul, 108
Goldstine, Adele, 127
Goldstine, Herman H., 127, 132

INDEX

Good, I. J., 131
Göttingen, 17, 39, 77, 135
Grohmann, A., 18, 21

Hamilton, Frank, 49
Hamming, Richard, 98
Handbook of Mathematical Functions (U.S. National Bureau of Standards), 68
Hartree, D. R., 127-128, 131
Harvard Mark I. *See* ASCC
Harvard University, 43, 48-49, 132; Computation Laboratory, 65, 67-69
Henschel Aircraft Company, 15, 18; HS 293 Flying Bomb, 38
Hilbert, David, 24, 135
Hinterstein, 38
Hollerith, Herman, 4, 47
Hydrogen bomb, 126-127

IBM Corporation, 43, 48-49, 52, 68, 100, 111, 123; Card Programmed Calculator (CPC), 69; Endicott, N.Y., plant, 49, 57; Poughkeepsie, N.Y., plant, 51; Selective Sequence Electronic Computer (SSEC), 69, 150; Type 601 and 603 Multipliers, 48-49, 51, 57, 122
ILLIAC IV, 98
Institute for Advanced Study, Princeton, 139; IAS Computer, 139-140
Institute for Applied Mathematics, Darmstadt, 37
Iowa State College, 105, 109-110
Iverson, Kenneth, 70

Jacquard, J. M., 46-47

Kepler, Johannes, 77
Kettering, Charles, 78
Küssner, H. G., 37

Lake, Clair, 49
Lehmer, D. H., 127
Leibniz, G. W., 17, 24
Leitz Optical Works, 39
Logic. *See* Symbolic logic; Propositional Calculus

M-9 Gun Director, 94
Manual of Operation for the ASCC, 52, 60, 64
Mark I. *See* ASCC
Mark II, III, IV (Harvard), 68
Mauchly, John, 105-110 *passim*; education, 108, 111; and the EDVAC, 138, 142; and the ENIAC, 110-112; proposal for a computer, 108
Memory, computer, 139-140, 145, 151; EDVAC, 138; mechanical, 18, 19; read-only (ROM), 146, 152; Z3, 30
Metropolis, N., 126
MIT, 93
Monroe Calculating Company, 48
Moore School of Electrical Engineering (University of Pennsylvania), 105-107; conferences held at, 132
Multiplication, machine, 16, 21, 51, 87, 121-122, 133-134

NACA (National Advisory Committee on Aeronautics), Langley, Va., 95
National Cash Register (NCR), 105
National Defense Research Committee (NDRC), 94
Northrop Aircraft Company, 69

Operating Systems, 96

Palmer, R. L., 51
Pannke, Kurt, 21
Parallel vs. serial computing. *See* Programming
Parity checking, 98
Pascal, Blaise, 3
Philadelphia, Penn., 104-106, 127
Plan Calculus (*plankalkül*) 39, 142-144
Plugboards, 47, 110, 116-119. *See also* Programming
Postfix notation, 36
Prefix notation, 89
Programming, 14, 81, 144-146; by perforated tape or film, 26, 56, 116; by plugboard, 47, 116-117; sequential vs. parallel, 45-46, 60, 91, 117-119, 138-139. *See also* Control, devices for

Programming languages, 23, 143-144, 147, 150. *See also* Plan Calculus
Propositional Calculus, 23-25
Punched card equipment, 4, 45-47, 51, 54, 109, 122; IBM 601 and 603, 49-50

RCA, 105
Registers, 54
Reich, H. J., 111
Relays: crossbar, 85, 87; electromechanical, xii, 22, 26, 29-32, 58-59, 84-87, 97, 123; electronic, 26; mechanical 21; notation, 22; and vacuum tubes, 6
Reliability. *See* Errors, computer
Richardson, Lewis F., 108
Russell, Bertrand, 24
Rutishauser, Heinz, 144

S1, S2 Computers, 38
Schreyer, Helmut, 18, 26, 28-29, 38; proposed electronic computer, 28-29
SEAC (Standards Eastern Automatic Computer), 93
Sequential vs. parallel programming. *See* Programming, sequential vs. parallel
Shannon, Claude, 84, 100
Shapley, Harlow, 48
Shockley, William, 99
Simultaneous linear equations, solution of, 109
Slide rule, 11
SSEC (Selective Sequence Electronic Computer), 69, 150
Static indeterminate equations, 11, 15
Steinmetz, Charles P., 77
Stibitz, George R., xi, 6, 73-75, 98, 100, 125; and Complex Number Computer, 81-84, 86-87; education, 78-79; first work on computing, 78-79; later activities, 94-95, 125
Stored program principle, 7-8, 57, 69, 121, 132-133, 137, 144-146, 150
Strowger, Almon, 75, 85
Subtraction, 53, 55
Symbolic logic, 23, 24, 84, 87. *See also* Propositional Calculus

Tables, mathematical, 45, 55, 58, 66, 102; function, 122; NBS, *Handbook of Mathematical Functions*, 68. *See also* Firing tables; Bessel functions
Teichmann, Alfred, 29, 37
Telefunken Corporation, 28
Telephones, 73, 99; and computers, 31, 97; dial, 75; switchboards, 81
TRADIC (Bell Labs Transistorized Computer), 99
Transistor, 99-100
Trigger circuit, 111. *See also* Flip-flop
Turing, Alan M., 8, 131, 134-136, 146
Turing, Sarah, 131
Turing "machine," 136

UNIVAC (Universal Automatic Computer), 147
University of Pennsylvania. *See* Moore School of Electrical Engineering
Ursinus College, 105, 111
U.S. Bureau of the Census, 147
U.S. Navy, 49, 51

V1, V2, etc., computers. *See* Z1, Z2, etc., computers
Vacuum tubes, 26-28, 74, 111-113, 125-126
Vail, Theodore N., 74, 75
Viète, F., 147
von Neumann, John, 6, 127, 137-139; computer architecture, 139-140

Walther, Alwin, 34, 37
Watson, Thomas, 48-49, 51. *See also* IBM Corporation
Watt, James, 4, 105
Weather forecasting, 108, 127
Weaver, Warren, 94
Western Union, 74
Whitehead, Alfred North, 24
Wiener, Norbert, 17, 93
Williams, Samuel, 84, 86-87, 92, 123
World War II, 28-29, 43, 93, 106, 126, 149

Z1 Computer, 25, 29
Z2 Computer, 29

Z3 Computer: cost, 30; description, 29-35; destroyed, 39; programming, 35-38; specifications, 34-35
Z4 Computer, 38-39, 55-56, 132
Z5-Z11 Computers, 39
Zürich, 39
Zuse, Konrad, xi, 6, 79-80, 109, 151; and army, 29; and binary system, 17-18, 47, 84, 110, 125, 132; builds prototype computers, 18-21, 24, 29; and concept of "reckoning," 14; education, 10-11, 15; first thoughts on computing, 11-14; and Plan Calculus, 141-143; and Plan Preparation Machine, 144; and Propositional Calculus, 22-23, 84; postwar activities, 39-40, 140-141, 151; and the Z4, 38-39

About the Author

PAUL E. CERUZZI is Assistant Professor of History at Clemson University in Clemson, South Carolina. He has previously published in the *Annals of the History of Computers*.

RAYMOND H. FOGLER LIBRARY
DATE DUE

BOOKS ARE SUBJECT TO RECALL AFTER TWO WEEKS

~~MAY 14 1987~~
~~AUG 17 1987~~
~~DEC 15 1987~~